# Crime, criminal justic probation service

Now more than ever it is vital for criminal justice professionals – and probation officers in particular – to have a thorough knowledge of criminal justice and their own role in it. *Crime, Criminal Justice and the Probation Service* introduces key facets of criminal justice to students and professionals, enabling them to rise to the special challenges they are currently facing.

Robert Harris, well known as an academic and researcher in social work and criminal justice, is also a former probation officer and teacher of probation students, with wide experience of writing about theory and policy in a manner accessible to professionals themselves. His book provides readable and up-to-date information about our knowledge of such areas as criminal statistics, victims, fear of crime and crime prevention; it also looks at controversial areas such as the treatment of women and ethnic minorities by the criminal justice system, the question of a sentencing council and the future of community corrections. In addition, Professor Harris presents an analysis of the role of the probation service in developing an integrated system of criminal justice.

A central theme is that all the professionals involved in the criminal justice system must work more closely together so that the mistakes of the past can be avoided in the future. The book therefore has a wide appeal not only to probation officers and social workers, but also to criminal justice professionals and administrators, including the police and the legal profession.

**Robert Harris** is Professor of Social Work at the University of Hull. A former probation officer, he researches, publishes and lectures internationally in the fields of social work and criminal justice.

# Crime, criminal justice and the probation service

Robert Harris

Tavistock/Routledge
London and New York

First published in 1992
by Routledge
11 New Fetter Lane, London EC4P 4EE

Simultaneously published in the USA and Canada
by Routledge
a division of Routledge, Chapman and Hall, Inc.
29 West 35th Street, New York, NY 10001

Laserprinted from Author's disks by Gilcom Ltd., Mitcham, Surrey.
Printed and bound in Great Britain by Mackays of Chatham PLC, Chatham, Kent

*British Library Cataloguing in Publication Data*
Harris, Robert *1947*–
    Crime, criminal justice and the probation service.
    1. Great Britain. Crime
    I. Title
    364.941

*Library of Congress Cataloguing in Publication Data*
Harris, Robert, 1947–
    Crime, criminal justice, and the probation service/Robert Harris.
    p. cm.
    Includes bibliographical references.
    1. Probation–Great Britain. I. Title.
    HV9345.A5H36 1991
    365.6'3'0941–dc20

ISBN  0–415–05034–0
      0–415–05035–9 (pbk)

91–3192
CIP

# Contents

# Acknowledgements

The feminine view appears to be that grumbling only makes things worse, whereas I have always held that a fine grumble makes things better. If I have not had a good breakfast, I argue, at least I have had a good grumble.

(J.B. Priestley: *Delight*)

Academics, though no slower than others to complain about their lot, spend their working lives in the company of scholars whose ideas provide almost constant stimulation. Of the many colleagues at Hull University who have influenced this book, chief among them are Clive Coleman and Adrian James, both of whom have stimulated and helped me, as have Keith Bottomley, Martin Copsey and Larry Harrison. Several former students, some of them excellent criminologists in their own right, have done so too: not only Keith McInniss and Robert Waters, whose influence on Chapter 6 is acknowledged there, but others too, including Mary Candlin, Jan Hardcastle and Ian Warner. At the Home Office I have received sound advice from Philippa Drew, George Mair, Satish Malik and Colin Thomas; Brian Fellowes made valuable comments on my schema; David Webb has enabled me to reduce the number of people whom I shall inadvertently offend; and Mick Ryan has been characteristically helpful in relation to the politics of probation. All of them are innocent of complicity in any errors and probably tried vainly to persuade me to avoid them.

Families are usually thanked with varying degrees of effusiveness on these occasions. Though I cannot match the memorable lyricism of Flowers in *Minorities and Criminality* (or in its companion volume on women, which just missed a citation), my own family know well how they have helped me. In fact, in a slightly unseemly breakfast time squabble when I was in full flight with the book, a strident demand was made by junior members of the family that the book should be 'dedicated' to them, though further investigation revealed that the request was made under the misapprehension that dedicatees received the royalties. Once it was pointed out that, on the contrary, historically the dedicatee paid the costs of publishing, interest waned dramatically.

Though, therefore, the book was, by chance, completed on the very day my elder daughter, Ruth, became a teenager, she, as well as Amelia and George and my wife Janet, must make do with love, gratitude and grumbles. But, dedication being in the air, perhaps one may be made to my parents, Carl and Lucy Harris, to whom I owe so much, and who gave me the happy childhood which we now know to be less common either than we used to think it was or than it should be.

# Prologue

> Nowadays they probably have leisure centres down there instead: cafeterias and wall-charts and video-games and everything to make learning easy. Why are they so keen to turn learning into a game? They love to make it childish, even for adults. Especially for adults.
>
> (Julian Barnes: *Flaubert's Parrot*)

Every book is an experiment, though the experiment may be of different kinds. Two of my books thus far have been experiments in the production process itself, an experience from which I learned that the stresses of book production exceed those of authorship, both emotionally and organisationally.

A third book, *Welfare, Power and Juvenile Justice*, which I wrote with my old friend David Webb, was an experiment of a more academic kind. Firstly, we aimed to fuse two distinct intellectual traditions, the British empirical and the European philosophical, using the former as a touchstone for the utility of the latter. Secondly, we aimed to write a book which pulled no theoretical punches, but which would be read by practitioners as well as academics and students. Our concern was to put to the test the possibility of transcending the 'how to do it' emphasis of the practice handbook which, for all its seductive simplicity, we felt often had as much long term utility as a *soufflé* has in sustaining the starving on a cold winter's day. In particular, we sought to challenge the crude reformism of much British vocational writing, assuming as it does the existence of a technical solution to every problem of theory or ideology. To say that some problems did not have solutions and that sometimes the best strategy in the face of the insoluble was simply to do nothing, however, was unlikely to be universally popular in the utilitarian age of the late 1980s. Even if Mr Gradgrind had been supplanted by his distant descendant Mr Fixit, the message was still the same, and analytical detachment not the mode of the moment.

Nevertheless, the experiment was generally successful. The book was well reviewed, most reviewers engaging enthusiastically with the complexities we were articulating. Even the reviewer who was distressed that people who trained professionals could argue that their capacity to effect change was limited, which seemed akin to suggesting that the applied theologian should skirt over the problem of pain in twentieth century Christian dogma, found the book engaging and readable. Yet there was a problem, not of pain but of action, as we acknowledged in the book itself when we described it as having cleared away the undergrowth before further work could begin. This book, which is, therefore, an experiment too, is part of that further work and, to the extent that it addresses professional action in a complex world, builds on *Welfare, Power and Juvenile Justice*. It is in part, though only in part, an attempt to develop a conceptual framework for the probation service of the future by developing a portfolio of criminal justice activities in which it could and should involve itself.

The book's main aim, though, is less theoretical, more basic, than that. In the absence on study leave of our Professor of Criminology at Hull, Keith Bottomley, I taught his Crime and Delinquency course. Though I had taught the subject some years earlier, in updating my notes I discovered that no textbook for British criminal justice professionals covered the necessary areas, and I accordingly resolved to write one. *Crime, Criminal Justice and the Probation Service* contains basic information for criminal justice professionals and also serves as a source book for those who wish to study particular areas in greater detail.

This, then, is a theoretical book about criminal justice, but written with professionals in mind. It is not, I hope, dull or even unopinionated (my opinions both about sentencing and the future of probation, for example, are strongly expressed), and it is centrally about professional action. But it is not a 'how to do it' manual, and as I proceed I cast doubt on some popular assumptions and ask some difficult questions. The chapters on race and gender, for example, far from being campaigning tracts in 'anti-racist' or 'anti-sexist' practice, review critically what we know about such questions as whether women's criminality is becoming more like that of men and whether black people are discriminated against by the criminal justice system. And I fear that to campaigners in these areas, some of my conclusions will be heretical.

I shall be your guide, then, on our journey, describing the landscape as best I can, sometimes portraying familiar terrain in a new light, sometimes seeking to stimulate discussion and controversy. Though I hope the journey will be stimulating and enjoyable, there are, alas, no more wall-charts or video-games there than on Julian Barnes's cross channel ferry; on the contrary, to gain the most from this book you will need to traverse some quite difficult territory, particularly in the later chapters, with an alert and sceptical mind.

So much, though, for the Prologue. The curtain rises on a scene both familiar and uncertain. We have been here many times before, but there are quicksands to ensnare us notwithstanding. Criminal statistics are not safe walking country, and if I eschew the saying about 'damn lies and statistics' it is only because I have so taken to heart the injunction of the late Mr Sam Goldwyn to avoid *clichés* like the plague. Let us begin.

# Chapter 1

# Criminal statistics – some themes and issues

... vilely drawn pictures brought home to the dullest intelligence an interminable succession of squalid crimes, women murdered and put into boxes, buried under floors, old men bludgeoned at midnight by robbers, people thrust suddenly out of trains, happy lovers shot, vitrioled and so forth by rivals.

(H.G. Wells: *Tono-Bungay*)

Sixty-seven percent of the doctors surveyed preferred X to Y. (Jones couldn't be persuaded.)

(Paulos 1989: 99)

Our widespread use of statistics is usually accompanied by an almost equally widespread mistrust of them. To live in an advanced industrial society without recourse to batteries of figures on most areas of life would be, literally, unthinkable. For this reason alone it is psychologically as well as socially necessary to assume that the figures we daily consume at least approximate to what (as this is not a book about philosophy) we shall call 'the truth'.

Most of the time this works quite well. Many statistics tell us simple, factual things: how many of us are married, own a dishwasher, intend to vote Conservative. There is no strong likelihood that we shall deceive the collector of the figures, and if the study is competently and honestly conducted the results will be good enough, even though they reflect only the 'truth' of a frozen moment in time. Hence the figures on marriage may be dramatically changed by a new tax incentive which encourages cohabiting couples to trip up the aisle, those on dishwashers by a health scare or those on voting intentions by a key policy change by any of the political parties.

Other kinds of official statistics are less simple, and criminal statistics are, for three main reasons, among the most misleading.[1] Firstly, most crime is a secret activity inaccessible to conventional forms of social enquiry. Secondly, variations in criminal statistics are variably, unpredictably, and sometimes only incidentally related to changes in the behaviour of the criminals. Equally if not more significant are changes in the processes which transform invisible criminality into visible crime; indeed it is these processes which the statistics measure. And thirdly, the essentially political nature of criminal statistics makes them, alongside other 'social problem statistics' such as health and employment figures, especially vulnerable to political manipulation. So just as a reduction in hospital waiting lists could indicate that the National Health Service was doing better *or* that people had so lost confidence in the adequacy of the system that they were not troubling their doctor with minor complaints *or* that there had been a shift in family practitioner referral practice *or* that the counting rules had changed, so do criminal statistics begin rather than end the argument. Borrowing the language of the tabloid press, how can we tell whether a crime wave which incorporates everyone from sex fiends to dole fiddlers reflects an increase in criminal behaviour, improved training for social security inspectors, a shift in policing policy, or a misleading figure whipped up by an interest group to 'prove' the failure of the Government's social and penal policies or the need for more police?

Criminal statistics are, therefore, *problematic*, and criminal justice professionals need a good working knowledge of their uses and limitations as well as those of alternative data-gathering strategies designed to complement the official approach. For probation officers in particular a grasp of this is especially important, for the members of the public with whom they will in the future be working increasingly closely are inevitably exposed less to the knowledge of the expert than to the headlines of the tabloids. As we proceed, therefore, you will see that I believe the criminal justice professional of the future should not only be able to give a balanced and informed account of crime and criminal justice to a wide range of members of the public but also encourage them to feel that crime is not a social 'fact' beyond their control, but a process in which it is desirable that they intervene.

Locating this chapter and the next early in the book is designed to indicate just how fundamental their content is to what follows. Nowhere can we talk confidently about 'crime' as behaviour; always our discussion is mediated by statistics which filter what we observe about crime itself. Sometimes I make this explicit, sometimes, for I do not want to bore you with too much repetition, it is unsaid. Always, though, we must tread warily, being aware of the contradiction in which the criminologist is trapped, of speaking about the artefact and calling it reality. In this chapter I shall be demonstrating the extent of the problem, in the next I shall show how attempts have been made to solve it. And for the rest of the book we simply proceed as best we can in a world where almost nothing is quite what it seems. It is a world which is fairly simple to those people who, on discovering my profession, buttonhole me on trains and at parties, and confidently inform me about the increase in crime, its causes and cures. But the more we penetrate the dark interior of the world of crime and criminal justice, the more complicated and mysterious it becomes.

## ON USING OFFICIAL STATISTICS

Though 'counting' has doubtless characterised all advanced societies for many centuries, most official statistics are the products of the rise of industrial capitalism in the eighteenth and nineteenth centuries. The first census took place, in the midst of political outrage, in 1801, and the bureaucratisation of government in the nineteenth century led to the development of distinct statistical divisions. The first international statistical congress took place in 1853 at the suggestion of Quetelet, and included criminal statistics among its ten topics for discussion (Wilkins 1980). This official measurement combined with the efforts of researchers and reformers such as John Howard, Charles Booth and Seebohm Rowntree to influence nineteenth century social policy.

Official counting has always been accompanied by a degree of scepticism (Pepinsky 1980), based either on the suspicion that the counting methodology is inadequate or that counting is a mystification, a self-seeking manipulation of data by the powerful. Only more recently has a more fundamental theoretical critique emerged which rejects the very basis of what is sometimes pejoratively called 'number crunching', arguing instead that a statistic is a social product not a fact. Once we move from the 'mere' counting of the obvious and uncontroversial (for example, the total number of pigeons sitting in Trafalgar Square at noon on Saturdays in November 1991) into areas of social definition or meaning, there is room for ambiguity and hence manipulation. It is not hard to count pigeons if we ensure the researcher is honest, can tell the time and knows what day of the week it is, can distinguish pigeons from ring doves and seagulls, can count, knows the boundaries of the Square and is clear whether to include walking as well as stationary pigeons and pigeons which land at a second past noon. With more complex categories the situation is less simple, and since the purpose of collecting statistics is usually instrumental not intrinsic, it is not often, to this school of thought, that we can be confident about the accuracy of the figures or the uses to which they will be put (see for example Irvine, Miles and Evans 1979).

Few informed commentators would today accept the commonsense view that in an area such as crime we need only to refine our data gathering, analysis and interpretations to get at what is 'right' and to form a rational policy on the basis of it. That is not, of course, the same as saying that there is no point in having the statistics. After all, as R.H. Tawney once memorably wrote, the impossibility of attaining a state of absolute cleanliness does not mean that we should roll in the dung heap. No, what we have to do is be clear in what ways statistics can help us and in what ways they can mislead.

Here, for example, are some problems with ostensibly uncontentious data. I begin, deliberately, with an example which has little to do with criminal statistics, but which raises some related issues. As you read it, try and think in what ways it is similar to, and dissimilar from, what you know already about criminal statistics. Note also that to be a critical and informed consumer of official statistics does not necessitate having more than a fairly elementary technical knowledge of statistics. Though such knowledge will make you a more sophisticated consumer, you can get a long way with a critical intelligence and a healthy scepticism. You will seldom be lied to by the statistician (and if you are, you will probably never know), but nor will you always be told the whole truth. Hence, to have your wits about you is essential.

*1. How many people are unemployed?*   Clearly 'unemployment' is not a 'thing' like a leg or a tooth or a castle, but a social definition. We should not, therefore, *reify* it but remember that because it is an artefact it can mean very much what significant definers of the word want it to mean. It may, therefore, have different definitions for different purposes. Do we define as an unemployed person someone who:

- is not in full-time paid employment?
- is claiming unemployment-related state benefits?
- is required, as a condition of receiving benefits, to be seeking work and available to do it?

Do we include or exclude in our definitions people on Government training schemes, the long term sick, housewives, students on vacation, people working in the 'black economy', prisoners, members of the House of Lords, people with large private incomes? A shift in definitions changes the figures and hence the 'social meaning' of unemployment. However clear the researchers may be in their definitions, not only may the popular presentation of their data not reflect this clarity but the definitional changes which are frequently necessary year-on-year in official statistics (whether through changes in law or policy or because one category has been found technically inefficient or politically inexpedient) gravitate against effective comparisons being made.

While it is, crudely, the aim of Government to minimise, and of Opposition to maximise, the numbers of the 'unemployed', neither actually has 'the true facts' on its side. Of course we should no more expect to receive the 'truth about unemployment' from ministers or Opposition spokesmen than we should expect to obtain a dispassionate account of a crime from the speeches of the defending barrister. Nor, strictly, do we get this 'truth' from *anyone,* because 'truth' in this simple sense very seldom exists. But the impartial expert analyst should at least set out both sides of the question to enable you to clarify your own opinion.

Nothing, therefore, is quite what it seems, and in an imperfect world we can only ensure that we have examined all sides of the question, been open to changing our views where those views are based on ignorance or error, and resisted the sometimes overwhelming temptation to distort the arguments of the other side. This distortion can take a number of forms, which range from simple misrepresentation to the more subtle process of taking an intellectually weak opponent's confusion as representative of the other side's case. From closing one's mind to new information it is but a short step to using the distorted version of the opposition case to confirm one's prior position. The old joke applies, that one should not use statistics as the drunkard uses a lamppost – for support not illumination. Though one can never attain true objectivity and impartiality, there are academic conventions which enable one to move closer to them.

One crucial question is for what purpose the statistics have been collected and to what use you as a consumer wish to put them. In the case of unemployment, because it is not a 'thing' its meaning shifts as the social and political context of its ascription shifts. If Government, concerned at the problem of unemployment among school leavers, responds by 'creating' work or training and makes undertaking it a condition of receiving benefit, we face a new definitional problem of who, actually, is unemployed: the school leavers doing the created work and receiving unemployment benefits, the jobless school leavers who decline to do the created work and hence do not qualify for unemployment pay, neither or both. A benefit-based definition of unemployment would include the first category but not the second, an activity-based one would do the reverse; a flexible one might include both and a rigid one neither.

Our first task, therefore, is to interrogate the figures. Remember, they are not measuring an incontrovertible 'thing' but an artefact which can change as its creators change their minds. As we look at the figures we must ask ourselves what might be their multiple meanings? What questions do they leave us with? Remember, the figures will almost certainly not have been falsified but will tell a partial story. As we proceed, therefore, we must ask not only what the figures say but what they do not say. Every table is its own detective story.

When we are clear what the figures do (and do not) say, we can decide how to use them. Let us return to our 'job creation' problem. If our interest is in calculating the present cost to the Treasury of unemployment benefits, we need to include the youngsters engaged in job creation schemes but exclude the youngsters not so engaged. But if we want to examine the cost to the Treasury of increasing the numbers of unemployed school leavers in a scheme (perhaps by introducing penal sanctions or, conversely, by making the schemes more attractive) the numbers in this latter group represent a crucial piece of data because they will tell us the size of the reservoir of potential, as opposed to actual, claimants.

But let us suppose that our interest is of a different kind and we wish to test the market for a day centre for unoccupied unemployed youths. In this case, our interest in 'unemployed' youngsters in job creation schemes is incidental, for they will be too busy to come to the centre. Our only interest in them is in the drop-out rate, for our potential consumers will include job creation drop-outs as well as non-participants.

It is necessary, therefore, to look behind the figures, regarding them not as providing answers but as posing yet more questions. It is part of the job of any professional to look beyond the figures, to become a literate consumer and to be able to give dispassionate and well-informed policy advice. But let us leave our unemployment problem and take another example, this time from the world of crime. Here I have chosen a category about which there has been surprisingly little statistical controversy.

2. *How many murders are committed?* It is obvious that there are serious problems in determining the trends in a whole range of under-reported offences – from shoplifting to soliciting, from drug offences to

embezzlement – but it is generally assumed that this kind of problem does not arise with murder. But even in this (still) relatively rare and seemingly straightforward area of criminality, all is not what it seems.

As unemployment is a social construct, so is murder a legal construct, a particular form of unlawful killing. In a strict sense, therefore, the question 'how many murders are committed?' is answered simply: the number of murders committed is the number of murders recorded. All murders come to light because a death is transformed into a murder only by a legal classification. But this tautology is a very pedantic answer to our question, which really should be rephrased as: how many unlawful killings which would justify being categorised as murder are committed? Because there are two main reasons why not all such killings are defined as murders, it is impossible to give a precise answer to this question. Firstly, the incident may not have been known about; and secondly it may, though known about, have been classified 'not-murder'.

Neither circumstance should unduly surprise us. So far as 'not knowing' is concerned, there are many non-persons in the Western world: teenage runaways, isolated 'down and outs', illegal immigrants, fugitive debtors. And because non-persons lead an unofficial existence, their lives are by definition marginal and isolated, their disappearances unnoticed and hence unremarked. Estimates about the numbers of adults who 'go missing' vary widely, and help us little in determining how many have been murdered. One text produces bizarre stories of numerous women's garments and unexplained dentures being found in the homes of known mass murderers (Radzinowicz and King 1979: 44–5) but whether the numbers of such murders in a year run into two, three or even four figures is simply beyond our knowledge.

But such cases are still, fortunately, statistically deviant, and in the more usual categories when the body is found, the social processes which define a killing as murder are, like any human activity, liable to error or manipulation. Even setting aside the legal ambiguities which increasingly surround the beginning and end of life, there are numerous opportunities for the redesignation of murder. Accident, self-defence, suicide and natural causes are four main alternative significations, and they can apply to a range of deaths from drowning to falling, from fighting to sudden infant death, from fire deaths to overdoses. They may be the result of successful deception or simple ambiguity. The official figures tell us nothing of such instances: their frequency and distribution (are they randomly allocated? do they cluster geographically? or characterise the behaviour of a particular class, sex, race or culture?), what role professional discretion plays in these designations, whether there are differences among the doctors and coroners who make these legal ascriptions and hence significations. In short, we have no idea from these figures what proportion of 'actual' murders are so defined or how characteristic of such 'actual' murders legally defined murders are. Do we in fact define as murder a systematically distorted subsample of 'actual' murders? Will, in fifty years time, the assurance with which the professionals inform the public that, contrary to popular images, most murders are committed in or around the home itself come to be confounded by new knowledge? Perhaps the best we can immediately hope for is, by being aware of what we do not know, to look with sceptical eye at what we think we know.

## OFFICIAL STATISTICS: A BRIEF CRITIQUE

If you have by now been persuaded that the 'figures' are problematic, you will probably be following one of two trains of thought. If you have a basic confidence in the tools of science to explain the human world (inclining, thereby, to a *positivistic* view of the utility of the statistic) you will be saying that the problems are primarily technical; that clarity of definition or books such as this one which spell out the intrinsic limitations of official statistics enable us to make rational judgements about the limits of this utility. Indeed, you may even go so far as to agree with the American sociologist who asserted:

> It is self-evident that the crime rate of a society depends upon the incidence of criminality among its constituent groups.
>
> (Ferdinand 1970)

I can scarcely think of a better examination question than to ask candidates to 'analyse critically' this piece of self-evidence. Those sympathetic to the quotation will find support from Leon Radzinowicz and Joan King, the first chapter of whose international study appears to have been entitled 'The Relentless Upsurge in Crime' on the basis of changes in recorded figures (Radzinowicz and King 1979). You may, on the other hand, have a more fundamental objection to the statistic, believing, with the *phenomenologists*, that the statistic is essentially deceptive precisely *because* it gives an air of 'fact' to a piece of social construction. As Bob Roshier has said in his excellent commentary:

> Admittedly, most positivists had acknowledged that there were problems with their data. However, after a statutory early chapter

outlining these problems, the implications were invariably ignored in the serious empirical analysis and theorising that took place later.

(Roshier 1989: 43)

But even the more extreme phenomenologists do not reject the view that official figures are informative. The dispute relates rather to what it is, precisely, that they inform us about. In a seminal critique of official statistics the American sociologists Kitsuse and Cicourel put the persuasive argument that whereas criminal statistics in particular are unreliable as indicators of the nature and extent of criminal behaviour, they do yield important information about the agencies which collect them. From this we can gain certain insights into the values and processes of the society from which those agencies derive. To Kitsuse and Cicourel, the utility of the official statistic lies not in its account of *behaviour* but in the processes which produce rates of deviance: the problem is that there has been a failure

> to distinguish between the social conduct which produces a *unit* of behavior (the behavior-producing processes) and organizational activity which produces a unit in the rate of *deviant* behavior (the rate-producing processes). The failure to make this distinction has led sociologists to direct their theoretical and empirical investigations to the behavior-producing processes on the implicit assumption that the rates of deviant behavior may be explained by them.
>
> (Kitsuse and Cicourel 1963: 132)

A concrete instance of this point is produced in a critical paper on labour statistics:

> An indication of the priorities which underlie the compilation of official statistics is the derisory attention devoted to industrial accidents and diseases, in contrast to those topics which primarily concern governments and employers. The subject achieves a single page in the *BLSYB* (*British Labour Statistics Year Book*) whereas wages and earnings take up 100 pages, and employment, unemployment and vacancies receive 180.
>
> (Hyman and Price 1979: 232)

What we learn from labour statistics, therefore, is that labour statistics devote little space to accidents and injuries. If, therefore, we want to learn more about accidents and injuries it is not to this source that we should turn. If, though, our interest is in broader questions such as the priority given to industrial accidents by the data-collecting agencies (the rate-producing processes) then the official statistics are an informative starting point for our enquiry. The processes by which details of particular industrial accidents are or are not recorded are themselves social phenomena but they are different social phenomena from the details of industrial accidents. The unit of attention, in Kitsuse and Cicourel's analysis, therefore, shifts from the ostensible object of study, which may be the number of crimes or industrial accidents, to the means by which, and the reasons for which, data about them are collected. Official statistics tell us about official statistics.

The analogies with crime and criminal statistics are self-evident. This celebrated case tells us little about crime, but a lot about how information about it is collected:

> the reorganisation of the New York city police department in 1950 resulted in a *recorded increase* of 400 per cent in robberies, 200 per cent in assaults with weapons and 700 per cent in larceny over the rates for 1948 and 1949
>
> (Hood and Sparks 1970: 37)

While nearer home:

> Between the years 1931 and 1932 . . . a dramatic increase of 222 per cent in the total figure of indictable offences in the London area was brought about by the simple expedient of abolishing the book listing items 'suspected stolen' and entering these instead as 'thefts known to the police' . . . (there is also) the example of male importuning in Manchester, for which there was less than one prosecution per year in the period 1955 to 1958. Then a new chief constable arrived, and prosecutions for this offence over the next four years steadily rose from thirty in 1959 to 216 in 1961.
>
> (West 1967: 34–5)

Conversely, of course, systematic exclusions from official figures can distort our understanding of the true nature of crime. Referring to the American crime statistics, Haskell and Yablonsky note:

> Offenses committed by organized crime in the course of its legitimate or illegitimate enterprises, even when reported to the police, are not generally included in the *Uniform Crime Reports*. This fact tends to distort the truth about crime in the United States since . . . organized crime takes about twice as much income from gambling and other illegal goods and services as criminals derive from all other kinds of criminal activity combined. Another

noteworthy exclusion is white-collar crime. Fraudulent advertising, combinations in restraint of trade, price-fixing to cheat the Government, violations of patents, and other white-collar crimes constitute a substantial amount of crime not included in the Crime Index. They are included only when arrests are made, and this is rarely done.

(Haskell and Yablonsky 1970: 38)

So again the official figures follow and reflect the practices and values of the rate-producing agencies. These in turn reflect the hegemonic values of the dominant interest groups of the society in which those agencies are situated. The official figures mislead us if we look to them for an accurate 'account' of criminal behaviour. But a key omission from these figures tells us both about the state and influence of organised crime in the United States in the 1960s and about the law enforcement strategies of the police and correctional agencies. Similarly, as Sutherland has shown, the opportunities for corporate offences increase as societies become more affluent, technologically sophisticated and interdependent with overseas economies (Sutherland 1941) yet white collar crime is difficult to detect, costly to process, collusively concealed and some-times politically sensitive (Sutherland 1949). The pursuit of complex frauds or industrial espionage involves disproportionate amounts of police and court time, acquittal rates are high, and public (and hence political) concern is less intense than with many blue collar crimes.

There is no simple relation between public and political concern about crime and the amount of illicit profit to be made from it. To the pragmatic 'sense' of the low ranking police officer that working class criminals are 'softer targets', therefore, is added a political push which focuses more on solving crimes which visibly disrupt the lives of identifiable people than on more distant, abstract and less immediate delinquencies. This is not, at least in intent, a class conspiracy, but the product of a set of seemingly pragmatic responses to 'the job' as characterised in police morality, culture, training and socialisation. But because the official statistics mirror this emphasis they can tell us little about Kitsuse and Cicourel's 'behavior-producing processes' but much about the 'rate-producing processes'. So while it would be naive to believe that criminal statistics could give us an authoritative account of the state of crime in the country today, they can, in this analysis, give us a very good picture of ourselves – our class structure, values, concerns, stereotypes, voting practices – through their portrayal of the activities of the criminal justice and penal systems.

There are, therefore, two conflicting analyses of official statistics. The one portrays them as deficient but going along the right road, able to provide useful information about the state of crime in Britain today provided we acknowledge obvious deficiencies in counting, the impact on the figures of police practices and so on; and the other suggesting that as an index of crime they are so fundamentally flawed as to be useless: indeed they mislead because they reflect the hegemonic values of the society which produces them. In this sense, while they hold up a mirror to that society they have little use beyond that, and it is only as a commentary on the 'rate-producing processes' that they should be valued. Perhaps when you have read this chapter you will be able to express a clear view; both views cannot, after all, be correct.

## CRIMINAL STATISTICS: THE FILTERING PROCESS

the government are very keen on amassing statistics. They collect them, raise them to the nth power, take the cube root and prepare wonderful diagrams. But you must never forget that every one of their figures comes in the first instance from the village watchman, who just puts down what he damn pleases.

(Sir Josiah Stamp, cited in Nettler 1974: 43)

The finest theoretical exposition of why criminal statistics have certain limitations is overlaid by the often chaotic realities of the police station and the magistrates' court: things are forgotten, lost or, of more interest to us, human error being after all ubiquitous and unpatterned, strategically ignored. Let us, therefore, concentrate instead on the processes by which an illegal act – of which countless thousands occur daily – becomes, against all the odds, transmuted into a criminal statistic.

If few pieces of criminal behaviour are translated into crimes, even fewer result in their perpetrator being sentenced by a court. Each act, once committed, becomes subject to a sequence of decision-making processes, a decision to proceed no further at any one of which filtering it out of the system. Different decision-makers take centre stage as the process continues, so for our act to proceed to conviction, decisions to continue must normally be taken, sequentially and often independently, by a relevant member of the public (a victim or witness of the crime, a confidant of that victim or witness, or someone else who knows that the crime has been committed), the police officer to whom it is reported, a more senior police officer, the Crown prosecutor, the magistrate and perhaps a jury. Because some of these decisions are taken independently of each other, some writers do not like talking about the criminal justice *system*, the word 'system' implying the existence of *feedback* among the component parts, when this is by no means invariably present in criminal justice (Locke 1990), preferring to speak of a criminal justice *process*. But as criminal justice is by no means devoid of feedback mechanisms (Moxon 1985) I shall, in this book, follow both logic and convention and speak of the criminal justice system.

**To report or not to report?**

The first decision as to whether to report our criminal act is, of course, made by anybody who is aware of its commission. There are some crimes where nobody (including the criminal) knows that this is so (Walker 1971). Clearly, if there are no witnesses and the offender either does not know an act is criminal or is unaware of having committed it, the act simply vaporises. Such instances are characteristically, though not necessarily, minor crimes; they may be acts on the verges of legality where an expert is needed to determine whether an act is a crime. Do *you* know, for example, whether you would be committing a crime if you:

- picked up and kept a 10 pence piece which you found on a piece of waste land?
- agreed to accept a 'discount for cash' from a workman you had hired on the implicit (but not explicit) understanding that this would avoid VAT?
- made a private telephone call from work without permission, to say you would be working late?

Unless you are a lawyer, probably you do not. In the first and third cases nobody is very likely to be concerned either way and the principle *de minimis non curat lex* would probably apply – the law does not concern itself with trivia. The second example, however, is of a different order entirely, and depending on circumstances you could be innocent of all charges or guilty of the very serious offence of conspiracy to defraud the Customs and Excise, and possibly (since it could reasonably be inferred that if VAT were to be avoided so would income tax be) the Inland Revenue.

There are many other circumstances in which one might not know a crime had been committed. One might be too drunk or otherwise drugged to know that one had killed a pedestrian, stolen from a shop or committed an act of violence; again, some forms of physical or mental illness lead to loss of memory or affect. But let us set these cases aside. No one knows a crime has been committed, so they do not feature in our present considerations.

Offences, though known about, may not be reported to the police for reasons which include the following.

- *The victim may not know an offence has been committed even though the offender does.* This can apply across a range of crimes, from violent or sexual offences against children to theft from shops, from one's place of work or from other members of one's own family to many 'white collar crimes' such as fraud and embezzlement.

- *The victim may collude with the offence.* Obviously where illegal but consensual sexual activity takes place, one party being under age but able to give informed consent, the ostensible 'victim' has not only tolerated, but in effect been party to, the offence. There are, however, less obvious instances of victim collusion than this. In another area entirely, for example, in many places of employment the prevailing linguistic, cultural and moral codes make a conceptual and moral distinction between 'reasonable pilfering' and theft (Martin 1962). Martin's work in Reading suggests that toleration of 'reasonable' pilfering represents an organisationally functional collusion between managers and employees to accept (though always within tacitly acknowledged limits) the continuation of relatively minor theft and fraud. The effect of this collusion is to create an environment in which offenders can 'neutralise' the moral impact of their crime by the 'everybody does it' technique (Sykes and Matza 1957; see also Braithwaite 1989). Hence, the crime being stripped of stigma or shame:

  > Embezzlement and stealing are often committed by trusted employees and workers with no criminal records, leading respectable if modest lives and participating actively in civic crusades of every kind, including those aiming at better control of crime.
  >
  > (Lopez-Rey 1970: 26)

- *There may be no victim.* There is another category of offence where there is literally no victim, except in the most abstract sense of the Crown. Certain Road Traffic Act offences, crimes against public property, importing illegal goods, the possession of pornography are all instances of this, and there are many more of them. Their detection is dependent, therefore, either on a report by a member of the public or on direct observation and arrest by a police officer.

- *The victim may be fearful.* Obviously victims of violence are especially likely to come into this category; and when to the variable of violence we add personal or social proximity, it becomes clear also that those people who are most likely to spend time in the company of their attacker are most likely to be so. This means that the victims of *domestic violence* – mainly but not exclusively women and children – are particularly vulnerable, and the sensitivity of criminal justice professionals to the frequently ambivalent reporting behaviour which reflects their situation is relatively recent.

  A similar point applies to prisoners. The lack of public, or even professional, interest in *crimes committed in prison* is astonishing. Indeed so invisible is this area of crime, and so socially insignificant the victims, that prisons are regularly assumed to provide effective protection against offenders. Yet prison life is daily characterised by forms of behaviour which would not be tolerated for one moment in a more visible, or higher status, community, and there can be few citizens more prone to victimisation than prisoners (for sensitising accounts, see Menninger 1966 and Wooden 1976. A serious study of violence against prisoners in the United Kingdom, though much needed, has still to be written).

  It is not only victims of violence, of course, who may be fearful to report a crime. Fear may not just be of assault but of blackmail or non-violent reprisals such as rejection by a community disaffected with the police. This problem stands independent of the nature of the crime: the stigma associated with 'telling' is evident from the mountain of pejorative epithets for the 'sneak', 'snout', 'nark' or 'grass' to be found in any dictionary of slang (even if one did not remember it well from one's own schooldays).

- *The victim may dislike the police or have been involved in illegality too.* Members of some working class and ethnic minority communities may feel they have little reason to see the police or courts as being on their side; and in other situations, though linguistically and stereotypically we may crudely regard 'criminals' and 'victims' as opposites, the reality is rather different. The typical victim is in many ways similar to the typical criminal – young, male, with minor convictions already, and a town dweller. As we shall see in the next chapter, one of the most startling findings of the *British Crime Survey* has been that people who declared themselves victims of crime were much more likely than others also to admit to having committed an undetected offence.

- *The victim may regard the offence as too trivial to report, or the likelihood of apprehension remote.* Doubtless like me, you have been the occasional victim of petty offences involving the loss of such items as pens and books. You may have been shortchanged in shops, and have suffered minor assaults. You will not on the whole have reported them because to have done so would have penalised you further by occupying your time fruitlessly. In such circumstances you probably railed briefly against the gods and then got on with life. So much victim behaviour is of this kind that it is analytically quite wrong to regard the non-reporting of crimes as deviant behaviour. On the contrary, not to report minor crime is perfectly normal, and the interesting question for the psychologists and criminologists is why people *do* report crimes. Clearly one motivator must be the hope or expectation of personal benefit – through insurance, criminal injuries compensation or direct payment from the criminal. Another may be that fear of repetition is greater than fear of reprisal and that the victim believes that reporting the crime will reduce the likelihood of repetition. It may also be that reporting crimes is a form of learned behaviour, justified in terms such as 'responsibility' or 'public spiritedness'. Certainly middle class victims are more likely to report minor crimes than are working class victims, even though (or perhaps because) they are less likely to be victimised.

The police certainly do not encourage the reporting of trivial infractions, and to imagine that the immediate and natural response of a victim is to 'tell the police' is a considerable oversimplification of a complex piece of personal or corporate decision-making:

> Thank God for shoplifters and those who do not report their crimes. . . . Managers often ask us about stock 'shrinkage' – 'What do you want us to report?' We say 'don't report everything, especially if it's not likely to be detected.' (Senior CID officer).
> (Bottomley and Coleman 1981: 25)

So far as corporate victims are concerned, some have a policy of reporting only certain kinds of offence, and when the victim is an employee many firms prefer a resignation to the cost and bad publicity of a prosecution.

The embryo criminal statistic, then, though conceived by the criminal act, is nurtured by the social act of *reporting behaviour*. Since it is rare for the reporting behaviour to be that of the police officer (the image of being caught red-handed with the swag being for the most part best restricted to the pages of the *Dandy* or *Beano)* and since it is not, at least outside the television studio, a daily occurrence for the penitent thief to prostrate himself before the bemused station sergeant to confess all, crime reporting is mainly a product of the relation between police and public. The act of reporting is typically the establishment of contact with the police by, and on the initiative of, a victim or member of the public. It is therefore at the police station that the next stage in the process takes place.

## Recording crime

When a crime is reported, the police normally fill out a *crime complaint form* which may or may not be translated into a more formal *crime report*. This crime report is the basis of a criminal statistic. There is, however, a shrinkage between reporting and recording which is primarily a product of police practices. Not all crimes in respect of which a complaint form is made out are transferred on to a crime report. Some are withdrawn by complainants, but more importantly certain decisions are made by the police at this point. They have to ask whether they believe the complainant, how lucid the complaint and how likely it is that a reported crime will be 'cleared up'. There are very high levels of discretion available to, and exercised by, quite low ranking police officers (Davis 1971: 80–90). There is also ethnographic evidence of a number of deviant practices by the police in relation to recording crimes (see, for example, Cain 1973; Bottomley and Coleman 1981) including 'cuffing' a suspected crime (metaphorically putting it up your sleeve) and only producing it if it results in an arrest. It is also clear that different recording practices exist in different police forces. In one study it was discovered that the very high crime rates in Nottinghamshire were a product not primarily of behaviour-producing processes, but of rate-producing processes: the Nottinghamshire force recorded crimes not recorded by neighbouring forces and took greater account of further offences admitted under interrogation than was the case elsewhere. So while Nottinghamshire's crime rate was genuinely high, it was exaggerated by the local force's accounting practices (Farrington and Dowds 1985).

It is important to remember, therefore, that a criminal statistic is not a simple, scientific measure but in part a strategic device. The selective recording of crimes can enhance the clear-up rate of the police force, while heavy recording can increase the credibility of bids for increased resourcing. Given that, as we have seen, petty crime is such a widespread though secret activity, the capacity of the defining agencies to vary the small proportion which becomes public is considerable. The bureau-professional descendants of Sir Josiah Stamp's watchman who does what he damn pleases are alive and well today.

## Clearing up crime

The notion of 'clear-up' is an important one in policing, though increasingly Chief Constables are coming to acknowledge that the 'clear-up rate' is not a reliable indicator of police efficiency. (For a balanced review of the uses and limitations of 'clear-up' see Burrows and Tarling 1982). Some of the reasons for this scepticism will by now be clear; other texts deal with the matter in greater detail (see, for example, Kinsey, Lea and Young 1986, Chapter 1). Nevertheless, the notion retains its *cachet* in the world of press and public opinion, and for that reason alone it remains politically significant. In a sense, the clear-up rate is for the police force what the success-rate is for the probation service: a fundamentally flawed but superficially attractive and hence politically crucial measurement tool. The major difference between the two is, however, that they are differentially vulnerable to manipulation.

Of course, for an offence to be 'cleared-up' an arrest must be made, and this has led to suggestions of personal bias based on variables which include the sex, race, attractiveness and demeanour of the suspect:

> Getting arrested is an interactional process. The police force, the policeman *and* the offender do make a difference . . . studies indicate that if you are apprehended committing a minor crime, being respectful to the policeman may get you off . . . If you are apprehended committing a more serious offense . . . being respectful to the police is not likely to make much difference.
>
> (Nettler 1974: 57)

An offence is 'cleared-up' when someone is proceeded against; a conviction is not necessary. Cautioning (in which an offender, having admitted an offence, is formally cautioned by a senior police officer, but not taken to court) is included in clear-up figures, as are offences admitted by a criminal, normally during interrogation, and 'taken into consideration' in passing sentence. Bottomley and Coleman show that 44 per cent of recorded property offences in their study were cleared-up by what is known in police jargon as 't.i.c.ing' and that this rose to 65 per cent for certain categories of offence, including theft from motor vehicles. Over half the 258 offences in this study which were cleared-up by t.i.c.ing first became known to the police during interrogation for

other offences. It is clear, therefore, that the extent to which interrogation techniques elicit high t.i.c. levels can radically affect the clear-up
rate.

Police forces receive guidance from the Home Office on counting
crimes and dealing with complexities such as these:

> An anarchist kills two people with one bomb. A referee is attacked
> by ten spectators. An advertiser causes a fraudulent advertisement to
> appear in sixteen issues of *The Times* and defrauds eighty people . . .
> How many crimes are involved in each case?

> (Walker 1971: 24–5)

But in addition to the plentiful scope which exists for the creative
application of these guidelines (now called *Counting Rules for Serious
Offences*), as Bottomley and Pease have shown the guidelines themselves
are couched in such terms as to make individualistic and hence variable
interpretations inevitable (Bottomley and Pease 1986: 38–9). Any
discussion of the 'clear-up rates' of different offences, therefore, must be
approached in the same spirit of cheerful scepticism appropriate to
much of the official data we have been discussing. In the case of 'clear-
ups', the 'rate' cannot be unyoked from the history and biography of
the individual statistic or from the purposes to which the statistic is to
be put. If, early in the process, low ranking police officers discourage
the reporting of crimes with a low clear-up probability then the clear-
up rate will be high; the maximisation of the potential of the
interrogation process to detect t.i.c.s will have a similar result.

Some crimes, including domestic violence, shoplifting and
embezzlement, are virtually cleared-up by being reported: to know of
the crime is to know the identity of the offender. But the fact that these
'automatic' clear-ups cross the categories of crime set out in official
statistics entails that the overall clear-up rates assigned to those
categories constitute no more than an averaging out. So, to take an
extreme case, the category 'theft and dishonest handling' includes theft
by an employee (which has an almost 100 per cent clear-up rate) *and*
theft of bicycles (which, as any student knows, has a remarkably low
clear-up rate). The misleading mean is one of the banes of the statistician, as the old story of the non-swimming statistician who drowned
in a pond with an average depth of three feet graphically illustrates.

The next journey for our statistic is from the police to the Crown
Prosecution Service, the nationally organised prosecution system,
introduced in 1986 to make prosecution matters independent of the
police. If the police have a suspect, it becomes the responsibility of the

CPS to decide whether or not to proceed. They typically do so firstly if they decide that to proceed is in the public interest and if there is, in their estimation, a 75 per cent chance of obtaining a conviction. The CPS has been much criticised by the police in particular for its supposedly conservative approach to prosecution. When the decision to proceed is taken by the Crown Prosecution Service, an offence becomes classified as cleared-up.

## CONCLUSION: OFFICIAL STATISTICS AND THE PROBATION OFFICER

We have covered much ground in this chapter, but nothing like as much as there is to be covered. My aim has been the fairly circumscribed one of posing some of the questions to be answered by the literate consumer of official (and in particular criminal) statistics. In doing so I have tried to move beyond the 'lies, damned lies' *cliché* of Mark Twain. I have not, however, gone systematically through the official statistics themselves, and to gain the maximum benefit from this chapter you should now study the most recent *Criminal Statistics*, perhaps reading them alongside the authoritative discussion in *Crime and Punishment: Interpreting the Data* (Bottomley and Pease 1986).

I have in particular raised the question of whether the official statistic is useful but inadequate, or whether it is fundamentally misleading and hence dangerous. Does it tell us about behaviour, or just about the agencies that collect the data? There is a fundamental theoretical controversy in social science behind this question. Clearly, in unsophisticated hands the official statistic does more harm than good, as it is never possible for it to give an unsullied account of criminal behaviour. Few if any experts today would do other than reject the simple positivist view that the official statistic can tell us the 'truth' if only we can improve the methods of data gathering and analysis.

But although the two positions we have discussed are conflicting and cannot, therefore, be 'integrated', there is a third theoretical possibility of reconsidering the relationship among criminal, reporting and recording behaviour. To the positivist the latter two simply reflect the former; to the phenomenologist the three are essentially separate issues all of them less important than the processes which contribute to the social construction of crime itself. It is, however, logically possible that a relationship of a kind exists between them but that its nature has still to be determined (see, for example, Cohen and Land 1984). As Hood and Sparks observe:

Only if it can be shown that a constant ratio of certain crimes is reported will it be possible to develop an index from official statistics ... Without the assumption of constancy in reporting and recording practices an uncertain amount of any fluctuations in recorded crime might be due to changes in reporting behaviour.

(Hood and Sparks 1970: 15)

This is not a new thought, the concepts of General Systems Theory having been introduced to crime analysis by Leslie Wilkins in the 1960s (Wilkins 1964), developed later by Jock Young in his study of Notting Hill drug users (Young 1971a, 1971b), and subjected to very readable, if somewhat knockabout, scrutiny later still, by Jason Ditton (Ditton 1978). The thought is as yet, however, still in search of a theory. If, though, a form of problem behaviour becomes accentuated, whether by frequency, gravity, or for some extraneous political reason, there is an immediate feedback effect on public attitudes (which affect reporting behaviour) and the correctional agencies (responsible for recording). Conversely, however, the actions of the enforcement agencies affect criminal behaviour, either by reducing it or, perversely, increasing it. Because there is no *simple* relation between behaviour and the recording process, however, it does not follow that there is no relation *at all* between them, and it may be possible to etch an *accentuation theory* which establishes a relation among the different parts of the crime and criminal justice process: deviant act, reporting behaviour and recording behaviour.

If, for example, we take the recently 'discovered' crime of child sexual abuse, we know that the increase in recorded instances has been sudden and exponential. We have no theory to help us understand whether this reflects a change in any one of primary deviance, reporting behaviour, recording behaviour, a combination of any two of them or all three. This ignorance has obvious and serious consequences for policy, law and practice, and an attempt to retheorise the official statistic is therefore probably overdue. If we follow this line of analysis, the dispute between the phenomenologists and the positivists as to whether the official statistic measures social control or crime has to be set alongside the separate question of what impact, if any, changes in reporting and recording behaviours have on primary deviance. This approach means that the criminal statistic may have an impact not only at the micro-level of its effect on individuals or the mezzo-level of its effect on agencies (police, courts, probation service), but more fundamentally on criminal activity. *If*, for example, it were to be established that the 'naming' and processing of child sex abuse or other domestic violence contributed to increasing instances of it (whether, crudely, by 'giving people ideas' or, more subtly, by legitimating the act as a common characteristic of family life, hence making it vulnerable to a technique of neutralisation), the statistic would itself become an aspect of the crime and criminal justice system. For this reason alone, to know and to think about criminal statistics and in particular the sociology of criminal statistics is a necessary part of the thoughtful professional's intellectual armoury.

But such knowledge has more day-to-day relevance too. If the 'job' of the probation officer in particular simply involved interviewing, assessing and treating 'clients', it could be done without this kind of discussion. But it will by now be clear that I do not see it in this way; indeed it is arguable that the 'clientcentricity' with which probation officers have for so long viewed their work has hampered their engagement with the local criminal justice system as a whole. Once we extend our conceptualisation of the probation officer's work into policy development, inter-agency liaison, public relations, crime prevention, combating the fear of crime, risk reduction, work with victims and potential victims, revenue generation, competitive tendering and resource management, an informed understanding of the overall context in which the probation officer operates becomes a prerequisite. Matters which have in the past been primarily for senior managers and the Home Office are increasingly becoming ones for more junior staff. It is unrealistic to assume that these tasks can be taken on with only the conventional 'client centred' skills and knowledge of the probation officer. In this changing work context it is going to be necessary for probation officers to deal increasingly with people other than the probationer who is still too often inaccurately referred to as the 'client'. Information about what we know (and do not know) about crime, what relation exists between fear of crime and vulnerability to crime, how crime can be prevented, what typically 'happens' to criminals is knowledge which it will be increasingly unjustifiable for probation officers not to possess. And understanding something of the life cycle of the criminal statistic is, as should by now be clear, an essential part of that process.

# Chapter 2

# Counting crime – beyond the official statistics

'Then the upshot of all your learning, sir,' – he said – 'is that one can never be quite certain of anything?'
'Exactly so!' replied the pensive sage with a grave shake of his head
. . . education is advancing at a very rapid rate, and the art of close analysis is reaching such a pitch of perfection that I believe we shall soon be able logically to prove, not only that we do not actually exist, but moreover that we have never existed! – And herein, as I consider, will be the final triumph of philosophy!'

(Marie Corelli: *Ardath: the Story of a Dead Self*)

Knebel, bored with the figures that studies on smoking perpetually produce, concluded: smoking produces statistics.

(Kothari and Mehta 1988: 200)

So the official statistics of crime tell us something, but not everything; what they in fact tell us is not always what they purport to tell us; they deal only with a minute proportion of the crimes that are committed; they are susceptible to chance fluctuation as well as deliberate manipulation; and, by focusing on indictable offences processed by the recording agencies, they give a misleading picture of the state of crime today. At the same time, our own understanding of these figures is vitiated by our lack of a theory of criminal statistics, though any such theory, if developed, could only be as sound as our theories of crime and criminal justice. Clearly, to study the official statistics, though necessary, is not sufficient if we are to gain an understanding of crime and criminal justice. In the absence of a *theory* to enable us to unyoke our analysis of criminal behaviour from our analysis of the official reaction to that behaviour, however, the sensible approach is to proceed empirically: perhaps we can create a *methodology* to enable us to do so.

With this in mind, a number of distinct approaches have developed, both in the United Kingdom and the United States, of which two interest us in this book,[1] the *self-report study* and the *victimisation study* or *crime survey* (for a fuller discussion on which, see O'Brien 1985). Both approaches have a surprisingly long pedigree, though, as Frances Heidensohn has shown, the impetus for the expansion of these studies lay in political, academic and public disquiet about the use of the American official statistics in the 1960s. This disquiet led to the institution of the Crime Commission by President Johnson in 1965, and to the consequent funding of a number of studies to provide better data to aid the 'fight against crime' (Heidensohn 1989: 162).

Though, as we shall see, there are methodological variations within each type of study, they all involve inviting individuals to report on crimes which have not, so far as they are aware, come to public notice. Self-report studies proceed by asking people what undetected offences they have *committed*, crime surveys by asking them about *victimisations*. Of the two approaches, by far the greater resources have been invested in crime surveys: in the United States the vast American National Crime Survey began in 1972, while in the United Kingdom, the British Crime Survey had its first 'sweep' ten years later. Both approaches have provided criminologists with rich and fascinating data, but neither is without its drawbacks.

## SELF-REPORT STUDIES

The claim of proponents of self-report studies is that they provide a 'Kinsey-type baseline' of criminal activity against which to measure the official statistics. There are some obvious problems with this claim, mainly that people may deny offences for strategic reasons, or falsely claim offences through braggadocio. They may not know they have committed a crime, or they may have forgotten having done so. On the other hand, if these problems could be managed, the potential for the academic or criminal justice professional of self-reports would be considerable. Let us consider some of the possible advantages.

An accurate self-report study would enable us to develop a much better understanding of the uses and limitations of official statistics. As we have seen already, we are presently unable to use them with confidence, yet they are regularly used inappropriately and mislead the public about the extent and pattern of crime. Our lack of just this kind of baseline knowledge has impeded both academic study and policy development. For this reason, the self-report study may appear the positivist's dream come true: a means of creating laboratory conditions and hence providing at least one piece of secure knowledge in a mutable world. From this knowledge, surely, we can proceed to discover that elusive grail, the 'truth'. The stakes could scarcely be higher.

Such knowledge would transform policy and practice, enabling us to target and shape our responses better by facilitating the measurement of the effectiveness of what we 'do' to offenders. No more would there be that awkward thought that, say, probation officers' 'successes' might reflect no more than the good fortune of the probationer in not having been caught reoffending. The lack of any clearly established causal relation between professional action and subject response is a major stressor for individual probation officers, a serious managerial problem for agencies (Clear 1985) and a restriction on knowledge development for the profession. Some areas of the probation officer's work today have scarcely advanced since the last century, in good part as the result of the lack of empirical verification of effectiveness.

A reliable self-report methodology would similarly enable us to understand the negative as well as positive impacts of social action on delinquent activity. The popular (though frequently misunderstood) theory of labelling (Lemert 1967) could be given its substantively legitimate place in criminal justice practice on the basis of precise empirical accuracy. Thus far, in spite of some attempts to theorise the labelling effect (see, for example, the small scale study of heroin users in Covington 1984) we rely on extrapolations: sometimes being apprehended and taken to court can extend (Farrington, Osborn and West 1978) or create (Klemke 1978) delinquency. But how fine it would be to be certain what we should and should not do in particular cases, how splendid to solve this problem:

> The problem with interaction and labelling theory is that they did not tell us under what circumstances we might and might not expect (a labelling effect).

> (Roshier 1989: 115)

We could learn about the impact of social problems such as homelessness, unemployment, alcohol misuse and family violence on criminality, thereby proceeding gracefully to hitherto unknown levels of rationality in criminal justice policymaking; and about the possible existence of systematic bias in the use of professional discretion by police, sentencers or probation officers, whether by race, gender, demeanour or physical attractiveness. New and tantalising vistas of positivistic pleasures would open before us if only we could put our faith in the complete honesty of the otherwise dishonest whenever they spoke to a researcher or completed a questionnaire.

Alas, life is not so simple, and to attempt to turn the messy and complex realities of existence into a Benthamite laboratory is to whistle in the wind. Of course this is not to reject the utility of the self-report study, simply to urge caution. Studies thus far have, however, provided us with broad indications about crime and who commits it, and there is sufficient consonance among different studies for some reasonably confident assumptions to be made:

> Where self-report studies *confirm* official statistics, observational studies, and surveys of victims, one can have some confidence in them. Where confessions of criminal conduct *disagree* with these other tallies of delinquencies, it will be political preference or 'social philosophy,' rather than good reasons, that determines which statistics one chooses. This is so because *asking people about their behavior is a poor way of observing it.*
>
> (Nettler 1974: 86. Italics original)

Few self-report researchers are unaware of the limitations of the mode, and most have taken sensible and responsible steps to reduce the likelihood of mistakes occurring. Self-report studies may be conducted by means of anonymous questionnaires or interviews, either of which may or may not be separately validated (Nettler 1974: 73–4). Early examples of the questionnaire approach include a classic study of 49 offence categories answered by 1020 men and 678 women which highlighted the existence of a vast reservoir of undetected criminality (Wallerstein and Wyle 1947) and a comparative study of convicted youths and students which suggested that that reservoir was greater among 'respectable' middle and upper class students:

> The court cases, as analyzed, were charged with fifty-five specific offenses, varying all the way from 'shooting spit-wads at a wrestling match' to murder. But they had no monopoly on such offenses; for the students, replying through schedules presented by our investigators, freely reported delinquencies of the same kind, largely without interference from the courts. A well-adjusted ministerial student said he had indulged in twenty-seven of the fifty-five offenses; and a successful pastor, also a student, reported committing twenty-eight.
>
> (Porterfield 1946: 38)

Such unvalidated studies are, however, of questionable reliability and validity, so some later studies have built-in a range of validation procedures varying from polygraphs (Clark and Tifft 1966) to the Cambridge approach (see, for example, West 1969a; West and Farrington 1973, 1977), which combines questionnaire *and* interview. West, in fact, mounts a particularly spirited defence of this approach, describing how he has avoided the main problems normally associated with it, notably non-response bias (a distortion of the findings by refusals of target respondents to take part) and respondent untruthfulness (West 1982: 164–8).

Interview approaches have varied from large scale studies with adolescents (Belson 1975) to more methodologically complex work (Erickson and Empey 1963; Hirschi 1969). (For a review of these and other self-report methodologies, see Nettler 1974: 90–6). The securest information from self-report studies is that:

● there is almost certainly an inverse relationship between social class and delinquency. The early view that class was not a significant variable in delinquency has not been subsequently sustained (see for example Gold 1966; Braithwaite 1981, 1989; though see also Williams and Gold 1972) and although because law enforcement agencies expect to find delinquency in working class areas they deploy their resources accordingly and therefore do find it, this of itself does not account for the behavioural disparity which actually exists. (For a more detailed discussion of this point, see West 1982: 166–7);

● though self-reports are inaccurate indicators of criminality, they consistently understate rather than overstate criminality: braggadocio is less significant than the combined effects of concealment and forgetfulness. Self-report studies, therefore, understate the amount of crime actually committed;

● once trivial offences are removed, there is a surprising relation between self-report and official records of crime. The Cambridge longitudinal studies have demonstrated that self-reported delinquents are less deprived and deviant than official delinquents (West 1982: 168). Though this difference does not refute the generalisation that working class youngsters are more crime-prone than middle and upper class ones, it does indicate that the concept 'working class' must be viewed as a heterogeneous grouping not a homogeneous entity, with the lowest stratum being most likely to be criminally processed.

Self-report studies tend, then, to confirm the view that minor delinquency is almost universal among the young and is probably best

left alone, since to process such cases officially would not only be
pointless but might just do more harm than good (Farrington, Osborn
and West 1978). On the other hand there does exist a cluster of serious
or repeated delinquents who are responsible for the majority of non-
trivial offences. Very few of these do not have convictions, and there is
a rough and ready correlation between the number of offences actually
committed and the number of official convictions obtained (West and
Farrington 1973; Shapland 1978). There is also a relation between
actual behaviour and negative behavioural ratings by others: offenders
with high self-report scores were frequently the same youngsters who
were rated 'troublesome' by teachers and classmates, who scored high
on other 'anti-social' indices, who were from families with criminal
parents and who had experienced poor parental supervision (West and
Farrington 1973):

> there are immense differences between boys who have a high rate of
> self-reported delinquent activities and those who have a low rate.
> The view that everyone is somewhat delinquent and that there are
> no meaningful differences between those who are slightly so and
> those who are markedly so can be firmly rejected.
>
> (Rutter and Giller 1983: 29)

For those whose academic training was influenced by 1960s
interactionism, it must seem that we have reverted to a pre-1960s
mode, with professional and commonsense knowledge, so dramatically
ruptured by the sociologists of deviance, once again coalescing. This is,
in fact, not quite the case. Though the 1960s saw an explosion of
creative writing, some of it, it is true, being now of largely historical
interest, not only did the ideas generated at that time push empirical
research in a new direction, they also identified official processes as a
necessary focus for analytic attention. This shift has been of considerable
significance in policy and practice. For example, the Children Act 1989
contains a presumption of 'no court order' unless it can be shown that
the benefits of social intervention outweigh the disadvantages. Whereas
in the pre-1960s days the possibility that social action could make things
worse was not seriously contemplated, the potential of the helper to do
damage is now an established piece of professional wisdom, challenging
us to refine our understanding of when professional action is iatrogenic
and when helpful.

One area where more thought is necessary is 'labelling' which,
probably by default rather than design, can encourage a tendency to 'do
nothing', or, if to do something, then to do as little as possible. Though

the notion of 'radical non-intervention' (Schur 1973) presumably has as great an appeal to the ideologically sophisticated as it does to the indolent or indecisive, the theory is, perhaps, a trifle crude and, in at least one significant sphere of criminal behaviour, child abuse, rather dangerous. Though I have myself suggested that to respond to an insoluble problem by doing 'something' is to commit the technocratic fallacy that all human misery has a professional solution (Harris and Webb 1987: 177), to make the reverse assumption is equally unjustifiable. It is tempting for the observer of juvenile court social workers and probation officers seemingly indiscriminately doing all they can to do as little as they can for as long as they can, to wonder whether the ultimate logic of their 'minimal intervention' strategies is not the dissolution of their own jobs.

Self-report studies have helped them win the battle over the marginal offenders. Everyone now agrees that youthful naughtiness is ubiquitous, and that generally the more advanced the society the more likely naughtiness is to be classified as delinquent. Accordingly, such children are better told off and left alone than turned into 'clients', 'patients' or 'prisoners'. The problem, however, is that this insight has been extended to include serious, repeated and committed offenders when the evidence is that many of them will not 'grow out of it' but will continue offending into adulthood. It is not obviously a professional triumph for the probation officer to persuade the police to administer an eighth caution, or a court to impose a minimal sentence, on an offender about whom there are grounds for profound pessimism. On occasions such as this, the different strands in the history and culture of the probation service (Harris 1989a) do tend to become entangled: the humanitarian impulse (or perhaps the inclination to champion the offender against the forces of law and order) does not rest easily with the duty to use what knowledge there is in order to contribute to the management of crime.

The question, though, is what to do instead. The sophisticated criminal justice professional will be aware of the empirical reality of the labelling effect, and also of the danger in applying the trends evident in quantitative research to an individual case. But a repeated offender has in effect labelled himself – or, in the style of the symbolic interactionists (Goffman 1968, 1971) been labelled in a host of more significant interactions than the one he has with his probation officer. A repeat offender from a large working class family living in a high delinquency urban area, whose parents are considered by the social worker to be 'unsatisfactory' at child-rearing and whose supervision of the children is lax, who is of low intelligence, who began offending at a young age, who offends alone and whose family has a history of drug or alcohol misuse is statistically rather unlikely to 'grow out of it'. Miracles do happen, of course, and there is a small but growing American literature on 'false positives', high risk youngsters who grow out of crime (for example Werner and Smith 1982; Jenkins and Brown 1988), but if you are optimistic you are so against the odds, and to suggest that a court appearance for a youngster with most or all of these traits or experiences will confirm his delinquency is akin to suggesting that to apply a pair of bellows to an outgoing tide will make it recede faster.

One of the securest pieces of learning from the self-report study is that you cannot avoid the responsibility of taking decisive action with a high risk delinquent on the ground that to do so would have a labelling effect. There is good reason not to 'criminalise' the naughty or silly child following an incident or two of petty shoplifting or of behaviour which commonsense suggests is uncharacteristic – perhaps the result of some personal or family trouble or just one of those pieces of inexplicable craziness which periodically afflict the most ordinary of adolescents. But this principle cannot justifiably be extended to committed young criminals whose conduct it is part of the professional's responsibility to check. In particular it will not do as a pseudo-theorised excuse for lenience.

## CRIME SURVEYS

if you are an American you have one chance in 400 years to be a victim of violent crime. But if you are a Negro or a Mexican-American the chance is one in 80 years; if a member of the white middle class, once in 2,000 years; if a white, well-to-do suburbanite, once in 10,000 years.

(Attorney-General Ramsey Clark, 1968. Cited in Haskell and Yablonsky 1970: 44)

Though Attorney-General Clark's comments are certainly out of date and almost equally certainly wrong in view of what we now know about domestic and sexual violence, they do graphically illustrate the central point that interpersonal crime is predominantly committed by working class people on other working class people.

Victim studies, like self-report approaches, received a considerable boost in the 1960s. As Frances Heidensohn notes, the official statistics in the United States (*Uniform Crime Reports*) were coming under increasing fire both in their own terms (as inefficient and unreliable) and from the new phenomenologists (Heidensohn 1989: 162). Crime rates and urban unrest were increasing and victims themselves were beginning to mobilise as an interest group which it was becoming increasingly difficult to ignore. For example, in a paper delivered to the first Restitution Symposium in Minnesota in 1976, it was argued:

> the act of victimization will cause the victim to question seriously the legitimacy and usefullness [sic] of the criminal justice system . . . the individual will consider his/her victimization a consequence of the system's failure to serve its function of protection. Therefore, the unresponsive system is not worthy of support.

> (Stookey 1976: 5)

The President's Commission on Law Enforcement and Administration of Justice (Crime Commission) commissioned a number of studies which heightened political and public sensitivity to the amount of unrecorded victimisation which existed. Its report *The Challenge of Crime in a Free Society* noted that the 'real' incidences of offences were between twice and four times as high as those cited in the *Uniform Crime Reports* – and this is almost certainly a serious underestimate (President's Commission 1967). At about the same time, the National Opinion Research Center was commissioned to conduct a crime survey of 10,000 households throughout the United States which revealed that 'as many as half of the people interviewed were victims of offenses which they did not report to the police' (Ennis 1970: 124) and, equally significantly, that the popular image of crime was inaccurate:

> About 40 percent of the aggravated assaults and rapes . . . take place *within* the victim's home; and about 45 percent of all the serious crimes against the person are committed by someone familiar to the victim. Random 'crime in the streets' by strangers is clearly *not* the main picture that emerges from these figures, even in the urban setting.

> (Ennis 1970: 126–7)

Ennis's study also drew attention to the phenomenon of intra-racial crime and the relative infrequency of victimisations of whites by blacks (even though blacks committed more crimes *per capita* than whites) and to the low levels of satisfaction with the criminal justice system expressed by victims. Though it contained significant defects in methodology, it produced some results which have been subsequently validated by more sophisticated studies; it also constituted a significant development in criminological research, encouraging further work (notably Hindelang, Gottfredson and Garofalo 1978), further funding of crime surveys by the federal Government and ultimately the introduction of the National Crime Survey in 1972 (Sparks 1981).

NCS was introduced with four components, of which the national household survey was the most significant. This vast study involved a stratified sample of 60,000 families selected and broken down into six cohorts of 10,000 each. Each family was interviewed twice yearly about victimisations over the previous six months, and remained in the sample for seven interviews of which the first, known as the 'bounding' interview, was disregarded in order to solve a technical problem called *telescoping*. In crime surveys, either because respondents cannot remember when they have been victimised or for cathartic reasons, they tend to 'telescope' into the period in which the researchers are interested any victimisation whenever it took place. This leads to an overstatement of victimisations in the first interview, and the bounding interview therefore establishes a baseline, with subsequent interviews asking about victimisations since the previous one.

NCS found that victimisation was very rare. In 1977 for example, violence was reported in only 3.4 per cent of households, and of these 75 per cent involved no physical injury. On these figures, the 'average' American would go almost 74 years before suffering physical injury. But of course victimisation is not evenly distributed, and NCS has produced useful data on spatial, social and temporal distributions of victimisation. High levels are found among adolescents and young adults, with the numbers declining with age, so that the 65 plus age group are least at risk; urban dwellers are more likely than suburban and even more likely than rural dwellers to be victims, males are more at risk than females, blacks than whites. Most crime is intra-racial, though black-on-white inter-racial crime is commoner than white-on-black. Most crime is not reported (even house burglary and robbery were slightly less likely to be reported than not), though decisions to report or not are influenced by commonsense notions of the seriousness of the offence:

> decisions to call the police are based mainly on a fairly rational assessment of the costs and benefits of doing this rather than on general attitudes to the police or the machinery of criminal justice.

(Sparks 1981: 22)

A central problem of NCS and almost all crime surveys is that of underreporting (for a parallel discussion in relation to the British Crime

Survey, see Hough and Mayhew 1985: 5–7). Firstly, there are definitional problems of whether, and if so how, to include minor crimes.
Secondly, the household basis of questioning means that the reporting
rate of intrafamilial crimes will be low. The crime survey is unlikely, for
example, to be a sound method of establishing spouse abuse, marital
rape or incest. Thirdly, there was a problem of 'time-in-sample bias'
whereby the longer people were in the study the fewer victimisations
they reported – presumably because of boredom, respondents having
been suitably catharsised by the preliminary disclosures. Fourthly, there
were cultural and class differences in reporting, with the white middle
classes reporting more victimisations than either the black or the white
working classes, almost certainly reflecting a working class tendency to
regard minor victimisations as part of the hurly burly of daily life.

In the United Kingdom, the first modest attempt at a crime survey
was undertaken in 1973 (Sparks, Genn and Dodd 1977) to be followed
by the British Crime Survey in 1982. This survey, coming as it did after
NCS, was able to solve a number of technical problems which faced the
American survey. For example, NCS dealt only with interpersonal
crimes, not with offences against corporations, or victimless crimes.
BCS dealt not only with victimisations but with undetected offences
committed by respondents to try to include white collar and other
crimes which would otherwise be omitted. NCS also lacked any
discussion of 'lifestyle variables', and since 'it is not illuminating to be
told that a man who never goes out of his house will never be robbed
in the street' (Sparks 1981: 42–3), BCS has paid considerable attention
to the actuarial basis of vulnerability to victimisation.

In the three 'sweeps' of BCS thus far, questionnaires were
administered to, and interviews conducted with, 16,000 households in
Britain, of which 11,000 were in England and Wales. The findings have
been reported in two ways. Firstly, the Home Office has published a
general report of the methods and main findings of each sweep (Hough
and Mayhew 1983, 1985; Mayhew, Elliott and Dowds 1989; see also
Hope 1984), and secondly there has been a series of shorter publications
focusing in greater detail on particular findings ranging from obscene
telephone calls to women (Pease 1985) and personal crime against
women (Worrall and Pease 1986) to violence generally (Hough and
Sheehy 1986; Davidoff and Dowds 1989), housing tenure and
victimisation (Hope 1986), autocrime (Hope 1987), burglary and
attempted burglary (Hough and Mo 1986; Lewis and Mo 1986;
Mayhew 1987); the impact of crime on victim behaviour (Mawby and
Gill 1987), the fear of crime (Maxfield 1984), lifestyle and the risk of

victimisation (Gottfredson 1984; Clarke, Ekblom, Hough and Mayhew 1985), and public opinion and victim attitudes to punishment (Hough and Moxon 1985; Hough and Lewis 1986).

Because BCS was not only a victim study but contained elements of self-reporting, it could address crimes unavailable to other victim studies, including illegal drug use (Mott 1985) and drunken driving (Riley 1985). Here, however, I focus on some key findings of BCS thus far and on the particular application of lifestyle approaches to risk of victimisation. I shall also introduce and discuss briefly two local crime surveys in Islington and Merseyside (Jones, Maclean and Young 1986; Kinsey, Lea and Young 1986) which offer a critique of BCS, and then examine a more fundamental critique of crime surveys. From all this I hope will emerge the importance of forming a clear view on the uses and limitations of the crime survey itself.

## British Crime Survey: some findings

BCS has covered five main areas: levels of victimisation, factors affecting the risk of victimisation, fear of crime, experience and expectations of the criminal justice system and self-reported offending (Hope 1984). All three sweeps suggest that victimisation is rare: the 11,000 households in the first sweep in England and Wales reported only 43 robberies, 15 sex offences (including one rape), 99 woundings and 541 burglaries. Excluding common assaults, only about 5 per cent of all offences were violent. On the basis of these figures the baseline for serious offences of sex and violence is so low that even if only one in ten rapes were recorded by the police, the number in each sweep would increase only from one to three in the 11,000 households (Hough and Mayhew 1985: 11).

This finding has not been without its critics. One study suggests that serious sexual assaults are even more infrequently reported than BCS suggests (Hanmer and Saunders 1984). An equally if not more serious omission is almost certainly incidents of domestic physical violence. This is for two main reasons: ineligibility and underreporting. Most cases of child abuse are excluded from consideration because the minimum age for a victim in BCS is 16; and the collection of data on eligible forms of intra-household criminality is obviously problematic in crime surveys whose methodology involves interviews conducted in the household.

Minor victimisation is very much more common, but still statistically unusual: the second sweep, for example, found that the commonest single crime was theft of milk from the doorstep – but even this offence had been experienced by only 10 per cent of households surveyed during calendar year 1983 (Hough and Mayhew 1985: 9). Autocrime was very common, with approximately 20 per cent of households including a victim of vandalism or theft of (or from) a motor vehicle.

Approximately two thirds of incidents uncovered by BCS were not reported to the police, and the more trivial the offence the less likely the victim was to report it. Nevertheless, a number of serious crimes also went unreported. The decision to report was, as in other surveys, class related, with non-manual victims more likely to report crimes than manual workers. These differences were probably a product of attitudes to the police and insurance – though this is insufficient to explain away class differences in reporting behaviour (Hough and Mayhew 1985: 23). Most property offences were indeed minor: half domestic burglaries involved losses of less than £100 and the damage to property incurred as a result of the break-in was less than £100 in over 90 per cent of cases. In spite of popular fears, burglars defecated or urinated on the furniture or floor in only 1 per cent of burglaries (Hough and Mayhew 1985: 27).

With the publication, in 1989, of the report of the third 'sweep' (Mayhew, Elliott and Dowds 1989) it is becoming possible to note some trends in victim-reported crime in the 1980s. In 1989, reports to BCS of household and property offences had increased by 21 per cent over 1982 (against an increase in the official figures of 26 per cent over the same 6 year period); theft of bicycles was a greater problem during the 1980s with an 80 per cent reported increase, possibly reflecting the increased trend for bicycles to be regarded as fashion accessories (Mayhew, Elliott and Dowds 1989: 62). Changes in burglary patterns are also interesting. Between 1981 and 1987 the proportion of unsuccessful (i.e. attempted) burglaries in BCS increased (possibly, the researchers speculate, as a result of improved home security). In the 'burglary with loss' category, BCS (combined with the General Household Survey) estimates an increase of 20 per cent in the six years, compared with an official increase of 125 per cent.

Ethnic minorities are more at risk of victimisation than whites. Asians in particular are at greater risk of vandalism and robbery or theft from the person, and especially vulnerable to attacks by groups of strangers. The pattern of personal victimisation of Afro-Caribbeans was different: they were more likely to know their offender and were much more likely than whites to be victimised by other Afro-Caribbeans. Women were more likely to be involved in offences involving Afro-

Caribbeans, both as offenders and victims, and woman-on-woman crime may be more likely in this racial grouping than others, though it remains even there a small minority. The researchers note:

> Asians seem more disadvantaged by their ethnicity. Their overall risks are generally higher than among whites . . . Race itself appears to contribute to higher risks for some crimes among Asians, and this is more often perceived by them to be the case. For contact thefts, it may be that – unlike Afro-Caribbeans – Asians are seen by offenders as passive or 'easy' targets.
>
> (Mayhew, Elliott and Dowds 1989: 49–50)

*Attitudes to punishment*

There has been much public interest in the apparently more tolerant attitude of BCS respondents to punishment than those of respondents to opinion polls. These attitudes derived from three research methods: a sentencing exercise (which showed respondents to be broadly in step with court practices), a knowledge check of current sentencing practice (which showed that respondents believed courts to be more lenient with burglars than they were), and by asking respondents how they would reduce the prison population (a question which produced a wide range of support for community service (86 per cent), compensation orders (82 per cent), shorter sentences for non-violent offenders (69 per cent) and fining (67 per cent)). This relatively liberal approach seems characteristic of victims as well as non-victims. Apparently there is:

> no support at all for the view that the courts are too soft for victims' liking. There is no substantial mismatch in terms of severity of sentence . . . There seems to be a clear desire amongst victims that offenders should make some redress for the harm they have caused.
>
> (Hough and Mayhew 1985: 46)

These findings should be approached with caution for three main reasons. Firstly, they starkly contradict those of some (though not all – see Shapland, Willmore and Duff 1985) other studies, and in particular opinion polls. Secondly, the third question presupposed but did not test a desire on the part of applicants to reduce the prison population. So respondents were not asked whether they favoured these alternatives to the prison but, presented with the desirability of reducing the prison population, were asked how they would favour going about achieving it. Thus:

The results may over-represent enthusiasm for liberal reform, as some respondents may have supported options which they saw as the best way of achieving an objective – reducing the prison population – to which they were indifferent or actually hostile.

(Hough and Mayhew 1985: 46)

Thirdly, the research inevitably took a very *rational* approach to its subject. But the characteristic response to crime is irrational, and it is possible that BCS's evidence is a product of its method of enquiry: when faced with a researcher and a battery of questions people perhaps play the role of rational and constructive respondent. What is beyond doubt, however, is that there is a widespread belief that courts are more lenient than they are. This means that public calls for 'tougher' sentences are frequently based on a false premiss: sentences already *are* tougher than many people believe, and it seems desirable, therefore, for criminal justice professionals to communicate that fact.

Though due caution is necessary, the figures do suggest that at the very least there is unlikely to be widespread public hostility to the idea of punishment in the community. The importance of the answer to the 'reducing the prison population' question is less whether respondents preferred prison or community service for particular offenders (an issue not resolved by these responses) than that restitutive alternatives were strongly favoured over non-restitutive ones. This is something about which I have written elsewhere (Harris 1989a: 29–30) and makes concern for the victim a necessary *leitmotif* for community-based punishments in the future.

## Victimisation and lifestyle: the BCS contribution

In this section I demonstrate one strength of BCS over other crime surveys: its analysis of victimisation and lifestyle. The lifestyle approach was popularised in this country by the American scholar Michael Gottfredson, during a productive attachment to the Home Office in 1983, which spawned an important study *Victims of Crime: the Dimensions of Risk* the following year:

the risk of victimisation for many major offences is probably less in England and Wales than in some other Western countries . . . but . . . most people have no accurate idea what the chances . . . are and how these chances might be expected to vary according to their own circumstances.

(Gottfredson 1984: 1)

Gottfredson's approach was to develop a situational analysis of criminality based on an actuarial calculation of the extent and nature of risk. Clearly one is 'at risk' of a particular misfortune only for part of one's life. If you insure against, say, physical injury such as breaking your leg, you are only at marginal risk while asleep in bed; if you insure against wrecking your car, you are barely at risk when it is locked in the garage. The first variable in an actuarial calculation is, therefore, the duration of your time at risk.

The second variable is the nature of your behaviour. You are more likely to break your leg if you go winter sporting than if the limits of your exercise are walking the dog. You are more likely to have a motor accident if you drive recklessly, have a sports car and engage in autocross or rallying than if you simply drive your family sedately to the country at weekends. And thirdly, you are more at risk depending upon who you are. If you are a young, inexperienced driver you are more likely to have an accident than if you are a middle aged academic (we are generalising, remember) because of the way you drive and where you drive to. These generalisations are by their nature unfair to individuals, but their probability is sufficient to ensure that the insurance companies stay in business.

To Gottfredson, for a crime to occur there must exist 'the confluence in time and space of the target and offender in the absence of effective deterrents' (Gottfredson 1984: 3). It thus becomes possible to identify likely victims and high risk situations by identifying likely offenders and situations in which crime occurs. But under what circumstances does this confluence occur?

Clearly though individual offences may result from sheer bad luck, the broad generality implies a degree of victim involvement in a particular interaction (see also Mawby and Gill 1987: Chapter 1). BCS produced some interesting findings on probability: violent crimes without theft, committed by strangers, happened most frequently outside the home on weekday nights; theft with personal contact occurred most frequently in the daytime, and public transport was a particularly high risk location. Household victimisations were different again: vandalism was largely nocturnal, residential burglary diurnal and early evening during the week and nocturnal at weekends. Flats and maisonettes were more likely to be burgled than houses, end terrace houses more likely than mid-terrace houses.

BCS confirms the views of most other crime surveys that, contrary to the stereotype, young males are most likely, and old females least likely, to be victimised. The survey also found that heavy drinkers were more likely to be victimised than others; that people who reported themselves as having committed an offence were seven times as likely to report a victimisation as those who had not; and people who reported themselves as having been involved in a non-crime-related accident were twice as likely to have been victimised as those who did not:

> The data strongly suggest that lifestyles conducive to victimization (of all forms) are also conducive to offending.
>
> (Gottfredson 1984: 17)

This may seem surprising, but if we pursue the idea of high risk situations and the necessity of a confluence of offender, victim and opportunity, it is not surprising that people are sometimes victimised by people pretty much like them. The Policy Studies Institute report into policing in London similarly found that victims were often stopped by the police:

> It is people who are repeatedly stopped who are most likely to be also victims. For example, among people who have been stopped by the police twice or more in the past year, 59 per cent have also been victims of some offence . . . whereas among people who have not come to police notice for any offence or suspected offence only 18 per cent have been victims.
>
> (Smith 1983: 314)

This is not, of course, to call victims 'undeserving' but to stress that for criminal justice professionals the data provide useful policy and practice guidelines in the spheres of crime prevention and fear of crime. This is an issue to which we return in Chapters 3 and 5. No sensible interpretation of these findings could imply that culpability should attach to the average victim; such a view would have to derive from the proposition that it was irresponsible to go for a drink with friends, to travel on buses or to go to a football match. At the same time, it is helpful to be reminded that offenders and victims are often the same people; that probation officers, in working with offenders, and in particular prisoners, are *ipso facto* working also with victims, and that some victims hold part of the key to crime prevention in their own hands. It is proper, therefore, for probation officers to explore with their charges sensible ways of examining their attendance at high risk locations, their behaviour when there, and their involvement in high risk activities out of which they may emerge almost interchangeably as victims or offenders. This is especially important for the supervisor of offenders in the light of Gottfredson's argument that similar social processes throw up accidents, offences and victimisations. In particular, Gottfredson notes the existence of *multiple victims* who are regularly but inexplicably prone to different kinds of victimisation in different circumstances. It would be remarkable if the caseloads of many probation officers did not include a number of people in this category, and to discuss what might be done about them is presumably professionally desirable.

People are variably able to minimise vulnerability, and the likelihood of most people becoming victims is so slight that the most practical advice is to take sensible precautions but not become obsessed with the problem. Fear of crime can be as debilitating as crime itself and more destructive of the social life of the elderly in particular, though often with little cause. Though elderly people's cautious lifestyle may contribute to their low victimisation rate, it is almost certainly not the whole reason: even when lifestyle is allowed for, the elderly still are less liable to be victimised (Clarke, Ekblom, Hough and Mayhew 1985). Yet lifestyle is certainly significant. For example, the relationship between going out at night and being victimised is so strong that though men are significantly more likely to become victims than women, this ceases to apply when victimisation rates of women who regularly go out both weekend nights are compared with those for men who go out on neither. In this case, the women are more likely to be victimised than the men. Since, however, most women who go out at night are not victimised, this is not to suggest that they should stay at home.

## Local crime surveys

Historically the survey, social reform and ethnographic traditions of criminology have been fused in a number of ways. Between the wars, the Chicago School (see, for example, Shaw and Mackay 1942) used a range of what have been described, not entirely unfairly, as journalistic techniques (Taylor, Walton and Young 1973: 110) to portray a social ecology of a turbulent city in transition, an approach which combines demography, geography and a case study approach which could hardly contain more 'human interest' (see in particular Shaw 1930; for a review of the contribution to criminology of the ecological approach, see Baldwin 1979).

Though it is possible that neither set of researchers would appreciate the comparison, part of the Chicago traditions of local ethnography, survey and social reform has resurfaced in crime surveys in Merseyside (Kinsey, Lea and Young 1986) and Islington (Jones, Maclean and

Young 1986). Whereas an obvious strength of the national survey is its broad overview of crime, a local survey can better explore the experience of living in a particular place at a particular time and can uncover dimensions of victimisation concealed in BCS. For example, the Islington researchers have argued that the racial dimensions of crime are inevitably underplayed by the impossibility of a national survey reflecting the demography of a multi-racial Britain which, though it contains proportionately very few blacks and Asians, nevertheless has high density clusters of ethnic minorities in particular localities. Local surveys have also suggested that crime against women is often concealed from national studies, whose methodology is insufficiently sensitive to extract painful or embarrassing information.

The local surveys have provoked both interest and controversy. Part of the controversy is essentially the private business of the analysing classes: the surveys represented the embrace of empirical methodology by traditionally radical criminologists who, almost but not quite for the first time (see, for example, Taylor 1981) challenged 'the left', in all its fragmented and demoralised reality, to take crime seriously. For theoreticians of the left to challenge the assumption that the objective concerns of the proletariat were with class warfare; to suggest that the manifest concern with street crime was a product not of false consciousness but of the daily experiences of working class people; and to point out that crime was no corrective measure against the property theft inherent in capitalism but an assault on the poor, the old and the black was a little indigestible for some of the class warriors of NW3. But the message was striking:

> 44 per cent of people interviewed in Merseyside had been victims of crime in the 12 months before our interview, and a quarter had been victims on two or more occasions . . . The poor not only suffer crime more often, but the impact on them is much more severe.
>
> (Kinsey, Lea and Young 1986: 4–5)

Part of the solution lay in the creation of trust between police and community. Mistrust of the police was reflected in negative behaviour towards them; this was reciprocated and the result was conflict policing strategies. This in turn led to a breakdown of the normal channels of information on which the police must depend if they are to be effective. Accordingly the re-establishment of confidence between police and community, for long a flagship policy of the centre parties and liberal professionals, was being advocated by researchers previously associated with the (fairly) hard left.

But behind this internecine warfare is the central message that the BCS argument that risks of crime are minimal ignores the reality of inner city life, where risks are ubiquitous and fear accordingly rational.

## Crime surveys: a critique

To the critique of the national by the local survey can be added a more fundamental reservation, that crime surveys generally have failed to develop the theoretical underpinnings necessary for their epistemology and methodology to develop (Johnson and Wasielewski 1982). Put like that, the criticism probably sounds rather arid and abstruse, but in fact it is not, and as will become apparent, behind the comment lie concerns which resonate with those of the Islington and Merseyside researchers.

Johnson and Wasielewski's position is that by focusing on inter-personal crimes, the crime survey contributes to an essentially ideological analysis which equates interpersonal crime with crime generally. As the work of Edwin Sutherland, already cited, makes plain, this is a serious distortion of reality (Sutherland 1941, 1949; see also Braithwaite 1989) which has the practical effect of implying that 'crime' is the province of working class predators, and ignoring the workplace crimes of executives or financiers or the crimes (whether pollutant, conspiratorial or health and safety) of large corporations. How might the crime survey acknowledge and address this partiality? To Johnson and Wasielewski, the next stage of theoretical development is to situate interpersonal crime in a context which embraces such offences as these:

> the public does react negatively to such actions as fraudulent advertising and sales practices, negligence in the safety of housing construction and maintenance, negligence in the safety of the work-place, and the sales of known dangerous products.
>
> (Johnson and Wasielewski 1982: 209–10)

Johnson and Wasielewski develop the concept *perceptual victimisation* which combines the normally distinct areas of victimisation and fear of crime; it also refines the notion of 'fear'. In conventional studies, 'fear' embraces both a specific and rational worry (associated, for example, with some high risk activity like walking alone at night along a 'bad' street) and a more generalised but irrational belief in the vulnerability of self and others to whom one has an attachment. Only the first of these is properly 'fear'. The latter they term 'concern', arguing after Furstenberg (1971) that crime concern has been inadequately addressed empirically and is undertheorised. 'Concern' in this formulation is a negative emotion applied without good reason in a manner conceptually distinct from the rational fear of the people of Merseyside. To conflate rational fear with irrational concern has a conservative ideological base and comes to justify more law and order, excessive political emphasis on the crimes of the poor, and insufficient attention to those of the rich and powerful:

> concern would appear to be an artificially 'created' anxiety. That is, it does not appear to be grounded in the actors' experiential world. It is a consequence of adopting meanings and interpretations of crime provided primarily by the state through the mass media which reflects the conservative definition of law and order.
>
> (Johnson and Wasielewski 1982: 212)

Fear is rational and adaptive, concern is negative. It is concern which leads parents to keep children away from the threat of 'dirty old men' and in the very environment, the home, where, ironically, they are statistically most at risk. It is concern that fuels racial discord, which unnecessarily lowers individuals' quality of life and which encourages the exponential growth of private security as people arm themselves (in the United States, literally) against crimes which are unlikely to happen. This, in Johnson and Wasielewski's analysis, is the underside of the crime survey. By generating concern among the citizens of Shrewsbury, Salisbury and Sanderstead it focuses popular attention on one very visible part of the 'crime problem', creating a situation in which these inhabitants of low crime areas believe themselves to be as much at risk of mugging, looting or rape as their counterparts in Liverpool, Lambeth and Lewisham.

## CONCLUSION

We have moved from the official statistics to a range of other-than-official ones. As we have done so, you have been exposed to a range of conflicting arguments, each one of which must have seemed to cut away the ground on which you were walking. Is nothing secure, nothing certain?

Some things, I think, are clear. The official statistics of crime tell us many things – about the agencies that collect them and about the criminal justice system which processes the people who commit the crimes – but rather less about crime itself. It is probably better to regard the official figures as an annual report on what the law enforcement agencies have been doing than as a state of the nation report on how delinquent we or our neighbours are.

The unofficial story of crime is told by the methods I have described in this chapter. It is a remarkable story, but still understates the amount of crime committed, and, if the local crime surveys are to be believed, it does so in a systematically, if unintentionally, biased way. By comparing the official and the unofficial crime rates we can learn much, not only about crime but about how it is recorded and what relation the official figures have to the closer approximations provided by the unofficial ones. The BCS has been of immense value in helping us understand more about the so-called 'dark figure' of crime, the subaquatic bulk of the iceberg, and the story it tells is in some ways reassuring: the deterioration in the crime figures is indeed partly artefactual; public attitudes towards criminals are not simplistically punitive, and reflect the view that reparation and restitution are appropriate ways forward.

But BCS may have its own distortions, and I introduced three distinct glosses on crime surveys to demonstrate what they may be. Firstly, there is the problem, which has surfaced as a major issue since BCS was designed, of intrafamilial physical and sexual violence. The methodology of the household survey is predicated on a notion of familiality which is transgressed by crimes of this nature; indeed crimes against children are actually excluded from its remit. Secondly, the local surveys remind us again of the problem of the misleading mean and that there are areas in which lawlessness is a regular experience. Locally based ethnographic approaches are necessary to identify the social problems of these areas, and in the next two chapters I shall begin to outline a possible role for criminal justice professionals in just this type of research. Thirdly, there is the more fundamental critique of Johnson and Wasielewski. While you may well feel it to have been a little overstated, it is not necessarily to be dismissed. Though it is hard to sustain the view that crime surveys are responsible for the conservatism in crime control which they identify or that they foster 'concern' (it is more likely that the reverse is the case) the omission from household surveys of non-household crimes is as striking, though inevitable, as the omission of intra-household crimes.

Much that has been covered thus far is essential background knowledge about the system for the criminal justice student or professional. From time to time I have made a specific allusion to the probation service, to make some specific point about how this knowledge might be directly useful. If, though, you are using this as a course textbook it would be sensible for you now to spend some time addressing certain questions. What, in the light of what you have read, are the main uses of the official figures? To what extent are the limitations of the official statistics corrected by self-report studies and crime surveys? What are the advantages and disadvantages of local, as opposed to national, crime surveys? What is your view of the Johnson and Wasielewski critique of the surveys?

All good examination questions, no doubt, but ones too of professional importance. Perhaps as we proceed their relevance will become even clearer.

# Chapter 3

# Fear, victims and community

'It's all right if you haven't been to Prison,' said the plump woman. 'It isn't what a man's happened to do makes 'im bad. We all happen to do things at times. It's bringing it home to him and spoiling his self-respect does the mischief. You don't *look* a wrong 'un. 'Ave you been to prison?'

(H.G. Wells: *The History of Mr Polly*)

I care not (in this place) what your principles are. Your principles may induce you to believe in the righteousness of burglary. I don't mind. All I urge is that a life in which conduct does not fairly well accord with principles is a silly life . . . What leads to the permanent sorrowfulness of burglars is that their principles are contrary to burglary. If they genuinely believed in the moral excellence of burglary, penal servitude would simply mean so many happy years for them; all martyrs are happy, because their conduct and their principles agree.

(Arnold Bennett: *How to Live on Twenty-Four Hours a Day*)

The criminal justice system has tended to operate in a fragmented way, with a relatively clear division of labour among the different agencies: sentencers sentence, prison officers turn keys, police catch thieves and keep the peace, victim groups look after their own and the probation service deals with the welfare and conduct of the offender. It seems neither likely nor desirable that this exclusivity will continue. Whatever other differences exist between them on criminal justice, it is the intention of both Government and Opposition that the system shall become more sensitive to the range of needs which exist within local communities, more involved in those communities and increasingly flexible and integrated (Home Office 1990a,c; Labour Party 1990). It is no longer sensible, therefore, to write a book exclusively 'for' probation officers. The trend towards interdependence means that jobs once performed exclusively by probation officers may increasingly become the tasks of others too, while conversely the probation service itself may increasingly become involved with community crime prevention schemes, victim support and the administration of punishment.

These possibilities should not, of course, be overstated, for the chaos of interchangeability would be in nobody's interests. But criminal justice is now too important and complex to be left to a range of agencies with different specialised tasks but few formal channels of communication. Firstly, therefore, while the probation service's predominant association with offenders makes it a less than obvious agency to provide a range of direct counselling for victims, we have seen already that the notion that victims and offenders live in opposing camps is false: many offenders are victims too. Secondly, the Home Office's expectation that the probation service will involve itself more with 'the community' has an immediate reintegrative implication, for the notion of reintegration (whether or not it follows some idea such as 'shaming') (Braithwaite 1989) implies an involvement with a potentially rejecting community as well as with an individual offender. And victims, as I have already stressed, are not always the individual recipients of interpersonal predatory crime, but may be members of chambers of trade, industrial concerns and other corporate victims in whose interests it is to take steps to reduce crime in the community. Thirdly, there are people with whom probation officers are already involved, such as the families of imprisoned criminals (Matthews 1983; Shaw 1987; Light 1989) whom we might term 'indirect' victims of crime (Conklin 1975), their lives having been adversely affected by it. Fourthly, to foreshadow a later argument, any involvement that probation officers may have with victims need not involve direct counselling: one is not insensitive to the problem of victims and offenders sharing a waiting room. It is no longer possible, however, to regard probation officers as providing only 'direct' services. They will also take on new duties in 'indirect service delivery' — developing and managing services provided by a sub-professional worker or volunteer. Using its new grant aiding powers, the probation service may well become involved in planning, coordinating and managing victim services, which are still driven in part by local interest as much as by need. Officers' training would in fact equip them well to take this task on. And fifthly, the clear indication from BCS that there is a popular preference for non-custodial punishments which involve reparation suggests that developments of such provisions cannot ignore the victim interest.

This chapter and the next will introduce some key notions with which the probation officer of the future may, therefore, have to engage. In this chapter I shall look at fear of crime and victims of crime. This will not only continue the discussion of the last chapter but lead us into the next chapter's discussion of crime prevention. There is an obvious theoretical logic in combining the discussion of fear with the discussion of the experience of those who actually experience crime. There is also, however, a professional logic in that systematic involvement in both areas involves similar forms of knowledge and skill – about crime patterns and risk, self-protection, resources available from other agencies and so on. Any ideological reservations which probation officers may once have had about involvement in these areas (for a flavour of such reservations see Walker and Beaumont 1981: 182 and *passim*) have presumably by now been dissolved by the results of the Islington and Merseyside crime surveys reported in the last chapter (Jones, Maclean and Young 1986; Kinsey, Lea and Young 1986). Probation officers' 'clients' after all are not just criminals; many of them come from the section of the community most likely to be victimised and, because of their social and economic marginality, most likely to suffer considerably if they are. I hope in this chapter to proceed beyond the crude notion that there is an inverse ratio between fear of crime and risk of crime and invite you to consider sensitively 'fear' as a multidimensional construct.

I also want to invite you to consider some quite difficult questions about victims. I will trail the key question now, but it will surface again later in the chapter. It has to do with victim participation in the criminal act. There are two popular but contradictory themes in 'popular' literature about victims. One is that self-protection is appropriate and necessary, the other that the victim of interpersonal, including domestic, crime is helpless and under no circumstances to be deemed 'responsible' for her own victimisation. The question is whether and if so how these perspectives are to be reconciled, whether one is right and the other wrong, or whether this is simply the wrong question to ask. Studies of victims have moved from the simple idea that victims precipitate crimes to the equally simple one that (especially when they are women) they are the passive recipients of male violence, their resistance broken by years of subordination. Is there a middle way between the extremes? For any professional dealing with, or sensitive to, the problems of crime victims, this is possibly the central question to address.

## FEAR OF CRIME

A man who travels a lot was concerned about the possibility of a bomb on board his plane. He determined the probability of this, found it to be low but not low enough for him, so now he always travels with a bomb in his suitcase. He reasons that the probability of two bombs being on board would be infinitesimal.

(Paulos 1989: 25)

You will remember that I introduced the 'fear of crime' issue in the last chapter, but only in passing and because it was impossible to disentangle it from our discussion about the problems of crime surveys. The authors I was citing made a conceptual distinction between 'fear' and 'concern' (Johnson and Wasielewski 1982): fear was a rational response to a personal assessment of risk (and the Islington and Merseyside surveys showed just how real that risk was), but concern was irrational, and promoted repressive measures against criminals and diminished the quality of life generally. We must now blur this distinction, however, or we shall be in linguistic difficulty when we pursue literature which does not acknowledge it. For the time being, therefore, 'fear' will normally embrace both 'fear' and 'concern' in the Johnson and Wasielewski formulation.

The concept 'fear of crime' is not so simple as it might appear, as our discussion thus far will have made plain. One study, for example, rightly observes that some of the questions designed to test fear of crime (which is not a piece of behaviour but an attitude or affect) do so by measuring behaviour and assuming it results from fear. The problem is of two kinds. Supposing, for example, 'staying in regularly at night' is taken as a behavioural concomitant of the affect fear. If it is a product of fear, the fear may be of several kinds: one might feel unsafe going out alone at night because of vague and free-floating anxiety, because of a belief (which may or may not be correct) that street crime is prevalent in the area to be visited or because of a belief that *should* one be attacked, however unlikely such an attack might be, the consequences would be so great as to outweigh the pleasure of going out in the first place (Mawby and Gill 1987: 13). On the other hand, there may be no association between staying in and fear of crime: one might choose not to go out for a host of other reasons which have nothing to do with crime, but which might appear shameful to the individual – a lack of money, a lack of friends to go out with, a lack of interests, a parental injunction to stay at home, a preference for watching television or shyness for example. But in such a situation one might use 'fear of crime' as a socially acceptable excuse for staying at home (Mawby and Gill 1987: 17). Researching a 'feeling' is very difficult, especially when that 'feeling' is really a catch-all notion for a range of different emotions, attitudes and beliefs.

A key question is whether fear of crime stands independently of crime itself as a social problem. This is an important issue for the criminal justice professional, for policy and practice implications follow. The belief that 'fear' is indeed a free-standing social problem has led to calls for 'symbolic reassurance' to be provided (Henig and Maxfield 1978) – such as increasing police visibility, better street lighting and better community interaction, for example through a Neighbourhood Watch Scheme.

The belief that fear of crime is independent of crime itself results from the assumption that fear is based on incorrect beliefs about risk. This assumption has its roots both in the argument that we tend to view 'the past' as a golden age and 'the present' as a period of rapid and irreversible moral and behavioural decline (Pearson 1983) and in the professionally widely accepted paradox that people who are statistically most likely to be victimised (young male working class urban dwellers) are least fearful, and those least likely to be victimised (elderly people, especially women) are most fearful. The view has led to calls for more information to be given on actual risks, and for the old and isolated to be advised to make new friendships or join mutual support groups. It has also caused some writers to suggest that the impact of elderly people's irrational fear of crime has led to undesirable and unjust social policy emphases:

> If the plight of elderly crime victims becomes even more visible nationally, more resources will be devoted to them at the cost of the poor, young, black males, who are in fact the most likely victims (and perpetrators) of crime.
>
> (Cook and Cook 1976: 644)

Certainly there are some serious errors in public knowledge about crime, and it must be proper for the professionals to be aware of all there is to know about local (as well as national) crime figures in order to provide authoritative information about them to individuals, groups and the media. It is presumably the job of agency research and information personnel to collect and disseminate this information to their colleagues. Increasingly, however, the view is emerging among criminologists that it is not quite as simple as that.

A number of factors contribute to this opinion. One has already been mentioned: that the local crime surveys claim that by aggregating and averaging national data, national surveys such as NCS and BCS fail to acknowledge the reality and address the implications of different crime rates in different localities. This leads to the systematic under-estimation of the impact of crime in inner city areas. Within this general underestimation is the particular inflexion that the experiences of women and ethnic minorities may be especially misunderstood. The negative domestic or sexual experiences of women may be especially impervious to survey methods, and the victimisation of ethnic minorities may appear more marginal than it is as a result of their heavy representation in relatively few localities (Hanmer and Saunders 1984; Kinsey, Lea and Young 1986). This could mean that women's fear of crime, which is higher than that of men, (41 per cent of women under 30, for example, claiming to be 'very worried' about rape), (Hough and Mayhew 1985: 35) is less out of kilter with the risk of victimisation than might superficially appear to be the case. Added to this is women's greater *vulnerability* to crime: they are likely to be physically weaker than men, more fearful of violence generally, and liable to be victimised in ways which would be very unusual in the case of men, who are seldom, so far as we know, subjected to sexual assaults, at least outside of institutions.

Vulnerability applies with at least equal force to elderly people, whose fear of crime seems out of all proportion to their risk of victimi-sation. Even if, as is probable, those criminologists who have suggested that the elderly are as liable to victimisation as others when they are out of their house are wrong (Yin 1980; Lindquist and Duke 1982; Stafford and Galle 1984), the potentially lethal consequences of violence for many old people are obvious. *Physically* they are less able to withstand assault, *socially* many are isolated or have peers whose own frailty is such that they cannot offer intensive support, and *economically* many are relatively badly off, and literally cannot afford the expense of being victimised. Many elderly people are objectively vulnerable, therefore, in a manner which makes fear a rational response. Indeed one writer has asked why we should assume that to reduce this fear is a proper policy objective. Might not success in doing so lead to undesirably risky behaviour on the part of vulnerable people? (Bennett 1990).

Even the assumption that most people overestimate the extent of crime has been called into question. For example, in a study in Tucson, Arizona, public beliefs about the prevalence of particular juvenile offences tallied almost exactly with the results of a self-report study administered in three high schools in the same city (Warr 1982). In spite of this finding, however, the weight of evidence is with the 'exaggeration theorists', at least in those parts of the United Kingdom where the local crime rate does not reach inner city levels. Certainly the second BCS sweep found that the risks of a number of offences, including 'mugging' (or robbery) and burglary were exaggerated, particularly in low delinquency areas. The reasons for this exaggeration are difficult to determine and may be indeterminable. International comparisons suggest that fear of crime is not universal and is greater in the UK than in many other countries. For example, fear of crime is lower in Australia (Braithwaite, Biles and Whitrod 1982) and the (then) Federal Republic of Germany (Van Dijk, Mayhew and Killias 1990) than in the UK or USA. In the United States, fear of crime remains high in spite of the fact that the crime rate there is now apparently falling, a fall only partially explained by the ageing population (Steffensmeier and Harer 1987).

The first BCS sweep also gives qualified support to the exaggeration theorists (Maxfield 1984). Women were more fearful than men but less likely to be victimised, and fear of all offences except sexual assault increased with age as risk reduced. But on the other hand vulnerability had an independent effect on fear, as did living in a high crime area and having been victimised oneself or having witnessed a crime. Respondents were asked how they behaved as a result of their fears, and it was found that on the whole people exercised sensible caution – contracting car aerials, bringing pot plants into the house at night, leaving a light on when they went out. But while only for a minority did taking precautions against crime seriously affect their lifestyle, predominant among that minority were women and elderly people, especially the inner city poor.

This in turn is consistent with yet another theory, this time of 'compounding', advanced by the left realist criminologists who argue that crime *compounds* other problems to contribute to what would once have been termed a 'cycle of disadvantage':

> The poor suffer from poverty above all – but also from bad housing, unemployment, pollution, nuisance, *and* crime. So crime is experienced more by people who are already suffering the impact of other forms of crime.

> (Kinsey, Lea and Young 1986: 70)

Fear of crime is, therefore, a real problem. Whether it is a problem independent of crime itself is controversial. Whether fear of crime represents healthy caution or unnecessary debilitation is not agreed.

Analytically, like crime itself fear is not a unitary phenomenon, and an all-embracing explanation is therefore impossible. There is, however, sufficient evidence of its complexity to discourage any simplified notion that it is intrinsically irrational. The fact that some people misunderstand the risk of crime does not justify us slipping into the easy assumption that *therefore* crime is not a problem.

Having said that, it is important not to go to the other extreme. The United Kingdom's crime problem is below the international average for the five year period up to 1988, and of our fellow EC countries the UK is safer than The Netherlands, France, Spain, the former West Germany and Belgium (Van Dijk, Mayhew and Killias 1990).[1] For all we know, crime surveys may themselves lead people to exaggerate their fears. It may seem to be tempting fate to tell a crime researcher you are not fearful of crime and that it does not cause you to stay at home sometimes, but the surveys do not tell us what people actually do, as opposed to what they say they do. A crime survey inevitably concentrates the minds of its respondents on crime, risk and vulnerability, but we do not know how frequently and in what circumstances the possibility of victimisation enters people's minds when they are not taking part in a crime survey. Nevertheless, in acknowledging fear of crime as a problem, in 1989 the Government commissioned an independent working group of lawyers, criminal justice professionals and media people to consider how to deal with this issue. The resultant report deals with the relationship between crime prevention and fear of crime thus:

> Crime prevention is being promoted at the cost of pushing up fear. For instance, both government publicity campaigns and commercial advertising for insurance or crime prevention devices can sometimes have a frightening effect. We strongly support action to prevent crime. But we insist that this will only be effective if, at the same time, more emphasis is placed on reducing fear.
>
> (Home Office Standing Conference on Crime Prevention 1989)

Of course, squaring this circle is not straightforward, and the dilemma that faced the Standing Conference also faces the criminal justice professionals to whom members of the public might reasonably turn for sound and expert advice. How might these professionals deal with the problem? It would clearly be wrong for probation officers, for example, to claim that fear of crime among those they meet is unnecessary. Firstly, it cannot be assumed that those who are given this information will make a proper distinction between fear and the exercise of proper caution; and secondly one cannot legitimately move from probability to an individual case: even in the unlikely event of only one rape really having taken place in the 11,000 households interviewed in BCS, one cannot be sure that it did not affect the household one is visiting, or that it will not do so in the future.

The relationship between crime prevention and fear of crime is contentious. One argument postulates a double bind effect: if one lives in a safe neighbourhood then one is not motivated to prevent crime, but if one does not then one is fearful of crime and the effect of fear can itself be debilitating. Another argument claims, conversely, that participation in community-based crime prevention activities reduces fear of crime for reasons which, though not entirely clear, presumably relate both to the expressive consequences of group cohesion and the confidence which derives from reconceptualising crime as something which can be tackled effectively (Kelling 1986). A third argument, however, is that community involvement in crime prevention increases fear of crime by focusing excessively on it, and also perpetuates stereotypes about criminals, closes neighbourhoods off from outside influences, legitimises racism and leads to the creation of de facto private vigilante squads (for discussions of these views see Abel 1982; Weiss 1987). And as we have just seen, a fourth argument, associated with the Standing Conference on Crime Prevention, stems from an examination of the relationship between crime prevention advertisements and fear of crime, suggesting that some advertisements, including those for private security devices, irresponsibly increase fear of crime in order to enhance motivation for crime prevention (Home Office Standing Conference on Crime Prevention 1989).

Probation officers can, however, ensure they know the local crime statistics and are able to give expert advice on what they mean. They can be sensitive to the fears of people they meet and develop skills to respond to those fears, the expression of which will frequently be accompanied by observations uncomplimentary to the probation service's criminal 'clientele'. They can ensure that they know which parts of the area are least safe, what local crime trends are currently developing, involve themselves more with victim support and neighbourhood watch schemes, develop skills in involvement in local crime prevention initiatives, liaise more closely with local police crime prevention officers, check that they are fully aware of victims' rights to compensation and restitution, and ensure that at least some of the programmes for supervision in the community which they develop contain a restitutive element.

Some probation officers sometimes do some of these things. The balance among them is a matter for local committees and management and is obviously resource dependent. Issues such as this are beyond my remit though it is worth stressing that the tasks I am outlining, though worthwhile, are not especially cheap. Some of them are, of course, simply attributes of current good practice, for how can a probation officer talk of reintegrating an offender into the community without working on significant and relevant members of that community as well as on the offender him or herself? Others, such as the development of information systems, are logical uses of the research and information officers now employed by many probation services. Others again are new, and presuppose funding being available for the extended role for the service which Government has in mind for it. The skills which probation officers on our best training courses are now acquiring are precisely those necessary for engaging with communities: developing case management skills, liaising with other agencies and volunteers, dealing with media interviews and working with people in crisis. And high on the list of people in crisis must be victims.

## THE VICTIM: THEORY, POLICY, NEEDS AND RIGHTS

It is not chance that the renewal of academic and professional interest in the victim has developed alongside the crime survey. The lack of interest in victims throughout the radical years of the 1960s and 1970s was, with hindsight, remarkable: if you disbelieve me, count how many references to victims you can find in the indices of British criminology texts published before 1980. There are no references at all in *The New Criminology*, one in *Critical Criminology* (Taylor, Walton and Young 1975) (a dismissive allusion to victim surveys), and even in Carol Smart's feminist study *Women, Crime and Criminology* there are only a couple of references, both debunking the theory of victim precipitation (Smart 1976).

Though Smart's neglect of victims is surprising, the women's movement having subsequently done much to sensitise theoreticians, policymakers and practitioners to the needs of female victims, that of the new criminologists is comprehensible. After all, concern for victims sat uneasily with the internally contradictory images of the criminal which the sociologists of deviance were propounding. To focus on crimes without victims (Schur 1965) was theoretically neater if one wished to construct a theory of law and policing as instruments of class oppression; alternatively it took but a modest sleight of hand to portray the criminals themselves as victims, striking out, sometimes in an inchoate manner, at the oppressive class system. Thus Jock Young, in pre-Islington mode:

Crime and deviancy from a socialist perspective are terms which encompass an uneven array of activities and behaviours – at times, behaviours which are quite inimical to socialism; at other times, rebellions against property and repression which are as justifiable in their consequences as they are primitive in this conception . . . But just as one must discriminate actively between crimes which are cultural adaptations of the people, and crimes which derive from the brutalization of criminal and community alike, so we must clearly distinguish the contradictory nature of many of these adaptive manifestations.

(Young 1975: 90–1)

## The victim: theoretical approaches

Historically, at least until the 1970s, interest in victims, where it existed at all, focused primarily on the 'kind of person' who became a victim or, more subtly, on the nature of the interaction between victim and criminal. Many papers from the 1940s onwards were reprinted in a collection published in connection with the first International Symposium on Victimology, held in Jerusalem in 1973 (Drapkin and Viano 1974a) and augmented by contemporary papers, including those presented at the conference itself (Drapkin and Viano 1974b,c, 1975a,b,c).

Much of the early literature was analytically crude, and is now of mainly historical interest (for a review see Heidensohn 1989: 160–1; for a feminist critique see Walklate 1989). Important ideas emerged embryonically in the early years but, trapped within an overdetermined clinical framework, were unable to be developed as part of a coherent social analysis. Mendelsohn, for example, has a potentially interesting concept in viewing offender and victim as a 'penal-couple' (Mendelsohn 1963) but can support it only by means of a simplified and moralistic six-part victim typology from 'completely innocent' victim to 'simulating victim'. In a paper first published in 1941, von Hentig, another founding father of victimology, speaking of the 'incredible depravity of many half-grown-up girls' (von Hentig 1974: 49) asks:

Are we permitted to say that in some cases criminality is a self-consuming process of antisocial elements in which criminals prey on criminaloids, killers on suicides or other killers, oversexed on oversexed, dishonest individuals on dishonest? . . . By separating in time the fatally 'harmonizing' parties, the formation of an explosive social compound can be averted. Remaining would be a potential perpetrator without a victim and a potential victim without a partner to whom he or she could turn to be victimized.

(von Hentig 1974: 51)

Clearly if victimology were to become a scientifically defensible discipline it would need a theoretical framework which transcended moralistic impressions based on clinical observation: though doubtless human pathology, like human deviance, is with us everywhere, the bad or mad behaviour of individual victims cannot be an adequate basis for a theory of victimisation. Yet nor are the issues which concern the victimologists to be easily ignored. We know empirically that crime is not randomly distributed; that violent crime is predominantly committed on people known to the criminal; that structural explanations of crime (as a characteristic, say, of the actions of men against women) are insufficiently sensitive to explain why it does or does not occur in specific instances; that it is possible for actual or potential victims to take steps to reduce the likelihood of victimisation; that criminals are proportionately more likely also to be victims than are non-offenders; and that there is an identifiable category of 'multiple victims' prone not only to criminal victimisation but also to other misfortunes such as accidents and injuries (Hough and Mayhew 1985).

Of course to say this is to skate on thin ice. Other writers, making a similar point, are quick to emphasise that their intention should not, in another phrase from criminology's days of radical liberation (Ryan 1972), be read as 'blaming the victim' (see, for example, the elegant footwork of Mawby and Gill 1987: 11–12). But 'blame' is a misnomer here. We cannot assume that in their social interactions everybody will be sensible all the time, and it is the responsibility of the state to provide a degree of protection for people who place themselves, or are placed by others, in positions of some risk. But the police cannot be everywhere, and ultimately effective self-protection must be necessary. But who is to give this advice? The police themselves have a large part to play, and are increasingly playing it. But it cannot be left to them alone: a range of criminal justice professionals need to provide information and advice on crime prevention and risk avoidance. Whether the victim argues with a drunken man, hitches lifts unwisely, leaves open a ground floor window of an empty house or fails to padlock a bicycle is in this sense irrelevant. Interpersonal crime involves an encounter between a potential offender and a potential victim in a situation where opportunity or temptation outweighs fear or expectation of capture. The victim plays a part in this, and sometimes though not invariably that part can be changed. In particular, people who are especially vulnerable need to be aware of their vulnerability and equipped with the most effective means available of preventing vulnerability becoming victimisation. Such means will include not only personal protective devices but information sensitively and expertly provided by professionals as to the possible consequences of their own behaviour. (I return to this issue in relation to female victims in Chapter 5.)

Victim pathology gives an inadequate and misleading picture of crime victimisation, therefore, but to reject clinical descriptions of individual victims as a proper basis for an explanatory theory is not to fall into the opposite trap of regarding victims as passive and helpless. Any sensible theory of interpersonal victimisation, however, requires integration with those structural approaches to victimisation which are now theoretically and empirically best developed. Feminist criminologists, crime surveyors (local and national), criminal statisticians and the second wave of radical criminologists have presented a clear picture of the very young and the very old, women, the black, the poor, and marginal people as disproportionately likely to be victimised and disproportionately vulnerable to the consequences if they are. This, however, is not a theory of victimisation but of social vulnerability: people who are vulnerable are predisposed to victimisation but not necessarily victimised. How is victimisation actually precipitated? There are factors which contribute to translating vulnerability into victimisation (Hindelang, Gottfredson and Garofalo 1978), and it is in this policy and practice-related area that the study of victims can best help us understand criminal actions and interactions. This is not, perhaps, best done by creating a separate discipline of victimology, for any decent theory of crime must include the victim in an equation which also includes offender, opportunity and those predisposing and precipitating factors which combine to turn a human interaction into a criminal one.

All this is too important to be left to the academics: knowledge about victims and risk is necessary for the professionals too. This is not to say that professionals should advise people not to take risks — one might as well forbid the sun to rise or the grass to grow. They should, however, be able to give reliable information and advice. This is partly a matter of 'knowing one's patch' — where the trouble spots are, who the troublemakers are; partly a matter of *broader theoretical knowledge* – the effects of group process, of alcohol; partly the *teaching of crime-inhibiting interpersonal behaviour* – reducing opportunity by the way personal valuables are held, establishing eye contact with potential aggressors, taking elementary safety precautions such as carrying anti-crime devices, ensuring that someone knows where you are; partly a matter of *intervention in relation to criminogenic environmental characteristics* – schools with high truancy levels, shops which sell solvents to children, lack of leisure facilities; and partly a matter of *analysing and discussing potential victims' leisure relationships*, which may well be akin to the relationships of offenders. To probation officers it cannot be said too often that the offenders they are supervising are frequently victims too.

But in addition to the offender and the victim, in street crime in particular there is often also a *bystander* (Sheleff 1974). If probation officers of the future are to take local crime seriously, they will need to address the proper role of the bystander. Do you know what legal obligations affect bystanders? Do they have to intervene? What if they injure the offender? Or are injured themselves? Do they qualify for compensation? Do they have obligations to report an offence? Or to be truthful if asked about it by the police? How do you discuss citizenship duties with bystanders? How do such duties balance with personal safety? Are there non-combative strategies of tension reduction which could be discussed with probationers? For if probationers are sometimes offenders and sometimes victims, you can be sure that they are also sometimes bystanders.

One of the few things which research does make clear about bystanders is that they frequently claim to misinterpret a crime which they are witnessing. Though there is an obvious likelihood of deception (including self-deception) in some cases, this is unlikely to be invariably the reason why bystanders seemingly so callously ignore distant screams or mind their own business when they witness street crimes. People do not want to look foolish. Yet if crime is to be checked there is a need for greater willingness to act decisively on such occasions. This need not involve 'weighing in' but a range of strategies such as conferring quickly with other bystanders, making a noise, summoning help, supporting the victim. Once it becomes clear that 'clients' are citizens as well as offenders, it becomes appropriate for the professionals, for all they may be told about 'focusing on the offence', to focus on good citizenship too: and good citizenship may be as much a matter of accurate interpretation of a situation and decisive action as of grand ideals and legal philosophy (Sheleff 1974: 118).

## The victim and criminal justice

For some time it seemed that almost any book about victims began with a value statement that the victim had been wrongly ignored by the criminal justice systems of the western world; and a brief historical anecdote which would typically begin with Old Testament, Babylonian, Saxon or Roman law and show how the 'fine' paid to the state superseded not only the blood feud of Icelandic saga but also the 'compensation' paid to the direct victim, how this had had negative consequences for victims generally, and how we were slowly redressing the balance but still had a long way to go (see for example Schafer 1960; Jacob 1976; Harding 1982).

That more recent studies can largely take for granted the reader's concern for victims is indicative of a major attitudinal change. Victims are now a cause espoused by most; they have mobilised into effective local networks and pressure groups, in some cases having the weight of broader social movements such as those campaigning for women's, children's, black or gay rights behind them; their cause also attracts support from conservative interest groups; police forces have victim liaison officers; victims are less likely to be 'blamed' for being victims; trainee professionals are discouraged (perhaps with excessive zeal) from paying attention to the VP (victim precipitation) literature.

To accept that the state has obligations to victims is to make an important and controversial statement. Indeed it is testimony to the political power of the victim lobby that the 1980s should have seen such unquestioning support for this position when the emphasis in other areas of social life was on self-help and personal responsibility. In part, of course, the policy has involved extracting money from the offender to pay to the victim, but the exponential growth in criminal injuries compensation, the resources allocated to victim support by the police and local authorities and the requirement that where compensation and a fine are ordered from an offender the former shall be paid first are significant investments. It is true that critics of the system have argued that provisions are too little and of the wrong kind; equally, many who have come into contact with the Criminal Injuries Compensation Board have left neither impressed nor happy; and we also know that victim satisfaction with the criminal justice system is very variable (Shapland, Willmore and Duff 1985; Newburn and de Peyrecave 1988). But in principle the state has accepted an obligation to ensure public safety and a consequent duty to compensate and support those in respect of whom it has failed to meet that obligation. This is a far cry from the round table discussion of 1959, in which concern was expressed about:

> the abandonment of individual responsibility through the introduction of a system of state compensation, and the 'sociological decadence that could come from that kind of thinking might be far worse than the economic consequences'.
>
> (Schafer 1960: 112)

The stereotypical but false image of the passive, innocent, vulnerable and deserving victim is a powerful one in the popular mind. Though courts have the power to disqualify culpable victims from compensation, for example, they seldom do so, in part for practical reasons but in part because of the outcry that has tended to accompany judicial pronouncements about victim precipitation (Miers 1978). We do not know empirically what relationship exists between that stereotype and the equally misleading one of the criminal, and whether the positive image of the one is paid for by the negative image of the other. If so, it is a high price to pay, not least because it is constructed on such a self-evident mistake. It must be clear to any criminal justice professional that criminals have few friends at present: the rehabilitationists are in retreat, the victims', women's and children's movements are emphasising the rationality of crime, offenders are almost never included in equal opportunities policies, a wide range of offenders are being excluded from any remotely sensitive job as a result of the problem of child sexual abuse; and in the midst of all this the victim is to be regarded as pure and passive. The slightest attempt to contextualise a crime, to discuss victim precipitation, to analyse male–female interactions is to fall foul of a new taboo in criminology. As Michael Ignatieff presciently observed:

> the public's awakening to the extent of sexual crimes against women may result in an increasingly intolerant attitude towards rapists. This is a familiar paradox of toleration in a liberal society.
>
> (Ignatieff 1978: 218)

And, many years earlier, George Bernard Shaw remarked:

> we are all brought up to believe that we may inflict injuries on anyone against whom we can make out a case of moral inferiority.
>
> (Shaw 1946: 13)

Government and Opposition are currently competing to meet the needs and extend the rights of victims (Home Office 1990b; Labour Party 1990). In the case of the Government this is almost certainly a politically necessary component of the strategy to increase the use of non-custodial penalties; the Labour Party document uses different rhetoric but contains little to suggest any radical divergence from the Government's position. Victims are presently in the happy position of being the beneficiaries of bipartisan politics. The Government has already given substantial increased resources to Victim Support Schemes and to the Criminal Injuries Compensation Board, it has laid down new regulations to protect the anonymity of rape victims from the initial offence onwards (in the light of the disgraceful behaviour of sections of the Press following the rape of a clergyman's daughter), and under the Criminal Justice Act 1988 there is a presumption of compensation. Though the first flush of enthusiasm for 'victim-centred' criminal justice schemes appears to have waned, and in particular there is now a general rejection of the ill-thought-out suggestion that victims should have a role in sentencing, it must be assumed that for the foreseeable future the victim will constitute a significant political, and hence professional, consideration in the administration of criminal justice.

## Victims: needs and rights

In the more flexible, not to say erratic, American criminal jurisdictions, there exist a great number of restitution schemes, many enthusiastically reported by their managers but rather fewer independently evaluated. There are 'creative restitution', 'restitution in probation', 'restitution centers', penal restitution structured around 'self-determinate' sentences (the harder you work in prison to pay your victim back, the sooner you get out) (all cited in Hudson 1976); there are Project Earn-It in Massachusetts, the Restitution Alternative in Maine, the Mississippi Restitution Center, the Tri-County Restitution Program in Minnesota and the New Orleans Parish Criminal Sheriff's Adult Restitution Shelter (all cited in Harding 1982; see also Stanley and Baginsky 1984: Chapter 8; and Harding 1987). And it would be a simple task to track down many more such schemes in the American restitution industry. I shall not pursue them in this book, but for the criminal justice professional, just to read about the ideas can be invigorating. However limited the evaluation, however partial the accounts, if they can stimulate and provoke thoughts about alternative ways of dealing with offenders they can have some use.

The UK system, though not devoid of restitutive creativity, has expended much of it on juvenile work (Rutherford 1986; though for examples of work with adults too, see Pointing 1986). There are as yet few effectively documented accounts of reparative or restitutive strategies. There has been some slight interest in 'mediation', which draws again on the American experience (Marshall 1985, 1987) and on work in Norway (Christie 1977, 1981) and involves informally adjudicated conflict resolution between victim and offender, sometimes using trained personnel in 'natural' communities such as schools to help them resolve their own problems without recourse to the law. A variation on this theme is the bringing together of convicted offenders and victims of crime (not necessarily *their* victims) which seems to have been useful (Launay 1985; see also Wright 1982: Chapter 10) but has not been closely evaluated. There is probably scope for probation officers to explore the possibility of experimenting with such schemes in consultation with local victim groups as well as with police, schools and penal institutions. Though there is no firm body of knowledge on which to build, this has not deterred the Americans, but a cautious approach accompanied by the systematic and independent evaluation of any scheme is strongly recommended, not least because mediation schemes do, in the wrong hands and the wrong circumstances, have an obvious potential for misfiring, and in a particularly public way.

The main work *for* victims in the United Kingdom has been done *by* victims in a number of national organisations, including Victim Support, which deals with some half million referrals annually. The growth of Victim Support has been remarkable from its modest beginnings in 1974 (planned, it is reported, over a drink in a Bristol public house in 1971) (Mawby and Gill 1987: 87); its work has been gratifyingly received by the vast majority of its recipients (Maguire and Corbett 1986), striking testimony to the fact that one does not need professional therapists to deal sensitively, humanely and practically with people in distress (see also Hoff 1978 and Parry 1990 for simple and usable accounts of crisis work).

Victim support schemes (and VSS is the best researched of the victim organisations) have on the whole remained true to their original planning: sound but simple professional administration but staffed almost exclusively by volunteers whose roots are firmly in their local areas, responding immediately to need and working on the basis of good relationships with the police.

VSS has characteristically enjoyed the blessings and the curses of relative independence. It has been free to be flexible and locally responsive, but it has not always been effectively administered locally (Maguire and Corbett 1986). It has relied on good relations with the police, and the system does not ensure that the most needy or distressed victims are referred: the process is haphazard and can be inefficient. In particular, where there is a disparity between police assessment of the 'seriousness' of a crime and the subjective response of the victim to that crime (as in the case of vandalism) referral is unusual.

There are also a number of offences where the impact on victims is beyond the capacity of VSS volunteers to manage, and where local variations in service militate against reliable relations either with specialist voluntary agencies (such as rape crisis centres or women's aid) or the statutory welfare services. Though VSS is not designed to take on long term therapy with the small minority of referrals who need it, it is hard for an organisation structured as it is to meet the needs of such people even by referring on. Nor are the volunteers necessarily of a similar background to the victim population. Mawby and Gill found some reluctance among volunteers to engage in mediation activities and a particular view of crime which reflected their age and class background:

> Their view of contemporary Britain was of a society in which crime featured as a major social problem, where moral chaos reigned, where criminal gangs ran amok in many cities, and where it was unsafe for women to go out alone after dark.
>
> (Mawby and Gill 1987: 212)

While such views may well catharsise victims in the aftermath of a crime, they do little for the longer term reintegration of the offender or for increasing community tolerance. Nor do they necessarily make for an easy relationship with probation officers who, if my analysis is correct, are going to have to become more involved with victims than hitherto. Mawby and Gill's study of probation officers in the south-west of England suggested that there was support for such a move, and that probation officers, in spite of the lack of enthusiasm of their trade union, were quite victim oriented (Mawby and Gill 1987: 185–98). In fact probation officers were almost twice as likely as the police to see reasons why victims should be referred to VSS (Mawby and Gill 1987: 195). Nevertheless, few of them could turn their generalised commitment to meeting the needs of victims into concrete information about the local VSS arrangements: only one in five had ever referred a case to VSS and almost none had ever had a case referred to them *by* VSS. The attitudes and beliefs of VSS volunteers were, in this study, closer to those of the police than to those of the probation service, and a number of volunteers were suspicious of probation's mission. Probation officers' only reservation about taking on more victim work, on the other hand, was resource driven. They had a greater belief than the police in VSS and were noticeably better disposed to VSS than were VSS volunteers to them.

This finding led Mawby and Gill to be pessimistic about the likelihood of closer working relations between probation and VSS. On the other hand, we know that as agencies work more closely together, attitudinal differences normally converge and boundary hostility diminishes except where the fear of take-over exists. In the case of probation and victim organisations, take-over seems unlikely. If VSS and other organisations are to make a greater impact on a wider range of crime victims, they need to become more central. At the same time, the probation service has been enjoined by the Home Office to become more involved in its local community; and it is clear that popular attitudes towards the treatment of offenders in the community indicate high levels of support for reparative and restitutive approaches. It is, therefore, neither desirable nor possible for probation and VSS not to form closer links, perhaps as contributors to the criminal justice fora of the kind I outline in Chapter 8 (see also Locke 1990) which will help determine the practices of the local criminal justice system in the 1990s and beyond. To assume that agencies with different ideologies cannot work together is surely wrong both in practice (ignoring, for example, the successful joint work in child protection of social workers and police) and in theory, for ideologies are not immutable but sustained or modified constantly by the functions, actions and beliefs of key agency personnel. The more discrete agencies are, the more discrete their ideologies will be; the more they work together, the more common ground they will establish and the more the unity as well as diversity of their various missions will emerge.

# Chapter 4

# The probation service and situational crime prevention

We have never regarded poor educational facilities, unemployment, broken homes, slums, poverty, or grossly adverse social conditions of any kind as desirable features of our society. We wish to get rid of slums, not particularly because they are productive of delinquency and crime, but because we think they are a despicable way for people to have to live. . . . In brief, the insights that we have gained from criminological research into the causes of crime and delinquency have not led us to want to do anything that we wouldn't have wished to achieve without such insights.

(Morris and Hawkins 1970: 51–2)

An enterprising New Yorker coped with a garbage strike by exploiting his knowledge that packages often are stolen from cars. Each day he wrapped his debris as though it were a present and left it on the seat of his unlocked car. It was invariably gone by morning.

(Bell and Bell 1987: 56)

To prevent, or at least reduce, crime is neither a new nor a precise ambition, and the figures we have been examining in this book, for all their deficiencies, make fairly plain that it has not been a very successful one either. It is, however, the most fundamental purpose of criminal justice, for only when it has failed do concepts such as punishment, treatment and reparation make an appearance.

Just as the health service, in part through the hegemony of doctors trained in the curative aspects of western medical science, has only recently come to acknowledge that curing illness is only necessary when positive health has not been successfully promoted, so has the criminal justice system paid less attention to the prevention of crime than to the treatment of criminals. Both health and criminal justice have concentrated more on reacting to problems than on identifying and tackling the circumstances which contributed to the problems in the first place.

This is understandable but shortsighted. Though there is room for as much disagreement about the causes of crime as there is about those of poor health, it is possible to proceed rationally by classifying different approaches to crime prevention and beginning the process of discussing organisational responsibility for contributing to it. Crime prevention does not 'belong' centrally in any organisation. The police have begun to invest in the field and have used their resources to advise victims and community groups on how to proceed, but their work is not always integrated with that of other professionals. Many people who are fearful of crime or victims of crime receive no advice on crime prevention beyond technical information about locks and bolts, alarms and dogs. We have no concept of crime prevention as a more general contributor to community health and happiness.

To have a vision – and at this stage a vision is all it can be – of safety from crime as a contributor to public health is to flag the inadequacy of a police-led approach to the problem. If the price of protecting our property from burglars is that we never leave it to go on holiday; if we worry when the house is briefly empty; if we do not buy pleasing pictures and furniture for fear of theft, spending the money instead on expensive alarm systems; if we have intricate locking and lighting systems which, because they tend to go dramatically wrong, cause us further worry – if this is our approach to crime prevention we may be secure but we are unlikely to be happy. It is this that we have earlier called 'concern' about crime.

Providing information which enables the public to distinguish proper fear from unnecessary concern is, as we have seen, part of any crime prevention strategy. The information is best provided in the first place by professional experts and disseminated through individuals, volunteers, community groups and the media. But alongside it must come sound and realistic advice on crime prevention: it is important that people maximise their power to protect themselves and their neighbourhoods, but under the guidance of professionals whose business is with enhancement of the positive as well as elimination of the negative. For this reason among others, if the probation service is to be asked to extend its work more into the community, it is right that its employees should themselves be versed in some of the rapidly developing literature on crime prevention.

Crime prevention is a catch-all concept for a range of disparate activities. I propose to make an initial distinction between *primary* and *secondary* prevention, the former involving preventing something from happening in the first place; the latter preventing something which has already happened from happening again. Primary and secondary prevention, then, constitute one axis of my model; the second axis comprises individual and social prevention, as Figure 1 makes plain.

|  | Primary Prevention | Secondary Prevention |
|---|---|---|
| Individual Prevention | **A:** Work with individuals identified as 'at risk' of offending or victimisation | **B:** Risk reduction/delinquency management work with offenders |
| Social Prevention | **C:** Generalised work on social amelioration; community development strategies | **D:** Situational crime prevention work in high delinquency areas: specifically targeted work combined with social amelioration |

*Figure 1* Crime prevention – a preliminary typology

Examples of Cell **A** work are fewer than once they were. The origins of primary preventive work with 'at risk' youngsters lie in late eighteenth and nineteenth century philanthropy (see, for example, Tobias 1967) and in particular the assumption that the 'devil makes work for idle hands'. There are numerous accounts of waifs and strays, from sentimentalised histories (see, for example, Hopkirk 1949) through sentimentalised novels to pseudo-science and professional literature such as this:

> Life demands so much more strength of character from the youth of to-day. He is given so much more freedom and so many more temptations assail him . . . Moral instruction may be given in many ways, but young people cannot be taught their social duties by abstract logic or through having their complexes unravelled by a psychiatrist; they require the practical lessons of Dame Bedonebyasyoudid.
>
> (Jones 1945: 19–20)

The moralisation, through education, treatment and opportunity, of the at-risk child has historically found expression in the industrial school movement, the youth service, the school psychiatric service, the early probation service, outward bound activities and, rather later, intermediate treatment, which initially involved the use of facilities 'in which other children can also participate, and not confined to children under supervision through court orders' (DHSS 1972: para. 15. For an excellent analysis of the attendant confusion, see Nellis 1990). Even where the children were subject to court orders, however, the 'preventive' strategy was frequently loose, with professional activities geared more to general relationship building than to the precise identification and elimination of delinquent behaviour. In one case, for example, on the assumption that delinquents were short of friendship, companionship, advice, were unclubbable and short of suitable adult company, volunteers were provided as surrogate friends:

> Several of the volunteers lived in the same neighbourhood as the adolescents involved in the programme. The result was that the latter often called on the volunteers for coffee, to take the dog for a walk, to play cards, to sit in the garden and chat, and to help with washing the car . . . They sometimes brought their friends with them, so that some volunteers got to know other children in the neighbourhood, including brothers and sisters not included in the IT programme, but who were possibly likely to get into trouble.
>
> (Jones and Kerslake 1979: 71)

It would be impossible to measure the effectiveness of such a programme in reducing crime, and in all probability the thought of doing so never really occurred to the organisers. The concern was less with the outcome of a targeted and planned intervention than with the expression of such social values as forgiveness, acceptance, reintegration and love. Thus it was 'the time the volunteers gave to the adolescents outside of our structured meetings and events which was probably of greatest significance to the youngsters' (Jones and Kerslake 1979: 70–1).

In the United States, the poverty programme of the Kennedy and Johnson administrations was, though much grander in scale and sophisticated in design, similarly founded on principles of social prevention. This programme was heavily influenced by the book *Delinquency and Opportunity* (Cloward and Ohlin 1960), the main thesis of which was that crime was caused by the dissonance between the American dream of success through economic individualism and the blocked opportunity structures which in fact existed. The programme accordingly sought to increase the participation of ghetto residents in local power structures, and injected massive resources into the areas themselves. The results were not what had been anticipated or hoped for: both crime levels and the social dissatisfaction of the intended beneficiaries increased:

> after five years of effort the reforms had not evolved any reliable solutions to the intractable problems with which they struggled. . . . Given the talent and money they had brought to bear, they had not even reopened very many opportunities.
>
> (Marris and Rein 1967: 222)

While there is a view that the impact of the British urban riots of 1981 and the ensuing Scarman Report (Scarman 1981) similarly contributed to the development of interest in social crime prevention in this country (see for example Stern 1987: 210), there was, in part as a result of the American experience with the poverty programme in general and the Mobilization for Youth programme in New York City in particular, a greater willingness to distinguish the problems of inner city regeneration from those of crime prevention. That poverty does not, in some simple way, 'cause' crime is beyond dispute: to eliminate poverty is not to eliminate crime. Indeed, whether poverty itself exists as a 'thing' to be abolished, or whether it is a basket containing a range of negative experiences, opportunities, attitudes and behaviours is itself a matter of longstanding academic controversy. Perhaps the construction and reification of 'poverty' have been, so far as crime and criminology are concerned, a rather pungent red herring. After all, as Gladstone has persuasively argued:

> The provision of better opportunities for work and leisure to give potentially delinquent youths better ways of occupying themselves may also be ineffective in that few crimes require much time or effort, and work and leisure in themselves provide a wide range of criminal opportunities.
>
> (Gladstone 1980: 8)

In Great Britain, factors such as the political scepticism of a radical Conservative government about the merits of 'throwing money at social problems', the increasing conflict between central and local administrations in the Labour-controlled metropolitan areas where social conditions were worst, the consequent pressure on resources and the increasing demand for value for money came conveniently to combine with an emergent professional view that preventive work was actually damaging to the youngsters. This political and professional consensus had, by the 1980s, come to make interventions of this kind of only antiquarian interest.

Similar arguments have helped restrict Cell C work, though it is true that individual probation teams use the notion of 'community involvement' to cover a range of disparate and potentially time-consuming activities, some closely and some tangentially concerned with crime prevention (Henderson 1986). A preliminary framework for generalised approaches to crime prevention via community amelioration has also been outlined by juvenile justice theoreticians and practitioners from Lancaster University (Thorpe, Smith, Green and Paley 1980: 106–13), but has not, so far as I am aware, been subsequently developed in practice. A new paradigm for the community involvement of the probation service will be needed if the service's work in the community is to be clear and comprehensible. The potential for the further development of the essentially *ad hoc* initiatives described by Henderson is probably limited; the scope for planned and monitored inter-agency work involving probation and other agencies is considerably greater.

Cell B work will be addressed in detail in a later chapter, for the management of delinquents in the community is likely to remain the central feature of the probation service's work, and the need for that task to be approached in a more informed, rational and systematic manner is paramount. Our present concern is with Cell D: situational crime prevention and the possible role of the probation service in relation to it.

## WHAT IS SITUATIONAL CRIME PREVENTION?

Situational crime prevention involves reducing or eliminating the opportunity to commit specific crimes. It does *not* make the empirically incorrect assumption that a causal relationship exists between social problems or human misery and crime, and that accordingly to eliminate the former will eliminate the latter. Instead, as Vivien Stern's account makes clear, it involves four stages:

> First would be an analysis of the situation, for example, supermarket, telephone kiosk, car park in which the offence in question occurs and the conditions which provide the opportunity for it. Second is the devising of measures which would make it more difficult. Third comes an assessment of how practical, effective, and costly these measures would be. The fourth stage is to select the measures which seem most likely to succeed.
>
> (Stern 1987: 212)

This, of course, is only the beginning of the story. Let us look in turn at the first two of these stages to help us understand what situational crime prevention means in practice, and what difficulties might exist in implementing a situational crime prevention strategy. The second stage will take us into the crucial areas of inter-agency collaboration and citizen participation (or community involvement). I shall then look at a number of objections to the strategy, and conclude by speculating on ways in which the probation service might properly involve itself increasingly in situational crime prevention.

## Analysing the situation

The first step is to determine what crime in what place is to be eliminated. When identified, this crime–place configuration is called a *target*. For a target to be appropriately selected, a number of conditions must exist. Firstly, the target must represent a crime-in-situation of sufficient frequency and seriousness to make it worth tackling. This may sound obvious, but it is possible for vociferous or influential individuals to steer local crime prevention strategies into channels which are either fantasies of their own about what *might* happen or into dealing with crimes which are either very infrequent or which affect only very few individuals. Either of these conditions will lower the motivation of the members of the community whose involvement is necessary. Secondly, the target has got to be amenable to situational crime prevention strategies. Not all crimes are. Child molestation is an emotive problem, but attacks on children in the street, though distressing, are rare and geographically random; most assaults take place in people's homes. Where this is not the case, however, – for example where there is a problem of child prostitution in a known area – situational crime prevention can operate. Thirdly, it is desirable though not necessary that physical features of the environment contribute to the problem. One celebrated instance of situational crime prevention was reported by Kate Painter, who demonstrated that improved street lighting in part of a 'problem' street in Edmonton, a working class suburb of North London, reduced both crime itself and also fear of crime, at least in the short term (Painter 1988: 2).

But, as Malcolm Ramsay has pointed out in a perceptive intervention (Ramsay 1989), it would be wrong to regard street lighting as a panacea for street crimes. Quite apart from technical questions such as how much lighting and of what kind should be installed and how it should be funded, he points out that most crime does not take place at night in dark alleyways and people's fear of crime is not restricted to specific times and places where there are no streetlights. In addition, streetlights can themselves be targets for vandals, lights shining through bedroom curtains can cause complaints of sleeplessness, and some streetlights can throw shadows which create new opportunities for crime. The 'streetlighting' hypothesis assumes, as much situational crime prevention does, a 'rational choice' approach to crime which should not be overplayed in the quest for simple answers. To overegg any pudding causes not only indigestion but dissatisfaction: improved streetlighting sometimes has a part to play in crime prevention, but only in relation to crimes which are prevented by light, and the number of those generally is probably fairly small.

The identification of a vulnerable target and making it harder to commit crimes against it is called *target hardening*. This typically involves the use of hardware: from improving locks on schools to fitting steering columns to cars; from installing janitors to using surveillance technology (for an account of a situational crime prevention strategy involving target hardening in two schools of significantly different design and with equally different levels of success, see Hope 1986; for a 'guide to good practice' in preventing school vandalism, see Ramsay 1989).

## Devising measures to make crime more difficult

Having identified as the 'target' a particular crime–place configuration, the next stage, as in any problem-solving process, is to decide what to do about it. So far we have concentrated on the crime–place dimension, not on the equally important question of who is going to be involved in the strategy. Certainly the police are properly and necessarily involved, but it is important not to confuse situational crime prevention with police crime prevention. Crime prevention is part of the daily task of the police, and they will approach it in any number of ways, of which the most prevalent involve strategies of increasing the visibility, acceptability and accessibility of the police to the public. In addition, the police periodically target specific crimes for preventive attention: attempts at improving motorists' car security strategies and at reducing truancy by introducing special truancy patrols (neither of which was especially successful), for example, are described in one research report (Burrows, Ekblom and Heal 1979).

Situational crime prevention on the other hand normally involves professionals and citizens working together, harnessing professional knowledge to community commitment. Though in practice professional agencies other than the police are seldom centrally involved, and the role for the public will vary, the police alone cannot normally commit sufficient resources to initiate and sustain community involvement; nor indeed do they possess the skills necessary to do so.

Nor again do they always have the authority to be successful alone. For example, they are seldom in a position to *require* any changes which will reduce crime to be made. Hence, a study of crimes in or against licensed premises in Newcastle and Southampton shows that the work necessary to reduce the number of incidents of disorder in city centre public houses can include changes to pub layout, music volume, supervision, staff training, closing times and transport availability as well as development of a more coherent and defensible policy of considering applications for liquor licences (Hope 1985; Ramsay 1986). The need was not simply for:

> piecemeal action to modify the more troublesome kind of setting in which drinking takes place but also for regular close liaison between major breweries . . . the police, local authorities and Licensing Justices, all of whom need to work together to have the greatest impact on the disorder which stems from problematic public houses and other licensed premises.

> (Ramsay 1986: 88)

Negotiations, therefore, involved local authorities, police, Licensing Justices and the liquor trade. Strategies adopted included pressure on public house owners to increase staffing levels and staff training (other research having indicated that poorly trained staff could exacerbate disorder); and behind the strategies lay the implied threat of police opposition to licence renewal applications. Pressure of this kind was necessary because of an obvious conflict between the crime prevention and the profit imperatives: the crime prevention measures would eat into profits without tangible benefit for the brewers.

Crime prevention is not, therefore, simply a matter of barbed wire, floodlights and new locks, nor is it without cost, and nor is it likely to avoid opposition from interest groups. So in the retail trade too, an attractive display designed to encourage purchase must also by definition encourage theft. Crime prevention is not, therefore, a simple matter of common cause being joined: a complex array of information-giving, persuasion, bargaining and conflict strategies needs to be adopted if the active cooperation of potentially interested parties is to be gained.

One writer who has made especially thoughtful contributions to the study of crime prevention is Ronald Clarke. Clarke has developed a three part categorisation of situational crime prevention: surveillance (for example by the introduction of video cameras in selected high risk areas and in department stores, and by the selective deployment of police manpower), design changes involving technical 'target hardening' (such as those introduced into telephone kiosks to make theft and vandalism more difficult) and environmental management (for example, making wage payments other than by cash, introducing containerisation in the docks, developing baggage screening in airports) (Clarke 1983: 233–44; see also Jeffery 1971: Part IV; LeBeau 1987). As the public house disorder example makes clear, however, any particular crime prevention activity may involve two or more of Clarke's types. To prevent such disorder it is likely that there will be increased police surveillance, and that public house staff will themselves receive training in making and reporting observations; there may well be target hardening strategies such as introducing fixed seats and protecting bar tills; and environmental management would take the form not only of the interagency liaison already described but adjustments to the volume and nature of music, increased provision of seating and adjustments to pub design in order to increase customer visibility. In this sense the typology is just that: not a description of a piece of social action called crime prevention but a classification of that action for analytic and policymaking purposes.

A major theme emerging from crime prevention strategies is the need for people from different agencies, or with discrete functions in the same agency, to work together, overcoming agency hostility, committing resources and sharing information (Stern 1987: 221–2). Typically this only happens effectively when the tangible advantages for those most directly involved outweigh the discomforts of change and the surrender of hitherto exclusive territory. The identification of a problem which adversely affects all relevant agencies and which is of sufficient gravity is, therefore, necessary. One key area of crime prevention where agencies have collaborated, however, is *child protection*. There the Department of Health requires local Child Protection Committees to deal with inter-agency matters such as joint training, collaboration, managing enquiries and developing inter-agency policies and procedures (DHSS 1988). But child protection is a special case, and for local agencies to be effectively and collaboratively involved in crime prevention generally, a similar requirement for local committees of criminal justice professionals is needed. I return to this point in Chapter 8.

Certainly collaboration is crucial. As a Home Office report makes plain, the most successful projects are those where collaboration is simple and where there exist strong system support and few partners. Potential for failure is heightened when initial enthusiasms wane, when the problem appears not to be susceptible to effective intervention, or when the particular collaborations necessary to achieve success are not successfully consolidated (Hope 1985; see also Yin 1986).

This, therefore, brings us to the issue of community involvement. So far we have looked at crime prevention schemes primarily involving inter-agency collaboration. But situational crime prevention, if it is to meet community concerns, must be more than that. In part it is a strategy, in part an ideology (that crime is a community, not simply a police, responsibility). And it has behind it a theory – that crime is related to opportunity: make it harder to commit and the level of crime will reduce. This may seem an obvious, if not tautologous, argument, but it is in fact controversial. If you take a different view – that much crime is, say, pathological, or, conversely, that it is systematic and planned – you will have reservations about crime prevention. In either case you will expect to encounter a *displacement phenomenon*: in the case of pathology because crime is expressive not purposive (the volume or persistence of the 'cry for help' not being noticeably reduced by Alsatian dogs or video cameras), and in the case of systematisation because crime prevention in one area will simply lead the criminal to commit the crime elsewhere. This is the phenomenon of displacement.

## COMMUNITY INVOLVEMENT, CRIME PREVENTION AND FEAR OF CRIME

The argument that to prevent crime is but to displace it elsewhere has been most fully considered in work associated with Ronald Clarke (Hough, Clarke and Mayhew 1980; Clarke 1983; Cornish and Clarke 1986). It has been responded to in an excellent paper by Gordon Trasler (Trasler 1986) who draws for his analysis on American work on displacement (Hakim and Regert 1981) and on psychological critiques of the 'rational choice' approach to criminality which Clarke has developed as the theoretical underpinning of his approach.[1]

In practical terms there is little fundamental disagreement about displacement: sometimes it happens and sometimes it does not. Situational crime prevention cannot prevent all crimes all of the time, but nor is it ineffective in reducing the total number of crimes committed. Cornish and Clarke note that among the successes of target hardening have been reductions in airline hijackings in the 1970s by the introduction of improved checking measures at airports, reductions in cheque frauds by the introduction of guarantee cards, and reductions in car thefts in Germany following the compulsory introduction of steering column locks in all cars. Against this, however, there are instances where displacement has undoubtedly taken place: in the United Kingdom, the introduction of a requirement that new cars only were fitted with steering column locks led to an increase in thefts of older cars. Unintended consequences are always likely in interventions in the social world, and to Cornish and Clarke the necessity is to understand how and why they occur and how to deal with them when they do (Cornish and Clarke 1986: 1–2).

Trasler, on the other hand, raises a number of objections. Some of these are theoretical, to do with the limited utility of rational choice theory, and I shall not deal with them here. Of more immediate interest to the policymaker and practitioner is the argument that displacement itself is very hard to identify empirically. We cannot *assume* that because a crime prevention measure has been introduced against, say, vandalism in one area and incidents of vandalism go up in the next area, displacement has occurred; nor can we assume that an increase in a different kind of crime is *not* a displacement. So, to take Cornish and Clarke's West German steering lock example, it may be that car thieves, instead of being diverted from all crime, were diverted from one form of crime into a different one, and this would not be apparent in any discussion of displacement.

Displacement can be of five kinds: spatial, temporal, tactical, target and type of crime (Hakim and Regert 1981). To identify displacement, therefore, is to acknowledge the complexity of the concept and the fact that the sum of what we can ever hope to know about crime is limited. To regard crime as wholly explicable in terms of rational choice would obviously be naive, and the main practical implication of the displacement debate is that situational crime prevention has a place, but not a unique place, in any attack on crime as a whole. The results of neighbourhood strategies based on the situational approach are too encouraging to jettison (see, for example, the NACRO schemes on high delinquency estates outlined by Stern 1987), but situational crime prevention cannot operate without supporting action such as individual crime prevention and risk reduction strategies, incapacitation of serious or repeated offenders and increased police efficiency. In particular, to make situational crime prevention too central a strategy is to set it up to fail and to encourage a fortress mentality which would be as unpleasant as it would be counterproductive. And though I am of the view that crime is not simply determined by social conditions, there is an obvious place for environmental amelioration as part of an overall social strategy towards attaining what the Home Office Standing Conference terms 'confident communities', or what I would term community health. To move towards a crime free environment would not, in the absence of other kinds of social reform, make us either healthier or happier, and in consequence we cannot entirely unyoke crime prevention from broader environmental objectives.

'Community involvement' is sometimes looked at askance by the theoretician who knows the problems involved firstly in defining it, secondly in translating any definition into social action, and thirdly in achieving and sustaining people's involvement. I do not propose to involve myself in that discussion here, for there is sufficient literature elsewhere to sate even the most compulsive consumer of the socio-logical critique of the concept community. I shall be more straight-forward and less sophisticated, defining 'community' simply as those people who, not normally being criminal justice professionals, live or work in a particular area and who wish, or can be persuaded, to translate their concern about some aspect of local criminal behaviour into action. Government is clear about the need for this commitment: the 'fear of crime' report devotes eight pages to the notion of 'confident communities' (Home Office Standing Conference on Crime Prevention 1989: 46–54); the Safer Cities and Five Towns projects instituted by the Home Office involve not only inter-professional collaboration but also community participation, as do Pubwatch, Taxiwatch, Crimestoppers and a bewildering array of local strategies (Home Office 1989: 23–34. For a helpful brief account of Safer Cities, see Ellis 1989). NACRO, the main voluntary organisation in the field, believes that community involvement and participation are 'the key' to successful crime prevention, at least so far as vandalism and burglary are concerned (Stern 1987: 214); the Labour Party too, though it foresees a pivotal role for local government, has similar aims:

> *the Labour Party will launch a comprehensive crime prevention initiative spearheaded by local authorities working in close partnership with the police, local communities, private enterprise and voluntary organisations.*
>
> (Labour Party 1990: 5. Italics original)

Community involvement, then, is generally held to be a 'good thing'; it is also one of the main planks of the as yet nascent crime prevention policies of the European Community (Council of Europe 1984). Equally it is deemed crucial in the United States, where research has shown that whereas citizen involvement, though varied in style and motivation, is vital for successful crime prevention, only about 10 per cent of Americans have taken part in it (Lavrakas and Herz 1982). The Lavrakas and Herz study (a telephone survey of a random sample of 1803 Chicagoans) also demonstrated that the most successful and persistent activists had become involved through participation in other kinds of neighbourhood group which turned to crime prevention from other social activities to address a perceived neighbourhood problem. Citizens who turned thus to crime prevention having joined their group for primarily expressive reasons were not dependent on tangible crime prevention for their continued satisfaction. Hence, they were less likely to become disillusioned than the instrumentalists who were involved in *ad hoc* crime prevention groups for which crime prevention was the sole *raison d'être*. Accordingly:

> Our finding that groups tend not to organize initially around crime issues and that many groups take on such problems after they have achieved some organizational maturity suggests that policymakers promoting community crime prevention programs should concern themselves with organizations already in place in the neighborhoods, including church groups and school groups as well as block clubs and community organizations.
>
> (Lavrakas and Herz 1982: 496)

In the United Kingdom, the best established form of citizen involvement in crime prevention generally is Neighbourhood Watch, the 1988 British Crime Survey suggesting that 14 per cent of households were members of a scheme. Though Neighbourhood Watch has not been extensively researched (though see Hope 1988) and our knowledge is threrefore patchy, we do know that schemes vary widely, having in common only the existence of a local coordinator, a community base and local police support (Mayhew, Elliott and Dowds 1989: 51). In the absence of systematic evaluation it is difficult to comment with confidence on what they do, and how successful they are. We do know, however, that there is an inverse relationship between prevalence of crime and the existence of a Neighbourhood Watch scheme (Husain 1988); membership appears to be associated with general security consciousness among members, but it is not clear whether membership promotes security consciousness, security consciousness provokes membership, or a mutual reinforcement phenomenon exists. Though most members are inactive, few schemes are, and very few have ceased to operate. It is possible that members of schemes are more 'fearful' of crime and that a fear-exacerbation phenomenon does in fact exist among members of schemes, at least in the United States (Rosenbaum 1988), though clearly membership itself demonstrates that they were not debilitated by fear, but were possibly experiencing the kind of signal anxiety which stimulates action and 'gets the adrenalin going'.

Neighbourhood Watch is essentially a case study in the ubiquitous phenomenon of the middle classes looking after themselves. No doubt the 'Neighbourhood Watch' banner has served to rally the concerned *bourgeoisie*, focus their worries and spur them to action. The occasionally expressed concern that the citizenry called to arms acts as a private army seems, from American research, to be generally ill-founded (Kelling 1986: 102). But the middle classes protecting themselves against crimes in relation to which their risk is low cannot constitute a major contribution to the development of a coherent crime prevention policy. Any such policy should presumably involve the active participation of those most at risk of victimisation, and some of the frustration which Government may be feeling about the as yet unfulfilled potential of Neighbourhood Watch is clear from the Home Office Standing Conference report:

> Neighbourhood Watch should be given a new look. The aim should be broader involvement in communities and their general quality of life . . . A new approach would offer a fresh opportunity to provide practical support for people whose lives are severely affected by fear of crime. . . . Curtain twitching may be appropriate in middle-class areas where outsiders might just conceivably be potential burglars. On a high-crime council estate, offenders may well be neighbouring children.
>
> (Home Office Standing Conference on Crime Prevention 1989: 51–2)

Neighbourhood Watch, which is useful in a rather specific way, needs augmenting by different and locally appropriate forms of crime prevention if policy is to develop coherently. But of course there are complexities in engaging in crime prevention strategies in those areas whose communities boast a considerable number of criminals. There are also sensitivities involved in crime prevention in high density ethnic minority areas, and the Standing Conference Report is, here and elsewhere, stronger on the 'what' questions than the 'how' ones. It may be, however, that the probation service can play a part, with the private and voluntary sectors, in encouraging crime prevention strategies in high crime areas where close police involvement is potentially embarrassing (see also Husain 1988) and where sensitivity to cultural and ethnic diversity is necessary.

## SITUATIONAL CRIME PREVENTION AND THE PROBATION SERVICE

The suggestion that the probation service should be involved in crime prevention is not new. It was promoted forcefully in a remarkably prescient book about the probation service published in the 1970s (Haxby 1978), and though Haxby's approach to crime prevention reflects the early notion of social (rather than situational) prevention, some at least of what he says is as relevant in the 1990s as it was in the 1970s:

> The probation service will, in my view, be making a great mistake if it dismisses primary prevention as being outside its terms of reference, or thinks that it is a task which belongs wholly to local authority departments. A service cannot focus on a social problem with such dimensions as crime and delinquency without being concerned with the pre-conditions which have such an influence on the incidence of the problem . . . Obviously it is preferable for different agencies to collaborate in developing policies of primary prevention. It may then be possible in certain areas or neighbourhoods to develop strategies which utilise the resources of all the agencies concerned.
>
> (Haxby 1978: 195)

At this time, crime prevention work was not included in the formal duties of the probation service. The Home Office's *Statement of National Objectives and Priorities*, however (Home Office 1984a), listed among the service's tasks:

> developing the service to the wider public by contributing to initiatives concerned with the prevention of crime and the support of victims, and playing a part in the activities of local statutory and voluntary organisations.
>
> (Home Office 1984a: 5)

Later the same year, in the revised *Probation Rules*, buried deep in Paragraph 37 ('other duties') appeared:

> It shall be part of the duties of a probation officer to participate in such arrangements concerned with the prevention of crime or with

the relationship between offenders and their victims or the community at large as may be approved by the probation committee on the advice of the chief probation officer.

(Home Office 1984b: para. 37)

This shift in policy provoked a short but useful paper in the probation officers' own journal the following year, which provided some basic information about crime prevention and outlined a possible role for the service in relation to it (Laycock and Pease 1985). It also caused the Central Council of Probation Committees to institute a working party on crime prevention (Central Council of Probation Committees 1987). Later a Green Paper on the future of the probation service noted:

the probation service must gear its work more and more towards crime prevention in its broadest sense. This involves firm and constructive work with offenders . . . it also involves joining together with the police, local authorities and the rest of the community in initiatives to prevent crime.

(Home Office 1990c: 6)

This Green Paper was quickly followed by a complementary discussion paper (Home Office 1990d) which not only took the issue of crime prevention and the probation service a little further, but also indicated, encouragingly, that the different Home Office departments concerned with supervision of offenders and with crime prevention were themselves engaging in discussions. Nevertheless, the fact that the single unsatisfactory paragraph explicitly about crime prevention concluded lamely that 'Crime prevention initiatives are, however being taken forward as a separate exercise' (Home Office 1990d: para. 2.11) suggests that there was still some way to go. Reminding readers of Home Office initiatives on crime prevention in 1984 and 1990 (by circulars advocating interdisciplinary attacks on crime) the document stressed the developing role in crime prevention of local authorities, business and voluntary organisations, and foreshadowed greater private sector involvement in the future (Home Office 1990d: paras. 2.6–2.8). More significant was the suggestion that there should be instituted:

A local committee on which would be represented the local authority, the major statutory agencies (police, probation social services etc), the voluntary sector, community relations councils and local businesses. Such a committee might then analyse local crime patterns to identify particular 'trouble spots' and types of crime committed by, for instance, young adults; look at local sentencing patterns especially in relation to the target group; and then devise a strategy for reducing crime committed by people in that group.

(Home Office 1990d: para. 2.7)

Could we not, though, some might ask, leave the probation service out of any such forum? To do so, argue Laycock and Pease, would be firstly to deny that those with experience of working with offenders have a contribution to make to preventing crime, secondly to deny to the probation service the broader perspective which a study of primary prevention would bring to its own work, and thirdly to prevent the probation service making a contribution, in crime prevention discussions, about the social costs of situational crime prevention itself (Laycock and Pease 1985: 45). A similar point is made by the Central Council Working Party:

> Despite our own uncertainty in this matter we kept being drawn back to the very marked feeling that a Service which supervised some 150,000 offenders at any one time and which prepared some 300,000 social inquiry and other criminal reports in any one year was bound to have a contribution to make towards crime prevention strategies.
>
> (Central Council of Probation Committees 1987: para. 24)

Though all these various thoughts are inevitably preliminary, and have to a degree been overtaken by events such as the move towards a mixed economy of community punishments, they do etch a rationale for the involvement of the probation service, outlining a possible rationale for probation involvement in the local criminal justice system and in relation to community attitudes towards crime:

> Nothing engenders punitiveness more than a sense of helplessness. If you want fewer burglars locked up, provide people with a sense, at least, of how they can understand and do something about burglary victimisation. Situational approaches are our best hope of this.
>
> (Laycock and Pease 1985: 47)

And, in similar vein:

> The probation officer who is insensitive to the impact of a client's offence on individuals and neighbourhoods does the client a great disservice. Equally the victim or the neighbourhood that is ignored by the Service will hardly feel encouraged to be tolerant and forgiving.
>
> (Central Council of Probation Committees 1987: para. 26)

The Association of Chief Officers of Probation had also, by 1988, identified crime prevention as a proper part of probation work, and its glossy pamphlet *Crime Prevention and the Probation Service* emphasised its concern not only with crime reduction but with victims, families ('a key element in the healthy development of society'), the community, drug and alcohol misusers ('to assist misusers to appreciate the harm caused by their abuse and to change their lifestyles'), as well as working with other agencies, central and local government and the courts. Clearly the world was the probation service's oyster, and all that was needed for it to 'take off' in crime prevention was adequate resourcing.

But again it was not so simple. The multi-agency effort involved in crime prevention work is neither simple nor unproblematic (Blagg, Pearson, Sampson, Smith and Stubbs 1988), the National Association of Probation Officers had long resisted crime prevention work, and the relatively *laissez-faire* management style of some probation areas gravitated against such a decisive involvement, as the Audit Commission noted in its inspection of the service (Audit Commission 1989). There are, however, signal advantages for the probation service in active involvement in crime prevention; equally it is entirely proper that it should be so involved:

1. Government is increasingly concerned that the probation service should see itself not primarily as a provider of services but as working in a more integrated way with local criminal justice networks. Such networks will almost certainly be in place long before the 1990s are out, and it is inevitable that much of their focus will be on crime prevention. It would be highly desirable for the service to determine what contribution it could make to those discussions and what roles in crime prevention it could properly play.

2. Among those roles might be included skills in *liaising with other professionals* (multi-agency work is, in good part as a result of the child abuse problem, now a central part of the best training courses and there is now a growing professional literature in this field) (Alaszewski and Harrison 1988); skills in *working with communities* themselves, including, as a result of 'knowing the patch' having a good grasp of local criminal trends, leisure facilities and criminals' lifestyles; a knowledge of the *impact of crime* on communities, but also of the *impact of communities* on criminals. In this sense the literature which speaks of probation as a 'bridge' between offender and offended against is appropriate.

3. It is desirable both for the service and for offenders that the service

engage with victims and potential victims. The idea that the probation officer 'represents' the offender as a 'client' is no longer tenable once we accept that criminality is on the whole not externally determined and that crime hurts communities. It is also important to remember that offenders are statistically far more likely to be victims than are non-offenders. It is also important to remember that, in spite of the stereotype, offenders are not generally committed and dedicated criminals; most of the time they are, in what is only seemingly a paradox, law-abiding citizens concerned to prevent crime. (Or to put it another way, most law abiding citizens are sometimes offenders.) Because some youngsters sometimes steal cars, burgle houses, steal from shops, it does not follow that they are unconcerned about the effect of crime on their families and themselves, that they are other than highly punitive in their sentencing philosophies or that they have taken the major step of self-identification as a 'criminal'.

Though it is inevitable and desirable that the probation service will diversify further in the next decade, there is now agreement that social work skills will continue to play a part in its activities. That those skills are themselves changing has been recognised rather late by ministers, to some of whom the image of social work remains that of the professional altruist, or perhaps radical activist – a picture which, as I have shown elsewhere, is a gross simplification (Harris 1989a). The impact of the proposed community care reforms on social services departments (Department of Health, Social Security, Scottish and Welsh Offices 1989) will in some respects resemble that of punishment in the community on probation officers (Home Office 1990d: para. 1.9). Multi-disciplinary work, community involvement, systematic problem-solving, managing indirect services, imposing statutory control, working with the law, helping structure otherwise unstructured lives, mediating interpersonal conflict, helping people in crisis, evaluating effectiveness are all necessary elements of both primary crime prevention and work with victims. Many of the skills are already there, and the key question is whether the use of them will be encouraged and hence resourced by Government.

# Chapter 5

# Women and girls, criminal justice and the probation service

Men are ugly. They are dirty. They say 'Come here my little girl, and I will give you something,' – then when I go to them they try and kiss me. And I will not kiss them, because their mouths smell bad. They stroke my hair and pull it all the wrong way. And when I don't like my hair pulled the wrong way, they tell me I will be a great coquette.

(Marie Corelli: *The Master-Christian*)

Besides the chances of not being prosecuted, there are the chances of acquittal; but I doubt whether they count for much except with very attractive women.

(Shaw 1946: 37)

Women and girls feature in criminology and criminal justice both as victims and as offenders. We have learned more about them in both those roles in the last twenty years than we knew *in toto* before the early 1970s. As victims, women are more vulnerable to crime and more at risk of it generally than we had previously thought; and in particular they are at risk of crime at the hands of people known to them, both in the workplace and, in particular, at home (see, for example, Stanko 1985, 1988; Mezey 1988; Smith 1989). Children, particularly girls, are similarly liable to physical or sexual assault, frequently by trusted parental figures (Finkelhor 1986).

In relation to women as offenders, interest has followed two different but related routes. Firstly, an argument emerged among early feminist criminologists (in particular Klein 1973; Smart 1976) that the theoretical vacuum in criminology about women's crime had been filled almost by default by crude forms of biological positivism rejected a generation earlier in relation to men. Whether or not this view was correct (and for an alternative formulation, see Edwards 1984: 81), it was an historically crucial development, leading to a new questioning of treatment strategies based on the assumption that women offenders were psychologically or biologically abnormal. These assumptions had, of course, found their apotheosis in the building of the 'new' therapeutic women's prisons such as Holloway and Cornton Vale (Dobash, Dobash and Gutteridge 1986). Secondly, the interest generated in this hitherto neglected area of study caused criminal justice theoreticians and policymakers to reject as simplistic the assumption that women offenders were treated leniently by courts (Edwards 1984; Eaton 1986; Allen 1987; Worrall 1990) and that the few who went to prison were sensitively cared for when they got there (Carlen 1983; Dobash, Dobash and Gutteridge 1986; Genders and Player 1987; O'Dwyer, Wilson and Carlen 1987).

In this chapter I shall consider women as, respectively, offenders and victims. I shall deal a little more briefly with girls, because I have already reviewed the literature on the treatment of girl offenders elsewhere (Harris and Webb 1987: Chapter 6), and in spite of a few subsequent additions to the literature (in particular Elliott 1988), the picture provided there is still current. Nor shall I deal in depth with the welter of recent literature on children as victims of child abuse, as this is a major and specialised topic in its own right.

I assume that devoting a chapter to this area is its own justification in a book written primarily for people who are or hope to become criminal justice professionals. The academic debate has indirect but profound implications for practitioners, in relation to how they address the needs and circumstances of women, whether those women are victims of domestic violence, the partners of child abusers, prisoners' wives or offenders themselves. There has been a burgeoning of interest in the 1980s and 1990s in the development of gender sensitive practice (for example in relation to writing social enquiry reports and the management of women in prison). This book is not part of that tradition but, in that it reviews the knowledge which underpins these endeavours, is complementary to it.

## GIRLS AS OFFENDERS

In *Welfare, Power and Juvenile Justice* David Webb and I showed that though the treatment of girls by juvenile courts was very variable, there was a greater reluctance to involve girls in court proceedings in the first place or to commit them to custody than was the case with boys. This variation was not wholly explained by differential offending behaviour. On the other hand, precisely because girls *do* offend so much less frequently than boys and because there is no concept of an 'offending girl' (expressed, for example, in such a saying as 'girls will be girls'), the notion that a girl delinquent has done something abnormal for her sex remains strong. This notion is, of course, periodically reinforced by the demonstrably distressed and disturbed conduct and character of a minority of girls who come before the court. The concept 'oddity' makes girls especially liable to a broader and less offence-focused examination than would be the case with boys and renders girls in the court system more likely to receive supervision-related (or tutelary) sentences focusing less on the prevention of recidivism than on general moral improvement. The girls in our sample were strikingly less delinquent than the boys (both in terms of prior record and of current seriousness of offence) and the experts assigned to supervise them were less precise about their strategies, more flaccid in their aims.

In this sense, both our literature review and our empirical study gave some support to those criminologists who argued that girls were being dealt with on the basis either of the outmoded assumption that their behaviour was the product of externally determined and identifiable causes or of a concern to regulate their sex morality. On the other hand we avoided making the crude assumption that girls and boys should be treated identically and that any difference was 'sexist' (for a blunt exposition of which view, see Allen 1987). After all, material differences between boys and girls in terms of power, ascribed status, vulnerability and behaviour are such that to regard gender as an irrelevant variable in court dispositions would clearly be simplistic. Further than this, however, the argument that it is 'unfair' to make supervision orders in respect of low delinquency girls rests on two main propositions, neither of them adequately empirically verified: firstly that being on supervision is more unhelpful than helpful, and secondly that the consequences for the supervisee's future of having been on supervision are predominantly negative.

There is no substantial consumer study of girls on supervision orders, and even research based on the vulgar approach of asking large numbers of girls to 'rate' the supervision provided by different supervisors is lacking. We have little knowledge, therefore, of how helpful or unhelpful supervision is found by consumers to be. Nor is there is any recent British research which identifies effective and ineffective individual supervisor characteristics or behaviours. So far as the *consequences* of supervision are concerned, the literature is similarly unclear. We know little about the impact of having been on supervision on employment opportunities and little even about what is inelegantly usually called the 'tariff-hoist' phenomenon (that to be put on supervision is to come closer to custody next time). Since, however, so few girls are committed to custody, any such effect is presumably marginal.

The criminal justice system deals with girls who defy their socially ascribed gender expectations. With working class boys, however, delinquency is normally viewed as a 'natural phase', and where no pathology is apparent the boy is simply punished and told to behave better next time. Only with some boy sexual offenders does the problem of 'double deviance' (Heidensohn 1987: 20) – of offending against both law and gender – normally come the way of the criminal justice system. Boys' gender deviance, which typically involves homo-sexuality or having 'feminine' interests like dancing, cooking or knitting which are popularly associated with it, is normally dealt with informally by other agencies of social control from parents and teachers to adolescent counsellors.

Double deviance cannot, of course, be wished away by the 'emancipation' of women, for to extend the range of things people *can* do is a different activity from changing a popular view of what they *ought* to do. That conventional views are typically embraced by the actors themselves, for example, is a central characteristic of almost any stereotype. One of the few available ethnographic studies of girl gang members notes that the aspirations of the girls ironically replicate and inadvertently parody those of their non-deviant sisters:

> The gang is not a counter-culture but a microcosm of American society, a distorted mirror image in which power, possessions, rank, and role remain major issues but are found within a subcultural life of poverty and crime. . . . Girl members as women want to be American, to be free, to be beautiful, to be loved.
>
> (Campbell 1984: 267)

Nor is it plausible to suppose that juvenile or youth courts will cease to act on their generalised concern about girls' welfare and their particular concern about pregnancy. But if the courts are, like many parents, to exercise closer supervision over girls than boys, it is preferable that they do so overtly and in accordance with the formal purposes of law. Our study found that social workers and probation officers recommended supervision orders on more marginal girl than boy offenders for less clear reasons; yet we also found, paradoxically, that, once the order was made, rather little work was done. This suggests not so much a concerted and efficient attempt by those 'powers that be' whom one periodically reads about to monitor girls, as a lack of clarity as to how to proceed in a case where the anxiety of the experts about what *might* happen so far outstrips any justifiable concern about what *has* happened.

We should not, of course, necessarily reject this approach. If for the sake of argument we accept the view (which, though popularly accepted, is not as yet definitive) that biological differences between boys and girls contribute marginally if at all to the stark differences in the criminality of the sexes, it follows that the forms and processes of social control to which they are subjected make a major contribution to girls' very low rates of serious criminality. This leaves us with two points. Firstly that there may be something to be learned experimentally from the social control of girls which can be usefully applied to boys; and secondly that should the social control of girls become less effective in the future, with the result that girls commit as many serious offences as boys, and women as many as men, we face a social catastrophe almost too awful to contemplate.

## WOMEN AS OFFENDERS

In this section I address two questions: has the greater recognition, and indeed extension, of women's rights of the last generation been associated with any changes in the nature or extent of women's criminality? And are women, when taken to court, treated differently from men? I fear that the answer to neither of these questions is as clear as one would wish, but I hope that by the end of this section you will be aware of the main dimensions of the debate and be able to identify the key participants in it.

### Recent changes in the nature or extent of women's criminality

Since the women's movement in both Great Britain and the United States began to constitute a significant political force in the early 1970s, there has been academic interest in whether increasing sex equality would lead to what has been termed a 'convergence' (Simon 1975) of conduct between the sexes in those areas, including crime, where there had hitherto been marked differences.

Once we try to answer this question empirically we run, of course, into the very problems of criminal statistics which I have already explained. Every indicator of criminality shows that women commit fewer crimes than men, though the controversy as to why this is so simply revisits the familiar nature versus nurture debate about the causes of human behaviour generally. The official statistics indicate that men are more likely than women to be sentenced for an indictable offence by a ratio of approximately 8:1 (Government Statistical Service 1990a: Table 12.12) and the ratio of men to women in prison is much wider, at approximately 28:1, a gap which has closed only marginally over a period of almost 30 years (Government Statistical Service 1990a: Table 12.15).

Nor is there strong reason to believe from other sources of enquiry that the 'official' count of female criminality seriously misleads. NCS data in the United States show a similar male:female ratio to the official arrest figures (Nagel and Hagan 1983: 102–4) and in this country BCS paints a similar picture. Further, the greatest fear-inducing crimes are even more predominantly committed by males than others, a fact which no doubt contributes to the popular view of female crime as trivial. Self-report studies paint a slightly different picture, with a closing of the ratios when crimes of all seriousness are conflated, but the maintenance of wide ratios for the more serious offences. There is much greater convergence among more youthful offenders (Smith and Visher 1980; Rutter and Giller 1983: 120–2), and though it is unlikely that this narrowing of the gap has continued as the subjects have got older, this view cannot be expressed with certainty from the data available.

There are also interesting American data from private agencies (such as the internal security departments of shops and employing organisations), observational studies and archival research (Nagel and Hagan 1983). The first of these sources supports the official data: there is a close relation between shoplifting arrests and reported incidents, and gender has only a minor impact on the decision to prosecute (though such impact as there is suggests that men are more likely to be prosecuted for high value, and women for low value thefts) (Feuerverger and Shearing 1982).[1] Similarly, employee crime is predominantly male, with such women's crime as there is again minor. Observational studies of street crime produce similar results, with female offenders being fewer in number and typically subordinate to a male criminal. This latter point supports Anne Campbell's findings in New York (Campbell 1984; see also Campbell 1981: Chapter 3), though another discussion, demonstrating the convergence of male and female adolescent behaviour in relation to minor subcultural criminality, notes that:

there is an adolescent subculture characterized by engagement in minor delinquencies such as the use of alcohol and marijuana, truancy, sexual behavior, and petty theft. Nearly all adolescents, male and female, report some involvement in one or more of these behaviors. In addition, for both sexes, we find a normative system which encourages such behavior and a social system of frequent peer activities.

(Figueira-McDonough, Barton and Sarri 1981: 44)

Women, though less delinquent than men, are, like men, more delinquent than the official figures suggest. There are some areas of more serious crime where there is virtually no female involvement; conversely, the gap between male and female delinquency is narrowest where the crimes are least serious. The most plausible interpretation of the fact that self-report studies but not crime surveys narrow the gap is that women respondents admit to offences which are victimless (such as soft drug use or soliciting), which have non-personal victims (such as fraud or shoplifting), or which, if they have victims, are so trivial as not to be recalled by them.

It also appears, as we have seen, that the criminal role of women is characteristically ancillary to that of men. Anne Campbell's work with New York gangs suggests that girls aspire to traditional sex roles within the overall context of the American Dream; Eileen MacLeod's work with prostitutes suggests that the ponce is typically male and dominates the women (MacLeod 1982: 44–51). In crimes committed with men the woman seldom appears to take the leading role, and this characteristic seems unlikely simply to be an artefact of police chivalry or strategic advocacy.

But is the pattern of female offending becoming more like that of men? The early belief was that it was (Smith, 1974; Adler 1975; Simon 1975). There is, however, an important technical controversy here, which turns on whether it is better to measure the *relative* or the *absolute* criminality of men and women (Steffensmeier 1978).

Suppose that in 1985 100 women and 1000 men were convicted of the imaginary offence of dibbling, and that in 1990 the figures changed to 200 women and 1500 men. Depending on how you express this data, you can show that the male:female dibbling ratio has fallen from 10:1 in 1985 to 7.5:1 in 1990 or that instances of cleared-up female dibbling have increased by 100 per cent over a five year period, while for men the increase is only 50 per cent. On the face of it, therefore, we need a theory to explain this dramatic increase in female dibbling. Perhaps liberated women have more access to dibbling opportunities; perhaps dibbling is a response to the new stresses involved in being a high powered female executive; perhaps (if you are from another branch of criminology) it reflects changing family patterns, with more pressures being imposed on single mothers by an oppressive and uncaring Government (for a memorably crude version of which view, see Cook 1987).

But interpreted differently, the data show that between 1985 and 1990 the increase in cleared-up dibbling involved 500 extra men and 100 extra women, thereby widening the absolute gap between male and female dibbling even further: not only is dibbling still an over-whelmingly male activity, but it is becoming more so, since 400 more men were dibbling in 1990 as against 1985, but only 100 more women. This point should make us cautious both of statistics generally and, more particularly, of the discussion about women's liberation and its relation to their criminality.

So whether the 'gap' between male and female dibbling in particular or crime in general has widened or narrowed depends, as academics are wont to say, on what we mean by 'gap'. Men *and* women are getting more criminal; because women start from such a low baseline they are getting criminal relatively faster than men but still, in absolute terms, more slowly. To suggest, therefore, that women's liberation has 'caused' women to commit more offences is to make the following analytic errors:

(a) it is to assume that the beneficiaries of women's liberation have become criminals, rather than the poor (for a refutation of which view, see Box and Hale 1984; Box 1987);

(b) it is to underestimate the extent of women's petty crime before the rise of the women's movement;

(c) it is crassly to posit the existence of a causal link between two distinct phenomena. The syllogism is: (i) women's rights are increasing; (ii) women's crime is increasing; (iii) therefore women's liberation causes crime (for an excellent theoretical discussion of this kind of fallacy, see Doyal and Harris 1986: 66–70);

(d) it is to draw from a *relative* increase in female criminality inferences which could only be drawn from an *absolute* increase.

## Do courts treat women offenders differently from men?

The question of court dispositions of women offenders also attracted little research interest before the early 1970s when the 'commonsense' view that women were treated more leniently than men came to be increasingly challenged. The picture that has since emerged is, of course, more opaque than before, possibly because courts act so differently in relation to almost all types of offence and offender that it is impossible to draw firm conclusions about differences *between* the treatment of men and women. The technical problem is the management of a regression to the mean. For example, if we were to discover that one court treated female thieves more harshly than males and another more leniently by the same amount, our aggregated but erroneous conclusion would be 'no difference'. Alternatively, if, as is undoubtedly the case, courts sentence inconsistently *within* genders, the basis of comparison is even more unsure, and a mean would conceal the fact that both men and women were receiving erratic justice.

This problem has led some reseachers to deal instead with smaller samples in greater depth, but this approach too has severe limitations. While it can sensitise us to what *can* happen by telling us what *does* happen in particular courts on particular days, it does not tell us whether the sentencing behaviour is typical or the courts representative. And the tendency of some researchers to use their observations primarily to draw attention to wider aspects of women's experiences does not make our quest any simpler. It does, however, raise a number of interesting questions to do with whether it is proper for courts to treat women more like men, men more like women, or whether, since there are such strong gendered lifestyle and opportunity differences, these should be reflected in court dispositions according to principles yet to be determined.

The issue of courts' treatment of women offenders cannot be unyoked from the earlier decisions which got them to court in the first place. There is some evidence, for example, that the police decision to arrest can be affected by gender assumptions, and that women who are older, white and deferential are more likely not to be arrested either than men or than younger, especially black, women who are less deferential (Visher 1983). On the other hand, a thoroughgoing theory which related arrest to gender deviance would, to be upheld empirically, require the police to be especially punitive to female violent offenders. Though a few studies have found this effect, Visher's did not, and she concludes that 'particular offense types are not labeled as sex-role traditional or sex-role deviant' (Visher 1983: 19. It should be noted that this finding has been misinterpreted by a British writer (Hudson 1987: 120) who claims Visher found the opposite to what she in fact found).

It would also be wrong to assume that police discretion in relation to extra-legal variables affects women alone. The decision to arrest or not is made by police officers many times a day. As we saw in Chapter 1, to be older, apologetic and 'respectable' is as advantageous for men as for women, and gender is only one of many variables to consider in the complex process of police arresting behaviour (Nettler 1974: 57). Similarly, in their review of 16 American studies of sentencing and gender, Nagel and Hagan show that that gender differences exist, with a preponderance of leniency in the case of women, but normally only where the offence is relatively minor, and the impact of gender on sentencing is much less significant than such legal variables as offence seriousness and prior record (Nagel and Hagan 1983: 128–34).

In Great Britain the knowledge base is much lower. One study of sentencing patterns in the cases of 300 male and 100 female criminals found that the apparent leniency accorded to women was largely explained by the fact that both their prior records and their offences, though superficially similar to those of the male group, were in fact less serious (Farrington and Morris 1983), but that extra-legal variables (such as marital status) intruded more in the case of women than of men.

The assumption that extra-legal variables are powerful indicators of sentencing philosophy in the case of women has been a strong theme in the British literature in this field (see, for example, Smart 1976; Edwards 1984; Eaton 1986; Allen 1987; Worrall 1987, 1990). Not all of this literature is analytically sophisticated (for a strong critique of Edwards in particular, see Smith 1988; and note also that Edwards's use of some of the references cited to support the critique of 'leniency theory' on p.185 is seriously misleading). It is of little value simply to claim that sex role stereotyping affects the sentencing of women. If we are to develop a theory to make sense of this we need to do so either by generating sufficient data to identify how sex role stereotyping also affects the sentencing of men (for example in relation to employment record or breadwinning responsibilities) or to identify precisely how it operates with women. And this, as Loraine Gelsthorpe rightly points out, requires us to consider agency decision making not as a crude exemplification of the ill-defined concept 'sexism', but in the same analytic framework we use to understand other forms of organisational decision-making. Ideology is daily mediated by the functions of the agency and the micropolitics of the agency staff (Gelsthorpe 1989).

It is also important to distinguish the dispositional behaviour of the sentencer from the strategy of the advocate: to present a female client in terms which provoke a chivalrous response from the sentencer is a common and sensible mitigation ploy. David Moxon's study of Crown

Court sentencing, for example, (in which there is strong evidence of greater leniency for women) shows that in mitigation:

> those factors which were advanced in a disproportionate number of cases involving women emphasised that the offence was out of character (which the differences in numbers of previous convictions tended to substantiate); and that the offender had been under severe domestic or emotional stress.

(Moxon 1988: 54)

Some progress has been made in these areas, but probably insufficient for it to be said that the feminist study of criminal justice in Britain has as yet moved beyond sensitisation into analysis and theory-building. This is partly a matter of a lack of empirical knowledge which is caused in part by the very small numbers of sentenced women and partly by the tendency of some writers to read more into their data than the data themselves justify.

For example, though Farrington and Morris have suggested that offence variables are used more strongly, and non-legal variables less strongly, in sentencing men than women, the study of the impact of, say, employment or 'good fatherhood' on male criminals is, as a number of criminologists (for example Box 1987: Chapter 6) have pointed out, as yet limited. And though juvenile justice researchers and theoreticians have debated the impact of sex-role stereotyping on the tutelary sentencing of girls (Harris and Webb 1987) the picture in the adult courts is more variable.

Hilary Allen on the other hand deals with the specific case of the use of psychiatry in the case of women (concluding, in what was decidedly not a consumer study, that though women 'do rather well out of it', nevertheless 'more of these women should be subjected to ordinary punishment') (Allen 1987: 120). This study, however, constructs an elaborate theory around the fact that proportionately twice as many women as men offenders are dealt with psychiatrically. Since, however, the numbers of women so dealt with over the last five years average only 333 (as opposed to 1359 men), since psychiatric disposals generally account for only between 0.1 per cent and 0.45 per cent of all disposals (Allen 1987: 3) and since her own sample was 'small and selected by non-random criteria' and 'cannot be taken as statistically representative' (Allen 1987: 15) her data tell us little about the treatment of women, and to generalise from them could be seriously misleading.

Studies of other courts (notably Eaton 1986) find that the treatment of male and female offenders *does* fulfil Allen's injunction of equality for the sexes. These courts, however, fall foul of a different argument, that they fail to allow for the structural inequalities to which women are subjected outside the courtroom. To Eaton the court is to be criticised for 'supporting the dominant model of the family', thereby 'contrbuting to the cultural reproduction of society and, thereby, to the continued subordination of women' (Eaton 1986: 97) whereas it should be seeking 'to consider alternatives to the prevailing social arrangements and thereby to challenge the divisions of class and gender which characterise this society' (Eaton 1986: 98). Since, however, as Eaton acknowledges, the transformation of the local magistrates' court into a revolutionary tribunal seems unlikely, at least in the short term, we are left with the tautology that institutions whose function it is to uphold existing structural norms have a tendency to uphold existing structural norms. One should not shoot the pianist because one does not like the tune.

The American literature, though stronger than the British, is still provisional. Nagel and Hagan pose the theoretical question of the relation between the two dominant images of womanhood which emerge from the research: woman as the proper recipient of chivalry, and the offender as the evil woman. On the one hand, in most instances women are treated more leniently than men at the dispositional stage; on the other, the offending woman by definition divests herself of those very attributes which provoke the chivalrous response. Interestingly, there is some evidence that the commonsense assumption that women's liberation would reduce chivalry is incorrect: one American study, to the patent surprise of the researcher, found the opposite (D.A. Curran 1983). Perhaps:

> the evil woman thesis is not contrary (opposite) to the chivalry/ paternalism thesis, but rather its corollary. Thus it may be that women are preferentially treated, compared with men, until such time as the basis for that preferential treatment − chivalry or paternalism − is rendered inappropriate. Then, by virtue of the seriousness of the offense charged, the lessening of the presumption of innocence, and the evidence of deviation from traditional female patterns of behavior, the woman is moved into the evil woman category, and preferential treatment ceases.
>
> (Nagel and Hagan 1983: 135–6)

One consideration addressed by the feminist criminal justice movement is whether the problem of criminal justice for women is a function of male system domination. If there were women in positions of power throughout the criminal justice system would there be measurable changes in policy and practice which would lead to the improved treatment of women?

Behind any positive response must lie three assumptions. Firstly, the value position that it is intrinsically desirable that the criminal justice system be broadly representative of the 'respectable' population as a whole. Secondly, that if this were to happen, improvements in the treatment of women would occur. Thirdly, that we know what these improvements would be. Of these three statements, however, only the first is unproblematic: presumably if the system is not availing itself of the ablest candidates irrespective of characteristics which include gender, it is not operating optimally. The assumption that to bring more women into the system would lead to 'improvements' for women defendants, however, is much more questionable, and would probably have to be sustained by the argument that the lot of women offenders would be improved in the long term by the political and professional empowerment of women professionals (certainly female offenders seem not to prefer to be tried by female magistrates in a manner comparable to that in which some black defendants prefer to be tried by black magistrates). This, though, is a value position disguised as an empirical statement, for we cannot know if it is true. And while this is not a reason not to do it, it implies that we should do it because we believe in it, not for an instrumental reason.

Part of the problem is that it is unclear what the 'better treatment of women' actually means. To Hilary Allen it is equality with men (meaning tougher sentencing for women); to Allison Morris it is dealing with women rather as they are now and treating men similarly (meaning more lenient sentencing for men) (cited in Smith 1988: 21); to Mary Eaton it is challenging the patriarchal structure of the family in capitalist society; to Susan Edwards it is a less personally intrusive form of treatment; to Barbara Hudson it is the apparently contradictory notion of individualisation not deployed on any kind of 'discriminatory basis' (Hudson 1987: 125). In truth, it is not always clear whether these contributions are research-based empirical analyses or whether the research simply serves to buttress the writer's presuppositions. So whether it is in fact in the power of the courts to satisfy Mary Eaton without a political restructuring is doubtful; that it is impossible to satisfy both her and Hilary Allen is beyond question.

Certainly there is a problem in defining operationally what the 'improved treatment' of women would be. It seems unlikely from the research that increasing the numbers of female magistrates or lawyers will achieve it, however, at least in the short term, and any longer term cultural transformation which a process of feminisation might achieve is literally unpredictable. A study of women probation officers in the United States, for example, found they were more benign about sex offending than their male counterparts, and that sex offenders processed by women probation officers were recommended for, and received, more lenient sentences than those processed by men. This was precisely because the women officers were more concerned about the 'extra-legal variables' surrounding the offence, operating on a continuum that ended up with the dictum *tout comprendre, c'est tout pardonner* (Walsh 1984). If it is the view that women will humanise the system by bringing in more traditional 'feminine' virtues (as one strand of feminism would claim), then the consequence of that may be more sympathy for (predominantly male) offenders, more concern with the social and family context of offending and greater leniency.

Nor does the greater involvement of women magistrates seem likely to effect a sentencing, attitudinal or cultural transformation in the courts. There is some evidence that women magistrates can be more punitive than their male counterparts towards women offenders (Farrington and Morris 1983); and work by Anne Worrall indicates clearly the difficulties experienced by women magistrates in dealing with female criminals, and the factors which perpetuate the existing structures within which the discourse between the 'deviant' and the 'non-deviant' takes place (Worrall 1987, 1990).

So far as the conduct of courts is concerned, therefore, there is little agreement among the theorists about what *should* happen. This lack of agreement distinguishes the gender from the race debate in criminal justice, for in the latter area there is broad (though not unanimous) agreement that race should not be a relevant consideration in sentencing, and that blacks and whites should be processed equally. But so far as gender is concerned this agreement is not present. Nor is there agreement about what *does* happen, and here we encounter once again our earlier problems with official statistics. If higher proportions of female than male defendants are processed psychiatrically, does this mean that courts falsely attribute psychiatric aetiology to female criminality? that they ignore psychiatric symptomatology among male defendants? that earlier decision-makers (police, Crown Prosecution Service) refer proportionately more psychiatrically disturbed female than male offenders to court? that disproportionately more 'normal' female than male offenders are filtered out of the system, thereby creating a psychiatric overrepresentation among the residue? or is it simply that a cohort of women offenders is likely to contain a higher proportion of psychiatrically disturbed members than a similar male cohort? These are empirical questions and they cannot be answered qualitatively or theoretically.

We are, however, left with the intriguing argument that while women are simultaneously less likely to be sent to prison by courts, the women actually in prison are less serious offenders than men (Matthews, Barnard and Stern 1988). Here the figures do not help us, neither supporting nor refuting the argument but emphasising that there are different patterns in female than in male crime (Government Statistical Service 1989a,b). There is, therefore, a legitimate sentencing question, but it cannot be answered by a simple comparison between males and females. Part of the problem is that prison reception tables show that the bulk of female prisoners have been sentenced in a 'catch-all' category of 'theft, handling, fraud and forgery' (44 per cent against 23 per cent of men in 1988), whereas higher proportions of men have been sentenced for violent or sexual offences (21 per cent of men against 14 per cent of women) and burglary (23 per cent against 6 per cent).The catch-all category, however, includes everything from minor shoplifting to major fraud, and in the absence of more detailed study of the crimes for which women have been imprisoned it is impossible to be decisive. It is true, however, that a higher proportion of women than men were imprisoned for non-payment of fines in 1988 (25 per cent against 20 per cent), that 133 women were imprisoned in the course of the year specifically for non-payment of fines for soliciting, and that lower proportions of women than men remanded in custody were subsequently custodially sentenced (46 per cent against 61 per cent).

Similar problems arise in relation to women from ethnic minorities, where the fact that over one quarter of female prisoners are non-white rightly causes concern. The limitations of ethnic monitoring, however, prevent us from undertaking a full analysis of the criminal records and offence seriousness of black as against white women prisoners. What is clear, though, is that there is a strong trend towards the lengthy imprisonment of women, disproportionately from ethnic minorities, for serious drug offences.[2] This trend is concealed in the reception figures, but becomes clear in the population tables which show that 28 per cent of all adult women but over 50 per cent of ethnic minority women held in custody on June 30th 1989 were being held for drugs offences. In fact, on that particular day there were at most only 197 ethnic minority adult women in prison in the whole of England and Wales other than for drugs offences, including 22 violent offenders, 1 sexual offender, 5 burglars, 13 robbers and 50 in the 'theft, handling, fraud and forgery' category (Government Statistical Service 1990b: Table 1.12).

## WOMEN AS OFFENDERS: A CONCLUDING NOTE

I have offered a critical analysis of the attempt to construct a theoretical understanding of women, crime and criminal justice. The literature I have reviewed indicates that the study of women as offenders is beset by lack of knowledge, and in particular by the largely unjustifiable assumption that the increase in female crime is wholly or partially explained by women's liberation. I rejected this view in its entirety.

I then reviewed the American and British literature on women and criminal justice. I have been critical of much of the British material, and am aware that my views will be controversial. It is interesting, however, that in Great Britain the debate about women and criminal justice has been conducted almost (though not entirely) exclusively within a feminist discourse. Only the excellent literature review by Lorna Smith and the sympathetic but critical study by Loraine Gelsthorpe stepped outside this particular analytic framework (Smith 1988; Gelsthorpe 1989).

This feminist hegemony has had many advantages, notably that it has sensitised the criminological community to an important and neglected area of study and has alerted professionals to the importance of developing a gender sensitive approach to women, but it has had its drawbacks too. Feminism, though a necessary, is by no means a sufficient explanatory framework for the study of women as offenders or as victims, and the fact that some of the more recent textbooks in this area are becoming very slightly repetitive suggests that the impetus for further theoretical work is diminishing. It is especially disappointing that so little theoretical development has taken place in Britain since the pioneering work of Dorie Klein and Laura Crites in the United States and Carol Smart in Great Britain.

It is clear that there are disparities in the sentencing of men and women, but gender is less significant a determinant of sentence than are legal variables such as gravity and intent, and the extent and nature of the criminal record. On the other hand there are differences in the criminality of men and women and it would be surprising if this did not have an impact on sentencing, of a kind which we as yet understand insufficiently well. The significance of gender as a sentencing variable diminishes with the increasing gravity of the offence, however, and we cannot, therefore, isolate it from other variables which contribute to leniency: after all, an apologetic mien, a ready admission, humility and professions of shame and remorse affect sentencing at the lower end of the tariff independently of gender. While it is true that non-legal variables are more likely to be deemed relevant in the case of women, David Moxon reminds us that they are as likely to be raised in mitigation by advocates as referred to by sentencers (see also Shapland 1981): domestic oppression has strategic as well as analytic value. The feminist analysis of the rather non-feminist world of criminal justice does need to be sensitive to the advocatory necessity of portraying the female defendant in a manner consistent with the 'chivalry/paternalism' framework and which insulates her from the danger of being dealt with as an 'evil woman'.

The use of tutelary disposals for women is, however, worthy of further attention. Our juvenile justice study was clear that such disposals were used earlier and for less reason for girls than boys (Harris and Webb 1987), and Moxon shows that probation was recommended more, and community service less, for female than for male offenders in his Crown Court sample (Moxon 1988: 55). This being so, it will be especially important for probation officers to monitor the effect on women of their increasing responsibilities for targeting and supervising high risk offenders in the community. On the one hand it appears that community service is an underused resource for female offenders, yet on the other the offence patterns of female offenders make many of them precisely suitable for punishment in the community: they are almost all non-violent, non-dangerous property offenders. Though it is impossible to forecast how community correctional services will develop, it will be important for the probation service to ensure that its facilities are amenable to use by women offenders. This will not necessarily be a simple task.

## WOMEN AS VICTIMS

Whatever uncertainties may exist about the offending behaviour of women and their treatment by the criminal justice system, the nature of women's vulnerability to victimisation is less ambiguous. We have seen already that women are more fearful of crime than men, and have considered whether, as some crime prevention theorists argue, this is irrational (because they are less likely to be victimised than men), rational (because although less likely to be victimised, they are more vulnerable to the consequences if they are), or whether they are simply more likely to be victimised than the available data imply.

This latter view, at least so far as inner city dwellers are concerned, has been forcibly expressed in the Islington Crime Survey (Jones, Maclean and Young 1986; see also Young 1988): some locations are genuinely dangerous and anybody who lives there is seriously at risk. In another context, Ken Pease has shown the frequency of obscene telephone calls made to women, indicating that the content of some calls suggests that the victim is in fact known to the caller. If this is correct, clearly realistic apprehension about future risk is a more appropriate response than annoyance at a piece of randomised unpleasantness (Pease 1985), though it must be stressed that it is rare for violent or sexual offences to be preceded by obscene calls.

The greater attention paid to rape and other serious sexual offences has, over the last decade, been associated with significant changes both in rape reporting and in the processing of allegations. The British Crime Survey has shown that fear of rape is common among women who have never been raped, and that it can affect their lives by necessitating avoidance behaviour which, if successful, ironically accentuates the view that women's fears are irrational (Jones, Maclean and Young 1986: 183). On the question of how many rapes are prevented by avoidance behaviour the statistics are, by definition, silent.

It is also a commonplace that while women's image of rape is characteristically of stranger rape, the risk is greatest from those known to the victim. This remains the case, for though reports of stranger rape are increasing, they are doing so at a slower rate than those of intimate rape (Lloyd and Walmsley 1989). The nature of stranger rape may, however, have become more unpleasant than was the case in the 1970s in that a greater variety of sexual acts is now reported, though no greater use of extraneous violence (Lloyd and Walmsley 1989: Chapter 6). We do not know, however, whether this finding represents changes in rape behaviour or in police interviewing or recording practices, or, indeed, in victim frankness.

The impact of the women's movement on political and public consciousness of the nature and extent of rape has been considerable. Rape crisis centres have provided practical support and offered new options to many women who have been raped, as well as advice in self-defence and rape prevention. The movement has contributed to rape being generally viewed not as an uncontrollable outpouring of male libido but as an act of violence and oppression (Box 1983). It has contributed to a legislative change which has guaranteed anonymity to rape victims and improved police practices in relation to rape allegations (Blair 1985; though for an indication that there is still considerable room for improvement, see Smith 1989: Chapter 10; Jones, Maclean and Young 1986: 175). It has exposed the myth that rape is either infrequent or the province of strangers (Stanko 1985, 1988; Anna T. 1988) and argued successfully for longer sentences for rapists (as specified in Lord Lane's guideline judgement in R v *Billam and others (1986)*).

Academic research has also played a part in uncovering the nature and extent of hitherto little-considered instances of physical and sexual violence. There is a growing literature on violent and sexual victimisation by friends, including boyfriends (Pirog-Good and Stets 1989), and it is clear from prevalence studies of physical and sexual dating violence that both are more widespread in middle class student, as well as working class, populations than has generally been believed (Sugarman and Hotaling 1989).

But it is in relation to victimisation in the home that the greatest understanding of women's vulnerability has emerged. This, of course, affects both women and girls. As we have seen, there is a substantial literature on the vast, specialised and complex topics of child abuse and sexual abuse (see, for example, Finkelhor 1986; Wolfe 1987; Wyatt and Powell 1988; Gomes-Schwartz, Horowitz and Cardarelli 1990). There are strong similarities between child and spouse abuse: both are coercive; both predominantly involve male violence on female victims (though not, of course, invariably: see Bolton, Morris and MacEachron 1989 for a consideration of boy victims of sexual assault, and Stets and Straus 1989 for evidence of the prevalence of female on male domestic violence); and the stereotype of the rape victim as 'leading the man on' resembles that of the sexual abuse victim as a Lolita or Salome archetype.

Equally significant is the recency with which both child abuse and domestic violence have been 'named' as social problems. Both have, by becoming 'public', opened up the family to a form of scrutiny which would have been unthinkable a generation ago, and which has begun to shift the patriarchal structure of the family from its position as a taken-for-granted assumption to a focus for analysis and critique. This shift will almost certainly continue to have major implications which transcend the subject-matter of this book.

It is, however, in the context of this shift, involving the further attenuation of the father's proprietorial relation to his wife and children, that the opening up of the question of domestic violence – physical and sexual – must be viewed. How we are to penetrate the relative privacy of the family, however, is not entirely clear. Obviously a household-based crime survey such as BCS is hopelessly inappropriate (Hanmer and Saunders 1984; Worrall and Pease 1986; Stanko 1988), based as it is on the assumption that a 'household' is a unitary phenomenon, liable to attack from without but not from within. But beyond the obvious strategic reluctance of a woman to report domestic violence to a researcher, subtler issues emerge. Firstly, the victim may not recognise her own victimisation, regarding periodic violence as an invariable aspect of daily life; secondly, where she does recognise it she may choose not to report it for reasons discussed in Chapter 1; thirdly, if she does report it she may be regarded with scepticism by the police for reasons also discussed in Chapter 1 (though see also Oppenlander 1982; McLeod 1983; and, for a slightly pessimistic account of the police's implementation of 'innovative legal measures' against domestic violence in New South Wales, Stubbs and Wallace 1988). Such experiences will in turn presumably inhibit her future reporting behaviour as well as that of any friends with whom she discusses them. And fourthly, the legal basis of marriage is such that not all the sexual violence to which a wife is subjected may be criminal.

It is easier to agree that there is a serious problem than to determine what to do about it. There is a clear implication that the police, who are most obviously the responsible agency, need to improve still further the training of their officers, to recruit more women and to regard domestic violence as a serious crime. This point, it must be stressed, involves consolidating considerable progress rapidly made by many forces during the 1980s. At least as important is the effective enforcement of injunctions and the protection of women who have reported domestic violence from repeat victimisations (Oppenlander 1982). These are major tasks, their importance cannot be minimised, and it is clear that many police forces are already giving high priority to victim liaison work. For courts too, the necessity of sensitively treating victims is obvious and part of a broader problem of judicial administration which involves the reduction of waiting time, improvements in waiting facilities, explanation of procedures and the avoidance of accidental but distressing encounters between victim and offender.

But this kind of strategy can only go so far in dealing with the problems of domestic violence (Buzawa and Buzawa 1990). It can solve the problem of the victim who, though she wishes to proceed with her complaint, is deterred from doing so by system-related concerns that she will be humiliated, disbelieved or vulnerable to further attack. It would, however, be crude to assume that such concerns are the sole or even main ones of most victims of domestic violence. For some victims an analysis of the victim–offender interaction may identify points of tension or provocation which can be extinguished with professional assistance and, preferably, the involvement of both parties.

For example, work by Charlene Muehlenhard on misinterpreted dating behaviours leading to date rape identifies specific contexts associated with a male belief that the woman is sex-willing (notably when the woman initiates the date, when the woman agrees to go to the man's apartment and when the man pays the dating expenses). Men appear prone to overestimate the sex-willingness of female dates, and specific behaviours by females are liable to be interpreted as 'lead-ons' by men and to provoke claims of rape justification (Muehlenhard 1989). To make this point is not to justify the rape but to show that there is information about risky behaviour of which it is helpful for potential victims to be in possession, and which it is, accordingly, desirable for professionals also to have. Such information, it need hardly be added, is as important in work with actual or potential male sex offenders as it is with female victims. In work with victims, however, professional intervention may replace or supplement criminal proceedings. We know there are victims who, in spite of reporting violence, on reflection prefer to tolerate it rather than terminate a sporadically violent relationship. For them the support of other women will often be invaluable, as will the confidence that should their experiences go beyond what they consider acceptable, the criminal justice system will at that point be available to them, and will not condemn them for not having complained earlier, or for having withdrawn a complaint.

There is a role for the probation service here, either as a provider of a direct service (though its present duty to attempt to effect a reconciliation between the parties is sadly restricted) (see Parry 1988), or as coordinator and possible funder of voluntary efforts. The work of Victim Support Schemes has, as we have seen, been of value but is geographically patchy; in many areas Women's Aid, also a valuable resource, does not exist, and its strong feminist orientation may alienate some of the working class women who might be most in need of its services. An improved network of help for victims of violence, including the *sensitive treatment* of women who wish to proceed with a complaint; the *effective enforcement* of court orders to protect women from further violence; a *safe haven* for those who wish to leave home; *informed professional counselling* for those who wish to work to improve their relationship; and *volunteer support* for women who wish to make the best of their situation are all necessary. But these facilities need to be provided reliably and consistently, not on the basis of chance, unrelated to the existence of demand. If the probation service of the future is to take on a broad role of working with victims, working with the community, liaising with other professionals and preventing crime, the reduction of domestic violence and the enhancement of choice for its victims is worthy of higher priority than it has received in the past.

# Chapter 6

# Race, criminal justice and the probation service

Whether a black criminal ends up in prison depends far more on the class nature of his crime than on his race, or for that matter any other of his ascribed characteristics. And the overrepresentation, relative to population, of blacks in criminal courts or prisons is largely a product of legislative and court decisions regarding which offense types most merit serious punishment, and of the fact that blacks really do commit such common law offenses more frequently than whites.

(Kleck 1985: 284)

It is commonly believed that the Negro in our country is more criminal than the white. . . . Lack of formal education, the deleterious effects of the contact of the illiterate and unskilled Negro migrant with the city life of the North, the injustice of our agencies of justice, poverty and a host of other conditions are brought forward as generators of crime. The important fact, however, is the belief in the Negro's higher criminality. Regardless of its basis in reality, it is a significant element in the creation of racial attitudes toward him on the part of the white.

(Sellin 1928: 52)

Two comments on important and emotive questions: do black people (whether defined as of African or Indian origin) commit more crimes than white people? And are black offenders discriminated against by the criminal justice system? To Gary Kleck the answer is 'yes' to the first question and 'no' to the second; to Thorsten Sellin, what matters is what people *think* is the case, for it is that which governs social and political attitudes to black people.

It has been argued by conservative commentators that some theorists regard even positing the possibility of differential crime rates between blacks and whites as racist, and that the academic careers of those who have done so have been jeopardised (Sagarin 1980a). Certainly this is not an area of study invariably conducted dispassionately and analytically, possibly because of fears about the political uses to which awkward findings may be put. For example, in an emotional discussion two writers from the Radical Statistics Race Group state baldly that 'to ask the marginalized or the poor in any society the question "why do they turn to crime" is simply to put the wrong question or, as Hall puts it "a practical obscenity"' (Carr-Hill and Drew 1988: 40). They then add, in a footnote apparently designed to whip potential deviationists into line, that the question is nevertheless sometimes asked 'even by those who should know better' (Carr-Hill and Drew 1988: 58). An alternative view might, of course, be that if anything in all this is offensive, it is the mistaken assumption that crime is normal behaviour among Britain's black population. The central thesis of this chapter is that it is not, and that it is better to discuss these issues in possession of the best information we have than to resort to either racist or anti-racist sloganising.

## BLACK PEOPLE AS OFFENDERS

*Pace* Carr-Hill and Drew, in no race do serious offenders constitute more than a minute minority of the population. It is important, therefore, in reading a book such as this, which suggests that a different (but still minute) percentage of serious offenders probably exists in the black and white populations, not to assume that the issue necessarily has major policy implications: almost all people of all races are not serious offenders. The likelihood of being murdered, robbed or raped by anybody is, in most parts of the country, negligible. If one is oneself white and unfortunate enough to be the victim of a serious crime, one will probably suffer at the hands of a white male: most of the British population are white, most serious offenders male, and most interpersonal crime intra-racial.

Studies of the comparative criminality of members of different races have focused on one or more of a number of factors: biological predisposition, cultural factors, the differential availability of opportunity structures, and demographic variables such as the age and class composition of a particular population. Once again we cannot discuss these issues in a simple, empirical way because we simply do not have sufficient hard data to enable us to do so. The *per capita* offence rate of blacks in the United Kingdom is almost certainly higher than that of whites, however, though less starkly than either official figures or popular stereotypes suggest (Rutter and Giller 1983: 161), but is a product of a relatively high crime rate among Afro-Caribbeans but a rate among people of Indian origin which is probably lower than that of the white population (Mawby, McCullough and Batta 1979).[1] Nevertheless, in North America, where the research is better than in Britain, the data, though they differ on points of detail, show clearly that most minorities (Africans, Hispanics and native Americans but not Chinese) are significantly more crime-prone than white people, especially in relation to serious and particularly violent crimes (see, for example, Reasons and Kuykendall 1972; Bienvenue and Latife 1975; Curtis 1975; Wilson and Herrnstein 1985; Flowers 1988; Braithwaite 1989).

In Britain, the overrepresentation of black people in the prison system is partially (though not necessarily wholly) explained by differences in offending behaviour. The Afro-Caribbean[2] prison population contains higher proportions of rapists, robbers and, most significantly, drug offenders, and lower proportions of 'other sexual' offenders, burglars and thieves than the white population (Government Statistical Service 1990a: Table 12.17), and the longer the sentence length the more disproportionate the ethnic balance. This, however, is not to suggest that 'black people are more criminal than whites', an unfortunate generalisation carrying the incorrect implication that criminality is normal in the black community generally. It is clear, nevertheless, that race, like gender, is a relevant variable in considering criminal behaviour. This being so, it is impossible to avoid the conclusion that criminality has certain soft determinants outside the individually chosen actions of individuals (Matza 1964).

Soft determinism implies constrained choice: people's individual, family, cultural, gender and class biographies incline them, other things being equal, towards certain options and away from others. Hence we can predict that a cohort of, say, a thousand working class men will commit more crimes than one of a thousand middle class women. But because the choice, though constrained, is real, we cannot predict which members of either cohort will offend in what way and under what circumstances. If there were absolute and unconstrained freedom, we should expect a random scatter of crime across race, class, age and sex[3] and should, as criminologists, be bereft of any predictive tools at all. But, given the fact that most blacks, like most whites, are not serious offenders, the determinism must be very soft indeed if it triggers criminality in such a minute proportion of black people. Indeed the very notion that black crime has different 'causes' from white crime is controversial: perhaps, as some liberal commentators believe, it is simply that a higher proportion of the black population suffer the disadvantage which characterises many white offenders, and that that disadvantage is compounded by racism. But in this area it is always tempting to let one's predilections – whether for racist or anti-racist explanations – run ahead of the facts as we know them, and my aim here is to review those facts and recount critically, and as even-handedly as I can, the arguments behind them.

How do we address this issue, given that the nature of soft determinism is controversial? Do we opt for *historical or economic determinism* which locates the cause of different kinds of behaviour in the past and present social processes to which members of different groups have been subjected? For *biological determinism* which decrees that there are individual constitutional differences between members of different racial groups? Or for *cultural determinism* which decrees that some combination of a motley range of factors from dominant belief systems – towards material acquisitions, for example, or family roles and patterns – are significant influences on criminal behaviour? Our theory of race and crime is only as good as our theory of crime itself, and there we are, as ever, building on foundations of sand. Let us deal briefly with at least the first three of these possibilities in turn. The issue of culture is a major topic in its own right, and will not be addressed here.

In the United States, where it is impossible to unyoke the recent history of the black people from that of slavery, a clear *historically determinist* argument can be constructed which equates crime in the ghettos with the subhuman legal position of black slaves on the southern plantations prior to the Civil War. Central to this argument is the fact that ghetto violence, for example, did not 'begin' with the Watts, Newark and Detroit riots of the mid-1960s. Intermittent racial violence had occurred in the north from the time of the migrations in the 1920s (Rossi 1970: 3–6) and had only been suppressed south of the Mason–Dixon before that through physical oppression by slave owners who were as bereft of civil duties as the slaves were of civil rights. Thus did Rap Brown, a militant black leader of the 1960s, cheerfully observe that 'Violence is necessary and it's as American as cherry pie' (cited in Button 1978: 3).

The increasing articulation of historical, racial and cultural injustice among the formally liberated black population and the removal of the more overt means of preventing its public expression combined with a sustained attack on dominant American values which had its origins elsewhere. These origins lay both in teenage affluence and the compulsory involvement of articulate white youths in the Vietnam war. Together the articulation of moral outrage by the civil rights and the anti-war movements created a powder keg which could be ignited almost by chance. In this analysis, therefore, a nexus of historical circumstances 'produced' the crimes committed in Watts, at a particular historical moment, making the individual black criminal a product of the history of slavery and emancipation. Though that criminal is by no means bereft of choice, that choice is a product of the 'person', and the 'person' a product of cultural history and oppression as well as individual biography and traits. Hence, in a celebrated passage on inter-racial rape unlikely to commend itself to feminist readers:

> Rape was an insurrectionary act. It delighted me that I was defying and trampling upon the white man's law, upon his system of values, and that I was defiling his women – and this point, I believe, was the most satisfying to me because I was very resentful over the historical fact of how the white man had used the black woman. I felt I was getting revenge.
>
> (Cleaver 1968: 14)

But this is not a matter of settling an historical score. All criminal justice systems have the function of upholding the formal relations among individuals and between individuals and the state enshrined in criminal law, and it is superficial to regard different legal systems as different in purpose as well as method. Michael Hindus, for example, in an excellent comparative history of criminal justice in Massachusetts and South Carolina, concludes that for all their bases in different forms of authority, the different kinds of social and political relations which they upheld and the reforms made in the one and resisted in the other, the fundamental purpose of each was the maintainance of white power:

> . . . somehow things were not as drastically different in the two states as they appeared. Deference and other forms of traditional authority operated to keep planters and patricians in power in both states. In the highly formalized, legalistic Yankee society, control of political power was part and parcel of this accomplishment. In South Carolina . . . the courts were kept ineffectual, dueling was clandestinely promoted, and slaves were tried either on the planta-tion or before neighborhood slaveholders, never in courthouses.
>
> (Hindus 1980: 253)

Though the objective reality of slavery as an historically specific and especially coercive form of white–black relations had passed, the culture of subordination, of which slavery was an extreme manifestation, continued. The legal system was, in this line of logic, but one expression of an oppression constantly replayed on a perpetual gramophone of individual, social and political interactions, until it became a constant experience for the black population.

In this analysis the contemporary criminal justice system also embodies forms of racial oppression which permeate the social and political fabric: whereas Hindus's historical analysis is a spatial comparison between different states, a temporal comparison also holds. Hence, to understand issues such as black involvement in crime and civil disorder, we must divest ourselves of abstractions such as 'white racism' (Rossi 1970: 8) and focus on specific and contemporary manifestations of power and oppression which exist both objectively and in the collective cultural subjectivity of those experiencing and imposing them. This subjectivity has itself of course to be comprehended not only appreciatively, but rationally, theoretically and historically if we are to be aware of the true nature of racial oppression. The apparent abdication of social responsibility involved in criminality hence becomes the repudiation of a social contract by a race which has not been a party to drawing it up, and which disputes its justice and legitimacy.

Like many abstract theories, this one is not amenable to empirical testing, and will presumably be supported by those who are predisposed to support it and rejected by those who are not. The politicisation of the rape of white women by black men may, depending on your stance, be an appreciative account of an otherwise individual act of violence or the *post hoc* rationalisations of a dangerous criminal. Similarly, the question of whether the same analytic framework can properly be applied to acts of individual criminality by black people and group insurrection (such as the Watts riots) is controversial, since to do so is to posit a distinct theory of black criminality, and one which might exclude those black offenders who do not come from a slave culture.

We do not know to what extent the culture and meaning of 'slavery' are central dimensions of the subjectivity of the Afro-Caribbean British population. Though it would be wrong to ignore the impact of slavery on those black people who are concerned to rediscover their African roots, explanations of black crime in this country more commonly derive from *economic determinism*, the experience of economic marginality in what Marxists would call the capitalist relations of production:

Wherever the number of available persons is in excess of the available positions, some form of exclusionary practice grounded in a process of signification is necessary. Thus, within the capitalist mode of production . . . the racialisation of a population establishes a hierarchy of suitability and the ideological basis for exclusionary practices.

(Miles 1989: 131)

In this argument the material basis of racism lies in a mode of production which itself depends on the availability of surplus labour, thereby guaranteeing a superior bargaining power to the owners of capital over the suppliers of labour. Racism is thus an epiphenomenon of class relations under capitalism, its main convenience the visibility of the 'pecking order' which it provides. It is not an inevitable 'given', though if racism did not exist it would be essential to the logic of capitalism either to invent it or to replace it with an alternative form of signification and hence exclusionary practice. This particular form of economic determinism, therefore, makes racism an historically explicable by-product of class relations under capitalism, related both to the British imperial past and to the immigration policies of successive post-war Governments. And it is perpetuated by an institutionally racist state apparatus, in particular the police force (Hall, Critcher, Jefferson and Roberts 1978).

The relationship between this piece of social theorising and crime is also tenuous. It does contain an implicit theory of crime, however, rooted in political resistance or marginality – perhaps opportunity or control theory, positing delinquency as a product of being outside the normal reward systems of conventional society (Cloward and Ohlin 1960; Hirschi 1969; Elliott, Huizinga and Ageton 1982) and so repeatedly experiencing reminders of disadvantage and discrimination. But though tenuous, the theorising is not meaningless, irrelevant to those professionals who encounter black offenders. Both these theories, whether or not they are 'true', have behind them a value position that to understand offence and offender it is necessary to perceive them not as dehistoricised and decontextualised, but as carriers of a set of historical, economic, racial and cultural experiences, shaken by the kaleidoscope of individual belief, affect and cognition into a pattern of behaviour at once unique and culturally recognisable. Unless the professionals engage appreciatively and culturally with black offenders they will never understand the fundamental logic of the criminal act. This is not, of course, to offer a banal 'excuse' but to outline a framework within which to understand something of the relationship between individual 'choice' and the collective pressures which affect and influence that choice. This is an abstract way of saying that people, who may be black or not, offenders or not, are at once individuals and carriers of a culture and tradition. If one is part of that culture and tradition oneself it is slightly easier to be sensitive to the subjectivity of the other; if one is not, one has to tread carefully, to listen and learn, but not necessarily to make simple assumptions or, alas, always to believe:

> (Black clients) were also thought to be more unreliable and unpunctual than white clients. . . . Probation officers need to be aware of the dangers of blaming culture for difficulties of punctuality. Surely such behaviour indicates the unimportance of probation officers to the lives of clients. Frequently they have just forgotten.
>
> (Staplehurst 1983: 31)

A third form of explanation, *biological determinism*, has proved equally controversial, though for different reasons. It takes a number of forms, normally subjecting black and white subjects to standardised tests of intelligence or personality, or to genetic tests for chromosome abnormality (for a review of this literature, see, for example, West 1969b; Wolfgang and Cohen 1972; Hirschi and Hindelang 1977; Rutter and Giller 1983: Chapter 5; Wilson and Herrnstein 1985: Chapter 18). Of these tests the IQ is the most effective predictor of delinquency. Blacks tend to score lower on IQ tests than whites, and offenders score lower than non-offenders irrespective of race (Wolfgang, Figlio and Sellin 1972). A male, low IQ black adolescent, especially if he possesses other attributes commonly associated with delinquency, has, therefore, a disproportionately high probability of becoming an offender.

But this finding is not easy to interpret. Firstly, the IQ test is one of attainment rather than potential, and what is being tested is specific skill not intellectual capacity. Secondly, there is the problem of differential motivation. Since delinquency is associated with poor school performance and attainment it should not surprise us that offenders score poorly on what must seem like scholastic tests. Thirdly, it does not follow that because offenders are more likely than non-offenders to be low IQ scorers, the majority of low IQ scorers are likely to be offenders. Fourthly, it is a well-known truism that some IQ tests are ethnocentric, and though for many years now the best tests have addressed this problem we cannot assume that any specific finding is free of bias. And fifthly, individualistic approaches of this kind are inefficient in explaining either changes in delinquent behaviour which take place over time or place or white collar crimes committed by high IQ offenders (Braithwaite 1989: 124). In short, the IQ test decidedly does not provide us with a theory of crime.

This, however, is not to dismiss the predictive power of the IQ test when viewed alongside other indications of social and scholarly disadvantage, for it is perfectly possible to make pragmatic use of a predictor without knowing why it is useful (for a general discussion of the distinction between predictive and causal research, see Morris and Hawkins 1970: 241–5). But because we do not know *why* there is an association among race, IQ and crime, nor do we know the most appropriate policy response to it. Several hypotheses are equally plausible, by no means all of them constitutional, and there is insufficient evidence to establish *causal* links between poor IQ and delinquency. The good social scientist should always enquire what caused the cause, and though we do not know what causes some people to obtain a low IQ score, the reason is by no means invariably congenital stupidity.

If anything, such evidence as there is points to the contrary probability: some IQ deficits can be made up by intensive training, and there is evidence that criminality can itself be reduced by such means. In particular, promising results were obtained in the Perry Pre-School Project, an enrichment programme for low IQ black infants which, in a longitudinal study, was associated with both school success and reduced delinquency by age 15 (Schweinhart and Weikart 1980). Though we cannot generalise from this single study (see Farrington 1985, and Graham 1989 for helpful literature reviews) it should at the very least not discourage professionals, who by definition work in areas where knowledge is uncertain, from encouraging offenders and their families to improve their educational attainment and hence gain better access to the conventional reward system. Since to do this is intrinsically desirable, if there is also a hint that it may just lead to reduced criminality there is every reason to propose it, to seek funding for it and, last but not least, to have it evaluated by a disinterested researcher.

But for all this, it is important to remember that serious black crime remains, like serious white crime, the province of a tiny minority, and may in fact, as Sellin implied in the epigram, be a less serious social problem than the perceptions of it held by the white majority. This is not, of course, to suggest that it is a trivial problem, and it is clear that it cannot be explained away by liberal commentators on the grounds of such demographic variables as age or class distribution (see for example Stevens and Willis 1979: 41; Flowers 1988). Nor can the argument, from the Radical Statistics Race Group, that crimes are differentially reported depending on the race of the offender (Carr-Hill and Drew 1988) possibly be a sufficient explanation of differences in *serious* crimes, though there is reason from the British Crime Survey to believe that it may have affected the recording of minor and middle range offences (Carr-Hill and Drew 1988: 33). Nevertheless, the question of what impact if any popular stereotypes of black criminality have had on the workings of the criminal justice system is a proper one to try to answer, and it is to that question that we now turn.

## BLACK PEOPLE AND THE CRIMINAL JUSTICE SYSTEM[4]

Until the early 1980s, to the extent that serious consideration was given to race and criminal justice at all, it was polarised into a squabble between those who believed there was a 'problem' of black crime and those who believed there was a 'problem' of discrimination against black offenders. It would be easy to speak now of the literature as having generated more heat than light, but the introduction during the 1980s of ethnic monitoring within the criminal justice and penal systems resulted from the establishment of a *prima facie* case of systematic discrimination against black offenders.

At the same time, mainly as a result of changes in research funding and the politics of higher education, many academic criminologists and researchers were moving away from theoretical, and in particular critical, criminology towards the empirical study of the workings of the criminal justice system. This in turn led to critical criminology, which had hitherto been theoretical (or rhetorical), being bolstered by the injection of empirical data, including consumer, and in particular victim, perspectives on crime and its social consequences. The impact on our perceptions of crime brought about by respondents to the Islington and Merseyside Crime Surveys conducted by left realist criminologists (and already discussed in Chapter 2) has been considerable.

That it is perfectly possible for there to be a problem of black crime *and* a problem of discrimination against black offenders is now widely accepted (see for example Lea and Young 1984; Reiner 1985). Although the causes of black crime remain a matter of dispute it is now clear that its consequences fall disproportionately on the black community itself (Flowers 1988: Chapter 2). And the existence of a relationship between stereotype and reality is again probable: black crime is relatively high, therefore effective policing involves targeting the black community, therefore more black offenders are arrested, therefore black crime appears even higher than it is, therefore even more intensive policing becomes a populist clarion call (Lea and Young 1984: 167).

The criminal justice 'system' is, as we have seen in Chapter 1, best regarded as a series of decision points, with some decisions made independently, but others resulting directly from previous decisions. It is possible, therefore, for racial discrimination (the unjustifiable adverse treatment of one group of offenders over another on the ground of race) to occur at some points not at others: at the point of reporting crime (by a victim or member of the public), recording crime (by the police), deciding to proceed to prosecution (by the Crown Prosecution Service), conviction (by the magistrate or jury), report writing (by the probation officer or psychiatrist), sentence (by the magistrate or judge), appeal (by a senior judge), during the process of the sentence, including fine collection or enforcement (by the court's enforcement officer), probation order enforcement (by the probation officer), prison allocation (by the Home Office), parole decisions (by the Parole Board or its constituent local committee) and post-release licence (by the probation officer).

These possibilities are, of course, empirically daunting and, because human systems are involved, there is no likelihood that one set of interactions between points of discrimination will yield a finding which can be generalised with confidence. Some courts may discriminate some of the time, so may some police officers, probation officers and fine enforcement officers; but few are likely to do so consistently, or on the basis solely of race.

At this point, I must insert my own equivalent of a Government health warning. It is an important principle in analysing a system through which individuals proceed sequentially that the decisions of later actors are determined by decisions already made. The further we move from the original crime, the more unsatisfactory it is to analyse any decision in isolation. Courts, for example, only sentence people whom the police have arrested and charged, and against whom the Crown Prosecution Service has decided to proceed. If one court imposes higher proportions of custodial sentences than another the researcher has to determine where in the total system the discrepancy lies: in disproportionately tough sentencing, in local CPS or police strategies to filter minor offenders from the system or in the nature of local criminality. After all, if in Court Area A the police caution more minor offenders than in Court Area B, we should expect Court A to imprison a higher proportion of offenders than Court B simply because it would be dealing with a greater concentration of serious criminals. It would be an error to speak of Court A as 'tougher' than Court B. We are as yet, however, some way short of having a systemic framework within which to analyse the criminal justice system *in toto*, and in this book I can only review the available literature, and that is mainly agency specific. And as it is in relation to decision-making by police, sentencers and probation officers that the research is strongest, I shall say something about each in turn.

In relation to the police, the key question is whether decision-making leads to the inequitable treatment of black suspects. A number of issues are conflated in this question, including: is there more intensive policing in black areas leading to the apprehension of a higher proportion of black offenders? Do policing methods in black areas serve to provoke crime more than in white areas? Are black suspects treated similarly to white ones – in terms of crime recording, interrogation techniques and the granting or withholding of police bail? These issues can be addressed in a number of ways. We can examine consumer attitudes to the police (Tuck and Southgate 1981; Field 1984; Gaskell 1986) and police attitudes to consumers (Smith and Gray 1983; Ainsworth and Pease 1987: Chapter 8); specific encounters between police and public (Smith 1983; Small 1983; Southgate and Ekblom 1986; Southgate 1987); the formal discretion afforded junior officers at the point of possible arrest (Davis 1971: 80–96) and the details of police decision-making in respect of whether to caution (Landau 1981; Landau and Nathan 1983); policing strategies identified in reports on the police and race relations (Scarman 1981); and issues relating to ethnic minority recruits expressed in such areas as training, numbers of recruits, recruitment campaigns, wastage rates, disciplinary proceedings (both against the recruits themselves and against other officers guilty of racist behaviour), support structures and promotion.

None of these approaches can, by definition, answer the very broad, and hence literally unanswerable, question of whether 'the police' discriminate against 'black people' (see Waters 1990: 47–58 for a general discussion of the issues). All of them can, however, throw a little light on a more precise area of police activity. The research tells us, for example, that consumer satisfaction with the police is lower among blacks than whites, but still reasonably high except in areas where there has been a record of urban conflict. The figures do suggest a degree of ambivalence, however: one study, for example, showed that 92 per cent of whites and 84 per cent of blacks had no wish to complain about the police, but noted that among the black community there was a degree of generalised discontent which appeared to be fuelled by 'rumour and hearsay' (Tuck and Southgate 1981: 44). Since there have been particular grievances about the discriminatory use by the police of section 4 of the Vagrancy Act 1824 (the so-called ' "sus" clause'), the repeal of this section may have served to enhance police–ethnic community relations (see, for example, Benyon 1986).

We also know that police attitudes became more positive in the course of the 1980s. PSI studies published in 1983 revealed widespread instances of discriminatory attitudes (though not necessarily behaviour) among the Metropolitan Police (Smith and Gray 1983), and the Scarman Report suggested there was cause for serious concern about police attitudes and tactics in Brixton (Scarman 1981; see also Pitts 1988: Chapter 7). More recently, however, the police have responded to these problems. There have been adjustments to training, interrogation and disciplinary procedures to discourage racist behaviour at an individual level, and operational adjustments to encourage the more sensitive policing of areas with large black populations. There is as yet no authoritative research on the impact of these changes in policy and practice on service delivery, however, and in this rapidly changing field it is wrong to assume that the findings of ten-year-old studies are accurate accounts of policing in the 1990s. Equally dangerous, as any provincial police officer will confirm, is to generalise about 'the police' from a study of the Metropolitan force.

So we know that the police have taken recent but active steps to respond to concerns about their practices with ethnic minorities, but not how successful they have been. Nor do we know precisely what impact on decision-making about black offenders the introduction of the Crown Prosecution Service in the mid-1980s has had. It would be wrong, however, to assume that plugging these gaps would of itself enable us to determine effective and appropriate policing policies. For example, 'softly softly' policing strategies in ethnic minority areas have been encouraged by some black community leaders, but we know too little about the views of black communities as a whole to be confident that they would meet with general approbation. It would not be difficult, for example, to mount a case that such strategies could themselves lead to the neglect of the problems of black victims, implying that the inner cities in general and black victims in particular were unimportant. Nor is the subtle intrusiveness of community policing or the recruitment of more black officers necessarily going to solve these problems.

Nor again can the strategic value of the 'race card' to black offenders be ignored. Any system is most vulnerable to attack in those areas where it has been successfully attacked in the past and where it is committing itself to change, and the prevailing discourse of 'anti-racist' policing makes it almost uniquely difficult for a predominantly white police force to respond to unjustified claims of racism without the denial itself being taken as proof of guilt: to deny the charge is to stand convicted of it. This phenomenon is not unique to this country:

> police in the Netherlands sometimes complain that members of ethnic minorities are quick to argue with police officers and that they complain they are being stopped and searched 'because I am a Surinammer, a Turk . . .' An illustration of this was a meeting by the police (in the Bijlmermeer) with members of ethnic minorities to discuss the problems in the police–ethnic minorities relationship. In the heat of the argument one Surinam boy said that 'you weren't allowed to kick police officers in Surinam either'. He was immediately called a traitor by many of the Surinammers present.
>
> (Junger 1989)

There is also a literature on *courts and sentencing*. In Britain the literature is rather slight, in America extensive. In neither case is there convincing evidence that racial discrimination in sentencing (RDS) is widespread, though there is a somewhat stronger argument that the consideration by courts of non-legal variables such as employment and family status can impact indirectly on black offenders. In the United States, definitive reviews of the research on RDS by Gary Kleck (Kleck 1981, 1985) have shown that with specific exceptions in some southern states, particularly in the capital sentencing of black-on-white rapists (see also Wolfgang and Riedel 1977), race is not a significant factor in sentencing. This is not to say, however, that there is no racial discrimination in sentencing (and for a contrary view see Thornberry 1973, 1979; Gibson 1977–8), but that the research into it does not, *pace* the claims of some researchers, justify the conclusion that any overrepresentation of blacks in prison, the gas chamber or the electric chair is a result of it.

Nor does Kleck's work imply that race is *never* a factor: sentencing variation among jurisdictions and indeed individual sentencers, and the ineffectiveness of existing accountability structures make it almost inevitable that a range of prejudices, including racial prejudice, will be acted out. This, though, works both ways, and in some jurisdictions black offenders appear to receive consistently *favourable* treatment from sentencers. If this is indeed the case, it is possible that the justice system may, though not demonstrating high levels of discrimination, be more arbitrary than might at first appear. If being black may help *or* harm a defendant, a statistical regression to the mean will simply conceal the degree of variability within the system.

But we should not overstate this hypothetical possibility. In his review of 57 studies, some of which claimed a significant 'race factor' in sentencing which was not borne out by the data, Kleck found that while black-on-white crimes *were* treated more severely than crimes involving other racial combinations, this was due to legally relevant factors, not the racial combination. A study of black-on-white rape in Oakland, California throws some light on this:

> Interracial rape on Oakland, according to our data, is overwhelmingly a stranger-to-stranger crime. Unlike intraracial relations, where the rape offender and his victim frequently make initial contact in a social context, such as drinking at a bar together, the access of black offenders to white women is obviously restricted. The crossing of interracial boundaries takes place at those points at which the white victim is most readily available and vulnerable. The dominant scene of interracial rape in Oakland is of victims being seized in public places, as they await transportation or walk in a street or park.
>
> (Agopian, Chappell and Geis 1977: 137–8)

Kleck approached his review of the literature by asking why there was a widespread view that RDS was widespread when the evidence suggested otherwise. His answer lay in a number of 'short-cuts' taken by academics and students when reading the research, combined with the commitments of the researchers themselves:

> To discover what the available evidence on a given question indicates, students and members of the general public depend primarily on textbooks and public statements of social scientists. Text authors and most other nonspecialist professionals in turn primarily rely on short statements summarizing the evidence which are contained in the literature review sections of journal articles and monographs written by specialists on the topic. If an erroneous image of the evidence on RDS had become widespread, it was likely

to be traceable to these brief summary statements. Therefore, I went back through a selection of them to see what it was about them which had conveyed such a misleading picture.

(Kleck 1985: 272–3)

Kleck extracted five common practices: *selective citation* (offering a biased selection in the literature review), *letting the evidence speak for itself* (stating certain 'facts', notably the overrepresentation of blacks in prison, and leaving readers to draw their own conclusions), the *'mixed bag'* (including irrelevant as well as relevant data), *research democracy* ('all studies are created equal', giving equal weight to the patently deficient and the methodologically sophisticated study in a field where it was the least rigorous studies which were most likely to support the RDS hypothesis) and *magnanimous neutrality* (describing as 'mixed' or 'ambiguous' evidence which predominantly contradicted RDS) (Kleck 1985).

But Kleck's interest was in the American criminal justice system. Perhaps there is firmer evidence of racial discrimination in sentencing in this country, especially if we stretch the concept 'sentencing' to include the decision to remand in custody? The evidence is by no means firm, but as Waters notes:

It is important to see the paucity of empirical research into sentencing and ethnic minorities . . . against a general background of an area that is not methodically researched, compounded by a loosely structured system of high maximum penalties, a wide judicial discretion and occasional guidance from the Court of Appeal.

(Waters 1990: 86)

Two rather small scale but much cited studies (McConville and Baldwin 1982; Crow and Cove 1984) suggest there is no clear evidence of RDS in Britain, though a small but complex study in West Yorkshire by Mair has cast some doubt on this view, with probation orders and immediate imprisonment being disproportionately used for white offenders, and community service orders and suspended imprisonment for blacks (Mair 1986). In a further study, Hudson reports an intermittent sentencing survey of eight London courts over a three year period, involving 8,000 sentencing decisions. Though custody rates were significantly higher for Afro-Caribbean males than their white counterparts, this largely reflected the disproportionate involvement of blacks in serious crime such as drug importation and robbery, where custody would have been inevitable irrespective of race.

Nevertheless, she also found significantly higher levels of imprisonment among Afro-Caribbean offenders sentenced for such 'middle-range' crimes as assault occasioning actual bodily harm (75 per cent against 50 per cent) and burglary (64 per cent against 49 per cent), though as these samples do not appear to have been matched they are not definitive. Minor Afro-Caribbean offenders were also more likely than whites to receive such 'interventive' sentences as probation and community service, and less likely to be conditionally discharged (Hudson 1989: 9). She concludes that race directly influences sentencing of middle range violent offences and indirectly (through the medium of unemployment) the sentencing of property offenders. She also suggests that black offenders have a shorter 'tariff' of pre-custodial sentences, entering custody earlier than broadly similar white offenders.

But the picture is not unambiguous, not least because of the lack of methodological details provided: indeed the paper has the air of 'work still in progress' about it. Hudson does, however, make a number of important points.

Firstly, there is an interesting relationship between discrimination and disparity in sentencing. Custody rates vary significantly among courts in her sample, with the highest rates generally occurring in courts which deal with the highest proportion of black offenders. It will be important, therefore, for future research on discrimination to note the impact of disparity on sentencing, and of much interest to undertake more research on disparity, to determine whether that disparity is chance or patterned. In that disparity among courts is encouraged to enable courts to reflect local concerns and crime trends, the possibility of an association between 'tough' sentencing policies and the existence of high density ethnic minority populations is worthy of empirical testing.

Secondly, the lower rate of social enquiry reports on black offenders (a contrary finding to that of Mair in West Yorkshire) was attributed to the greater likelihood of black defendants pleading Not Guilty and being sentenced without a report to obviate the need for a further remand, presumably frequently in custody. In addition, for reasons about which one can only speculate, black defendants are apparently more likely to elect trial by jury than to accept summary trial. All this creates a complex issue. It seems desirable (a) that social enquiry reports should be available on defendants irrespective of race, (b) that no pressure beyond the incentive of the 'guilty discount' should be exerted to encourage Guilty pleas, and (c) that there should be no delay in sentencing following conviction. Yet the combined effect of this process is that a group of disproportionately black offenders is being sentenced in the traditionally firm Crown Courts without a guilty discount and lacking the explanatory benefit of a social enquiry report which might contextualise both the offence and the plea. There is little research on the effectiveness of (predominantly white) barristers in extracting relevant information from, and mitigating effectively on behalf of, black offenders, but the process is unlikely always to be straightforward, and the omission of a social enquiry report, with its potential to translate the offender's world into language comprehensible to the court, may therefore be serious.

Much of this is speculative, but it will by now be clear that to consider sentencing in isolation from other parts of the criminal justice system is difficult, and to regard it as an exact science, susceptible to any quantitative methodology which presupposes consistency, is incorrect. This makes the widespread local monitoring of court practices vital, and for there to be developed a forum for feedback on comparative strategies, and for discussion of individual cases, involving all members of the local criminal justice system.

The *probation service* has also been much studied in relation to its work with black offenders, for example by Taylor (1981), Pinder (1982), Whitehouse (1983), Green (1987) and Waters (1988, 1990). The main probation associations have developed policy proposals to ensure the equitable and sensitive treatment of offenders from ethnic minorities. Some of the issues raised have been extensions of the importance of 'good practice' generally – of such principles as clear communication, sensitive listening, developing creative responses to unusual need – others have involved challenging the ethnocentricity said to permeate much professional practice. Other exigencies have included increasing the numbers of black probation officers, mediating on behalf of black offenders with the less *sympathique* elements of the criminal justice system, and enhancing professionals' awareness of their own racism and increasing their knowledge of how diverse cultural patterns intersect with the absolutism of the English criminal code.

Particular attention has been given to the social enquiry report, the writing of which is not only the commonest justification for the first encounter of probation officer and defendant, but also the means of communicating information about that person to the court, and so contributing to the sentencing process. An early paper by Whitehouse, based on a number of training events in the West Midlands, began to identify the potential significance of the most innocent sounding comments and, by implication, drew attention to the different levels of ethnic sensitivity which existed among the criminal justice agencies. Could one conceive of the police or prison service, for example, agonising over the racism supposedly inherent in a passage such as this?

The family members have been mutually supportive and the parents are respected by their children. However, my colleagues have found that both parents have tended to be strict and have relied on physical punishment during the children's formative years, although at the same time there has been considerable affection within the family.

(Whitehouse 1983: 46)

Later studies of the probation service's work suggested that any problems of discrimination could not be laid primarily at the service's door (Mair 1986; Waters 1988, 1990), and that though the service itself was not immune from the institutional racism (Miles 1989: 50–62) of even the most liberal institutions in white society (Green 1987), examples of good practice were not infrequent (Staplehurst 1983). Waters's work on social enquiry reports sought to transcend the subjectivity of Whitehouse's earlier approach by making use of the comments of a 'multi-racial panel' (Waters 1990: 106–13) on a range of reports on black offenders in which there was:

evidence of both forms of race bias, positive and negative, but generally speaking depicting probation officers' reports on black (and Asian) defendants in a more positive light than earlier writers . . . The high number of recommendations for probation-oriented disposals, the concurrence rate between recommendation and outcome and the obvious attempts by report-writers to elicit sympathy are all indications of a more pro-active approach by probation officers which does not accord with the notion that the courts or the probation service are ambivalent or seek to exclude ethnic minorities from probation intervention.

(Waters 1988: 92)

## CONCLUSION

There are, as I have argued, severe limitations in analysing the impact of a system as a whole on one aspect of its throughput – black offenders – by reference solely to the practices of some of that system's parts. On the evidence that we have examined, neither sentencing nor probation work in isolation offers a plausible explanation of the high representation of ethnic minorities in the prison system. Since, as we have seen, higher proportions of black prisoners have committed serious offences than have white prisoners, we can certainly reject any suggestion that blacks are generally being imprisoned for trivial misconduct.

The position with the police is less certain: much of the evidence is out of date and we do not know what impact the flood of directives from the Home Office and senior command has had on the day-to-day behaviour of front-line officers. Further, the question of the 'proper' policing of ethnic minority areas is not one to be answered in a facile manner. Neither 'strong arm' policing which alienates the community as a whole nor 'softly softly' policing which fails to protect ethnic minority victims from ethnic minority criminals should be embarked on lightly. Part of the correct strategy must surely be for the police to continue and further develop their formal and informal links with ethnic minorities, so increasing their credibility and enhancing the confidence of the community as a whole. The difficulty of doing this should not be underestimated, however, and the frequent complaint from the police that they are being scapegoated for broader problems of race relations is probably correct.

There *is* a 'problem' of black crime and it would be foolish to deny it. The evidence from the United States that this is so is overwhelming; the evidence from Britain though less than overwhelming, is still strong. Theoretical criminology does not tell us why this is, or accordingly what to do about it. We know, however, that the main losers by such crime come from the black community itself: black crime is no more a Robin Hood activity than white crime. Both predominantly involve the poor victimising the poor: the problems of the inner cities lie where they fall – in the inner cities. To excuse or romanticise the predatory black criminal ignores these realities and implies that lower standards of behaviour can be tolerated from black people than from whites.

The responsibility for dealing as knowledgeably and sensitively as possible with black offenders is one for all agencies, however, for the danger of the stereotype is ever-present, not only for sentencers and the police but for probation officers too. Stereotypes cannot, of course, be avoided in any area of life: they are crucial means by which we recognise new situations and determine actions. We know that for social workers the 'what type of case is this?' question (Giller and Morris 1981) is essential to survival. My own stereotypes about, say, Italian drivers or Scottish weather are confirmed every time I cross a street in Naples or spend a wet weekend in the Highlands, and no doubt I reinforce them by filtering from my mind the occasional courteous Neapolitan driver and the slightly less occasional fine day in the north of Scotland. Simple prejudices of this kind are probably neither here nor there, but stereotypes matter much more when the signification is done by professionals, and when the imbalance of knowledge, power and authority is so great.

The danger of the stereotype is of two main kinds. There is a specific sense which involves the misapplication of a generalisation to a particular circumstance and a general sense in which deviance or pathology is attributed to alternative, and culturally explicable forms of social behaviour. The specific stereotype is best dealt with by professionals acquiring and applying a sceptical, enquiring, empirical mind, and being alert to the danger of forming conclusions on the basis of *a priori* assumptions rather than empirical enquiry, of succumbing, that is to say, to the tyranny of routinisation. That this particular book does not deal directly with this issue does not make it unimportant, and good professionals will doubtless study some of the better practical handbooks to supplement it (in this area a good starting point would be Nicolson and Bayne 1990).

The general stereotype stems from a lack of the cultural pluralism which, to borrow and adapt a phrase from C. Wright Mills, only an anthropological imagination can induce. Many studies of so-called 'primitive' societies, their linguistic codes (Kluckhohn 1949), social rituals, values and religious practices indicate the underlying utility of the seemingly bizarre. As societies evolve, so do these practices, to respond to new demands and circumstances in a manner which makes internal cultural sense. The imposition of disruptive change from without creates resistance and is generally counterproductive. Studies of black youth culture in Britain or America, for example, demonstrate that characteristic 'criminal' subcultures are comprehensible (if not always functional) responses to the experience of racial discrimination or even oppression, in an alien mainstream culture (see, for example, Brake 1985: Chapter 5).

The fundamental problem, therefore, is of fair treatment, and though the question has been posed as to whether, in an unequal society, equal treatment of blacks and whites is proper (Pinder 1982; Waters 1990) equality before the law is at least a less damaging starting point than any conceivable alternative. The danger is that, in the belief (which may well be correct) that disproportionate amounts of serious crime are committed by black people, 'good' policing comes to involve targeting black areas, sentencers respond to individual black offenders on the basis of racial stereotypes and the liberal and radical professionals, bewildered as to what anti-racist strategy to adopt, find themselves denying that which is patent and defending the indefensible. Since, for reasons I have tried to show in this chapter, quantitative research into specific parts of the criminal justice system can produce only a limited amount of generalisable data, there is a serious need for academics and researchers to develop a systemic approach to the study of the criminal justice system as a whole, perhaps of the kind which has been more fully developed in relation to juvenile justice.

A crucial part of this strategy, however, must be the close monitoring of local criminal justice systems by the various professionals themselves, as well as the development of closer links between all parts of the local criminal justice system. The existence of a statutory forum to bring together sentencers, police, probation officers, community groups and minority interests themselves would be a desirable means of dealing with the issues of public safety and civil liberty discussed here, and it is a matter to which I return later.

# Chapter 7

# Sentencing practice and the social enquiry report

. . . a standard set of 'relevant' factors become imbued with some meaning, and this is routinely presented as a form of individualized justice. Social enquiry reports for example typically concentrate on a set of home circumstances and psychic features of the offender and these are weighted according to the theoretical orientations of the report writer.

(Bean 1976: 91-2)

Now, there are but few cases in which the offender is without some extenuating circumstances . . . In fact, there is no crime in which it is not easy to discover them. It requires but a slight investigation and they swarm on all sides. In short, the only criminals who appear to us to be without excuse, are those for whom we have not taken the trouble to find it.

(Garofalo 1914: xxv)

There is an extensive literature on sentencing and a smaller but still considerable one on social enquiry reports. The literature on sentencing falls into a number of categories, which we will term the philosophical/analytic, the empirical, the informational and the reformist. They address respectively the principles on which academic philosophers assume sentencers base their decision-making; what those sentencers actually do; middle range theories of what the job entails – the statutes enforced, sentencing powers and obligations, the role of superior court guideline judgements, issues of gravity, intent, culpability, persistence and so on; and what the commentators believe *should* be the proper process of sentencing. These four categories are ideal types and not mutually exclusive (for example, Nigel Walker's superlative *Sentencing: Theory, Law and Practice* (Walker 1985) manages to combine at least something of all four in its 510 pages) though they do draw on different forms of knowledge. In this chapter I shall firstly discuss, and provide selective references on, aspects of three of the areas (the informational element does not lend itself to a brief account and is best pursued in one of the specialist texts cited in this chapter), and if at the end of this section you have a mental 'map' of the key issues and themes, my aim will have been met.

Secondly, I turn to social enquiry reports. Again I shall briefly introduce the key literature and consider how sentencing and social enquiry relate to each other. By the end of the chapter you should have gained some understanding of how social enquiry reports have developed historically, and how they might develop in the future.

## SENTENCING: IN THEORY, PRACTICE AND PRINCIPLE

Sentencing can be viewed in rather different ways. To the moral and political philosophers whose writings dominated early theoretical discussions about the principles of criminal justice, it is a practical application of the right (or obligation) of the state to punish the wrongdoer. Taken thus, to extract the practical activity from the assumptions which underpin it would constitute a flight into mindless technicism, an abdication of justice itself. The first category is, therefore, a *philosophical* debate about the right act of the state in response to a crime, and sentencing itself is a second order concern, a matter of implementing that right act.

The debate is well worn, and though Michel Foucault argues, with characteristically creative historical method, that a political theory of punishment can be discerned in early examples of medieval torture, the imposition of pain on the body of the condemned man being a precise reflection of the man's own treachery against the sovereign (Foucault 1977), it is with the Enlightenment and the social contract that the study of punishment really begins. This point, however, is in danger of tempting us into the realms of political philosophy, a temptation which both brevity and lucidity demand that we resist. In brief, however, the nature of the state's 'right act' provokes intense controversy, and it is to the question *what is the right act of the state when faced with a crime against its laws?* that the commentators have produced fundamentally different answers.

To one school of thought, the *retributivists* (see Honderich 1969; Walker 1969; Bean 1981; Prins 1982), rightness is best expressed as denouncing wrong (and so reinforcing right) by imposing a punishment regarded in contemporary society as proportional to the harm done:

Even if a Civil Society resolved to dissolve itself with the consent of all its members – as might be supposed in the case of a People inhabiting an island resolving to separate and scatter themselves through the whole world – the last murderer lying in the prison ought to be executed before the resolution was carried out. This ought to be done in order that every one may recognise the desert of his deeds, and the bloodguiltiness may not remain upon the people; for otherwise they might all be regarded as participators in the murder as a public violation of justice.

(Kant 1887: 198)

In this view, to impose a penalty proportional to the nature of the crime is not only the right but the duty of any society. Though expressed by Kant metaphysically as expunging 'bloodguiltiness', the position, or a variation on it (Walker 1969: Chapter 1) has many contemporary adherents (for a celebrated theological defence of retributivism and an attack on humanitarianism, see Lewis 1948/9). The attractiveness of retributivism lies in its application of a 'scale' of penalties which prevents a therapeutic or otherwise discriminatory overreaction. To the extent that it involves the punishment fitting the crime not the criminal, it is the most basic form of 'justice' conceivable, and as we shall see when we come to discuss sentencing reform, the clarity and specificity of the retributive approach make it an attractive proposition for those writers keen to develop more open and account-able sentencing structures (Pease and Wasik 1987). It does not, however, deal with the substantive question of how the 'scale' of justice is to be translated into practical reality: how much a rape, burglary or assault is 'worth'.

A more recent offshoot of retributivism has been reparation. The argument that the fundamental 'conflict' between criminal and victim has been 'stolen' from them by the state (Christie 1977) reminds us that part of the origins of punishment by the state lay in the attempt to create social order by the removal of private feud and vengeance. Retribution replaced informal measures of reparation when the reparative process spilled into uncontrollable disorder by creating the concept of the state as victim. The contemporary argument that the reinstatement and enforcement by the state of a 'paying back' process from offender to victim is a proper way to proceed within criminal justice (see, for example, Wright 1982), therefore, replaces a retributive relation between offender and state with a reparative one between offender and victim. Many retributivists, therefore, would accept reparation in principle, for the concepts of balance and proportionality are common to both, and, in the splendidly ambiguous community service order, are almost interchangeable (Advisory Council on the Penal System 1970; Young 1979).

Retributivists have, however, been criticised on grounds which include their insensitivity to individual circumstances, the fundamental injustice of their concern to impose equal penalties in an unequal society, their lack of compassion and forgiveness and, because in that by imposing pain equivalent to that caused by the crime they would have the state act as badly as (or, since the pain is so much more calculated, worse than) the criminal not in a morally superior way, their moral bankruptcy.

A different position entirely is that the right act is to impose the penal measure most likely to *deter* the offender (and, in a slight variation, to deter others) from future crime. This view, deriving from the Utilitarian philosophers (in particular Bentham 1789), is that punishment, in that, by deliberately imposing pain it departs from the obligation to increase the sum of human happiness, is intrinsically undesirable. It can be justified, therefore, only to the extent that it prevents future criminality imposing even greater unhappiness. Whereas to the retributivists the 'right act' involves the deliberate but measured imposition of pain, to the deterrent theorists the imposition of pain is a necessary evil. A punishment which either does not reduce crime or is greater than that needed to achieve its end[1] is, therefore, a wrong act.

Deterrent theorists have also been criticised. It is said that by rejecting the propriety of punishment they ignore the inevitability of revenge which the criminal code was in part instituted to control; that they leave the door open for arbitrariness and injustice by permitting the punishment of an innocent person (on the ground that to punish such a person may, if it prevents other crimes, meet the criterion of increasing the sum of human happiness); that they relegate the relation of state and individual from a moral to a purely technical one; that they prevent the creation of any consistent relation between crime and punishment; and, in that very few punishments demonstrably stop crime, that their approach means that frequently no response to crime is permissible (see Walker 1985: Chapter 7 for a sophisticated discussion of a number of these criticisms).

A third approach holds that the proper function of the state is to *prevent* criminals from offending by execution or physical incapacitation. This is sometimes called prophylactic theory. It has in the past found expression in preventive detention and the extended sentence, and has re-emerged recently as a possible means of achieving economic and effective crime control. This more recent interest has been in selective incapacitation, reflecting both the concern to experiment with crime prediction and the fact that most crime is committed by a small number of people whose long term removal would therefore have a disproportionate impact on the crime rate generally. By selective incapacitation, the argument goes, the maximum 'value' (expressed in terms of crimes prevented) can be extracted from each prison place, and the accurate measurement of the benefits as well as costs of prison becomes possible (Greenwood with Abrahamse 1982; for a powerful critique of selective incapacitation theory, see Von Hirsch 1985).

That there is room for prophylaxis in the penal system is uncontroversial (even the arch-reformist Karl Menninger accepts the existence of some form of 'facility' for 'professionals') (Menninger 1966: 251), but, like the appropriate balance in the retributivists' scales of justice, this does not take us very far towards agreeing from whom we should be protected, for how long, in what conditions and at what cost. After all, though there will be little controversy in relation to extreme cases, we could probably argue all day about which lesser offenders should be just above, and which just below, the prophylactic cut-off point. Indeed the entire thrust of the British Government's current policy of encouraging community-based sentencing is to dissuade us from incapacitating non-violent offenders.

Or should our primary concern be with *reforming* the criminal and not with punishment at all? Karl Menninger is unequivocal here, but does not argue for reform at the expense of other possibilities: only that the other possibilities should follow the failure of the reform attempt. For some, the 'blurb' on the dustwrapper of *The Crime of Punishment*, which perfectly summarises the theme of the book, will make chilling reading:

> The author proposes some startling remedies. He would . . . replace punitive vengeance with scientific assessment. On the basis of such assessment, many useful devices could be employed for effective rehabilitation. Failing rehabilitation, permanent detention or other controls should be made certain.
>
> (Menninger 1966)

To critics of reformism, this represents the apotheosis of control, achieving the ultimate aim of the totalitarian state by creating a world in which criminals no longer *want* to offend. Of course, in spite of the possibilities inherent in technological advance (Harris and Webb 1987:

Chapter 7), the medium term probability of such control being effectively imposed on any social system is slight (Harris and Webb 1987: 64). Agencies charged with enforcing social control are seldom efficient or even unambiguously motivated to do so; the intended subjects of control have, like other worms, an occasional tendency to turn (one should never underestimate the power of the powerless to subvert the controlling ambitions of the powerful); and in any liberal democratic society, the value of conformity exists in counterpoint to that of privacy. The case of child protection, for example, shows clearly that excessive control can unexpectedly trigger resistance both from those subject to, and those imposing, the control (Harris 1990b). It is, after all, central to British culture that the spectre of *1984* is to be resisted.

This philosophical/analytic approach, though intriguing, is incidental to the practice of sentencing. Not least among the practical limitations of this mode of analysis are that most of the sentencers themselves have almost certainly never heard of it, that there is no simple relation between any one of these approaches to the 'right act' and any specific penalty, that it is as inconceivable in the practical world of the courtroom as it is socially undesirable that any one of them should hold sway at the expense of the others, and that if one did, it would be a clear ground for appeal, either against harshness or against leniency. Sentencing is an essentially eclectic activity (Thomas 1970; Walker 1985: 117–21).

It is important, therefore, to distinguish the proper concern of the academic commentator to develop a frame of reference within which to analyse what courts do or should do from the separate issue of the practical conduct of the sentencer. The approach outlined here will assist in the former but not the latter. Though professionals in the criminal justice system will periodically come across references to retribution, deterrence, prophylaxis and reformation and should therefore have some acquaintance with what they mean, only a minority will need or wish to explore them in greater depth or to engage in discussions about, say, the relation between retribution and reparation, or between reformation and rehabilitation, on which much has been (and could here be) written.

## SENTENCING: AN EMPIRICAL APPROACH

Sentencing in England and Wales is primarily the business of the lay and stipendiary magistracy and different tiers of Crown Court judges. Numerous texts on the English legal system explain the structure and powers of the courts more fully (see for example Berlins and Dyer 1982: Chapter 2; Prins 1982: Chapter 6; White 1985: Chapter 1). But the aims of sentencing are, beyond the unhelpful abstraction of 'doing justice', neither clear nor agreed (Thomas 1970; Ashworth 1983; Walker 1985: Chapter 8); and, this being so, there are obvious problems in evaluating to what extent they are met (though for excellent reviews of the 'effectiveness' literature, see Lipton, Martinson and Wilks 1975; Brody 1976). Even the apparently simple quantitative approach of examining the relative reductionist capacity of different sentences presents problems. Firstly, as we saw in Chapter 1 the measurement of reconvictions is insensitive and unreliable; secondly, as there is little agreement among researchers about the criteria for success, comparison of different studies is difficult if not impossible (Hood and Sparks 1970: 175–86) and thirdly, the quality of the studies is once again variable (Harding and Koffman 1988: Chapter 8).

No study provides clear indications of what sentences are 'effective' with what kind of offender. This should not surprise us, for the scientism of criminal justice research in the 1950s was based on the extraordinary belief that a single event in the life of a human being – a sentence – would determine the pathway of his or her future criminality. Though, as we shall see in the next chapter, we are by no means devoid of predictive tools, they typically relate to such demonstrably powerful and prolonged personal experiences as parental criminality, patterns of child rearing, the quality of parental supervision (Riley and Shaw 1985) and substance abuse. The idea that an offender's future criminality should be predictably affected by a middle range sentence imposed, say, two years earlier is no longer credible.

Of course we can use other criteria to evaluate sentencing effectiveness. We can if we wish look not at the impact of sentence on future criminality but at the level of sentencing for particular crimes (the question of proportionality) or at the relativity of sentences imposed by different courts (that of consistency) (Walker 1985: 108–17). We can look at the factors – mitigating or aggravating – which encourage sentencers to depart from the norm (Thomas 1970) and argue about whether this is proper, or reflects inappropriate class, race or gender bias. We can argue about the costs of punishment: in the absence of clear behavioural consequences of sentencing is not the cheapest penalty the best? If we take this rather attractive line, we can certainly examine with interest the actions of a Government which, in the 1980s, imposed stringent cash limits on almost all public sector agencies, but continued to permit prison to be available as an open-ended resource for sentencers irrespective of the absence of either value for money criteria for its use or performance indicators for the sentencers themselves.

Sentencing as an activity, then, is largely devoid of agreed aims and objectives, impervious to the most obvious forms of measurement and evaluation, and conducted differently by different practitioners of the art. Sentencers are subjected to only the crudest form of accountability or quality control through superior court guideline and appellate judgements. Sentencing principles passed down the judicial line are frequently misunderstood or ignored by sentencers in the inferior courts (Henham 1986) and the act is conducted often without even the most basic information about how neighbouring courts typically handle similar cases. Sentencing is not only a 'human' (Hogarth 1971) but frequently an idiosyncratic process. Even in the Crown Courts:

> sentencers have very little to guide them in terms of hard evidence as to whether the ends they seek will be achieved by the means they employ.

> (Moxon 1988: 77)

Against this background it is not surprising that in the last chapter we returned a 'not proven' verdict on the question of racial discrimination in sentencing. Systematic discrimination can only be shown to exist in a process which is generally consistent. Courts exercise discretion on the basis of different principles, largely unaided by sentencing guidelines of the kind available from sentencing commissions or panels in a number of overseas jurisdictions (see, for example, Ashworth 1983; Tonry and Zimring 1983; Pease and Wasik 1987). In magistrates' courts, which carry responsibility for the great majority of lesser sentences, the emphasis is on establishing a consistent local sentencing policy (Tarling 1979; Tarling, Moxon and Jones 1985; Harris 1987):

> magistrates are little constrained by either statutory guidance or by informal instructions and regulations. Instead, they rely for the most part on their own wisdom and experience and on the codes of practice dictated by custom and habit. Inevitably, this means that differences in sentencing policy will arise between different courts and between different magistrates.

> (Tarling 1979: 43)

Differences among Benches, then, are greater than those among magistrates on the same Bench. Though there are always a number of 'rogue' sentencers, the strongly localised nature of magistrates' justice in

England and Wales, combining judicial function and social network, generally involves the relatively smooth transmission of a culture. Similarly, local training events help inculcate sentencing norms (see, for example, Burney 1979; Berlins and Dyer 1982; King and May 1985). Magistrates, therefore, undergo a process of socialisation which mediates idiosyncrasies and creates, on a local basis, a set of assumptions, attitudes and behaviours which have their most obvious practical manifestation in sentencing practice:

> The degree to which a magistrate will allow his personal attitudes to find expression in his behaviour depends, in part, on how he defines the expectations of the law and of 'significant others' in his social environment. This means that whilst attitudes of magistrates act as filters through which the world is perceived selectively, these filters can only partially screen out what is objectionable in that world.
>
> (Hogarth 1971: 78)

The 28,000 magistrates in England and Wales are responsible for almost all sentencing, with Crown Courts dealing with only a minute percentage. But of course Crown Court sentences reflect the nature of the offenders before them, and Crown Court judges are responsible for the majority of prison days to which offenders are sentenced. This fact alone makes them worthy of study, but to conduct studies of Crown Court sentencing has not always been easy. Hence we have been largely restricted to studies using methods which require minimal cooperation and 'official' (and approved) accounts from sentencers themselves (for example, Lymbery 1989; and in an especially illuminating account, Devlin 1979: Chapter 2). David Moxon's Home Office study of 2077 sentencing decisions in 18 Crown Court centres is the first empirical account of general sentencing practice in the Crown Court available to us. Part of the reason is not hard to find:

> I was invited to direct a research project into sentencing in the Crown Court, being carried out by a team of four researchers at the Centre for Criminological Research in the University of Oxford. In the event, that research came to an abrupt end after only one year, when the Lord Chief Justice, Lord Lane, refused his permission for the project to proceed beyond a 'pilot study'. That decision effectively prevents access to systematic knowledge about the approach to sentencing of those who pass sentence in the courts which deal with our most serious crimes.
>
> (Ashworth 1983: xix)

Moxon found a high degree of predictability of Crown Court sentencing and, by means of multivariate analysis, was able correctly to predict the outcome of 80 per cent of cases and identify the most potent predictors of particular sentencing outcomes (see Moxon 1988: 68–9). Additionally, in the context of the Home Office's espousal of non-custodial sentencing where possible, Moxon, following other theorists (for example Wasik and Von Hirsch 1988), considered a number of options to reduce the level of Crown Court sentencing. Though challenging the argument (put most forcibly by Bottoms) (Bottoms 1980, 1989) for the abolition of the suspended sentence, he argued for a refinement of its use, with some suspended sentences (and indeed short unsuspended sentences) becoming conditional discharges, intensive probation or unit fines (Moxon 1988: 74).

Overall, our knowledge of sentencing is patchy. It is an imprecise art; it is unlikely systematically to discriminate against any category of offender because it is too unsystematic generally to be able to do so. At the level of magistrates' courts there are considerable variations in sentencing, some of which relate to the insularity of the locally based magistrates' court system. Even where there is no justification for the differences, however intrinsically undesirable they may be they have less dramatic consequences than Crown Court variations because the maximum sentences available are so much lower. Moxon's Crown Court study is reassuring to the extent that there is an 80 per cent concordance rate between prediction and sentence, though this still means that potentially one sentence in five is a 'rogue'. Overall, however, sentencing levels in Britain remain heavy, and the sensitive balance between government policy and judicial independence is one which will need to be the subject of continuing discussion. This discussion must needs involve the judges, some of whose fears of a totalitarian state waiting around the corner are unjustified and, indeed, strategic:

> It is out of the question that bulletins should be prepared or contacts organized for the judges by any government department. If such tasks really need to be undertaken, it must be on the initiative of the judiciary and by means of arrangements which it alone creates.
>
> (Devlin 1979: 52–3)

The relatively successful training events provided by the Judicial Studies Board, introduced following the Bridge Report and in the face of much judicial hostility (Bridge 1978), combined with some rather constructive recent appointments to both the senior and the junior Bench, have contributed to reducing these concerns. Certainly it is now easier for researchers to gain access to sentencers and at least some aspects of sentencing are now open to external discussion and scrutiny. But the long history of secrecy which has surrounded sentencing has meant that our baseline of knowledge is low and our understanding of what sentencing principles judges actually use limited.

Critics of sentencers too, many of whom are themselves criminal justice professionals, are often seemingly confused about their own expectations (beyond showing the rather human response of expecting sentencers to agree with them in particular cases). There is an inevitable tension between pushes to consistency and flexibility, between predictable and compassionate sentencing. Probation officers, asked their view of the 'right act' in sentencing a white rapist may draw on different principles from those they apply to a black robber, and if their own approach to sentencing is eclectic it is hard to argue that that of the sentencers should not be.

We must, however, be clear what precisely we mean by eclectic sentencing. It has at least two distinct meanings which are sometimes conflated. The first kind of eclecticism I shall call *community sensitive sentencing*. It involves the abandonment of 'principle' (at least in the sense in which I am using the word) and its replacement by an approach which simply mirrors the often inchoate views of that amorphous mass the 'community' as to what should be done with this or that offender. Though it presents certain practical problems, mainly to do with what the said amorphous mass collectively believes, and though it is certainly anathema to academics who, as will by now be apparent to even the least conscientious reader, are never happier than when creating typologies, the approach is arguably a central feature of magistrates' justice. If the vast majority of sentencers are volunteer recruits from the serried ranks of clergymen, housewives and pork butchers, and if the main concerns about them are how 'representative of the community' they are, it follows that something other than jurisprudential sophistication is required of them, and the main place for sentencing principles is as *post hoc* justifications for any decision already, and pragmatically, taken. In this sense the sentencing principle is theoretically replaced by a principle of community responsiveness, though in practice, as we shall see in the next section, the 'community' is a far less significant influence on sentencing than the socialising processes of the local Bench itself.

The second type of eclectic sentencing, which I term *selective sentencing* is a more sophisticated activity, consistent with the formal definition of 'justice' that it is the principle that there should be principles (Peters 1970: 123). Selective sentencing acknowledges that courts cannot always follow one sentencing principle, and allows a place for all of them so long as the means of selecting among them are coherent and consistent. The process of selection is aided by statutory requirements and superior court guideline judgements, but fundamentally requires the sentencer to engage in the sophisticated intellectual activity of establishing *metaprinciples*, or determining a principle by which to choose among conflicting options.

If my analysis is correct, it is likely that the first of these two forms of eclecticism characterises lower court decision-making and the latter, though possibly occasionally honoured in the breach, is an aspiration for the higher courts, and in particular the appellate court. But as we shall see in the next section, matters are often simultaneously simpler and more complicated than that.

## TOWARDS SENTENCING REFORM?

'Guidance or Guidelines?' is the subtitle of a valuable collection of essays whose main title is, appropriately, *Sentencing Reform* (Pease and Wasik 1987). Guidance is 'the use of judgements made in respect of individual appellants which are used as vehicles to enunciate principles of more general application' (confusingly, this includes 'guideline judgements') (Wasik and Pease 1987: 3); and guidelines involve an advance, usually research-based, classification of offence and offender, deriving not from an application in a particular case or cases, but from earlier sentencing practice, a value-judgement or some combination of the two:

> The classification yields, for any possible offender, a presumptive sentence. In the case before him the sentencer may decide not to impose the presumptive sentence, but if he does not do so he is obliged to justify his decision. This justification may well be the subject of appeal to a higher court. The guidelines themselves are subject to regular review to take account of changing circumstances.
>
> (Wasik and Pease 1987: 3)

Critics of guidelines have argued that a guideline based on some combination of description and prescription, but with the force of law, while it would have the benefit of making explicit that which was otherwise implicit, would not otherwise represent any great advance on the present situation. The argument is that while it may suit some to shift responsibility for identifying sentencing principles from judges to researchers, we should still face the problem of how the guidelines were to be developed. The likelihood of research defining the 'right act' in a way which subtly fuses moral propriety and predictive efficacy is remote; and the judges, for all their frustrating tendency to block the Government's attempts to implement a coherent penal policy, do at least represent an independent element in a process which might otherwise fall into the hands of Government placemen.

It is important in considering the question of guidelines not to confuse the general issue of the independence of the judiciary with the particular contemporary conflict between a Government which wishes to reduce the prison population and a judiciary which reserves its right to differ. It is possible to agree with Government's objective but not its method. It is also important, in considering any move to standardised guidelines, to remember that individualised sentencing originated partly as a means of mitigating the harshness of deserts-based sentencing (see for example Greenberg and Humphries 1980; Forst 1982). Is it possible to standardise sentencing without being insensitive to the individuality of the offender and the uniqueness of the criminal act?

We do have some baseline knowledge about the use of sentencing guidelines in overseas jurisdictions. In the United States a number of attempts have been made to reform sentencing generally, and of these the establishment of a *sentencing commission*, particularly in Minnesota, has attracted the most attention (Tonry 1987). It involves the introduction of presumptive guidelines based on a 'just deserts' philosophy which excluded consideration of such extra-legal variables as marital status and employment record, a system of appellate sentence review and the presence of a standing commission to monitor and fine tune the system. Procedurally the result has been close conformity to the guidelines; but substantively it has led to increased imprisonment, albeit more consistently applied. There were also, as ever, unintended consequences: as judicial discretion (on sentence) decreased, prosecutorial discretion (on charge) increased. The system moved towards a retributive approach with a tougher scale of penalties for serious offences than hitherto, and the price to be paid for greater standardisation was more use of imprisonment.

Concerns of this kind have led Andrew Von Hirsch to argue for a less numerically precise system of guidelines in Britain, based on the Swedish system of 'penal value' (Von Hirsch 1987; see also Wasik and Von Hirsch 1988; Bottoms 1989). Such a system would involve what Bottoms calls 'penalty-scaling within a desert-based approach' (Bottoms

1989: 94), while permitting a continuing role for social-work-related activities by probation officers. Such a notion is the most obvious means of humanising a retributive orientation; it is consonant also with another concept, *just welfare* (Harris 1985) which, as we shall see later, argues that compulsory welfare activities should themselves be locked within a deserts-based framework: that offenders should not be required to receive more intrusive social work than their crime warranted. For courts to sentence in ignorance of the social context of the offender as well as the details of the offence would be manifestly absurd, though how that social context should be addressed in sentencing remains controversial (for an excellent discussion of this point, see Clear 1978).

It is precisely this question of how complexities such as disadvantage and discrimination should be addressed that necessitates a public debate on the closed world of sentencing. Whether one is a liberal who believes that social disadvantage should mitigate sentence or a conservative who, associating it with high recidivism prediction scores, argues that it should aggravate it, one can presumably agree that the matter is best discussed openly. And it is here that the question of a sentencing council comes in.

Influenced both by the 'presumptive sentence' approach of states such as Minnesota and by the Sentencing Council proposed by the Australian Law Reform Commission, Ashworth has advocated a broadly similar approach to the structuring and confining of judicial discretion in Britain (see, for example, Ashworth 1983, 1987, 1989). Arguing the need for a *via media* between the extremes of the present rather arbitrary system and a total system of presumptive sentences, Ashworth proposes a sentencing council chaired by the Lord Chief Justice, containing sentencers from all levels of the system and a number of other criminal justice professionals. Recommendations from the Council would be issued as Practice Directions and backed by the authority of the Lord Chief Justice:

> The English habit of muddling through without being explicit about the priorities and preferences embodied in sentencing practice must be abandoned. Issues such as the sentencing of persistent offenders and multiple offenders and the claim that a guilty plea should be regarded as substantial mitigation are awkward issues which are most comfortably avoided. However, they have to be faced and deter-mined every day by sentencers, usually without much appellate guidance.
>
> (Ashworth 1983: 448)

If associated with a broader set of discussions about criminal justice policy at central government level – preferably but not necessarily as part of the functions of a Ministry of Justice – such a council would establish clear policy principles to be discussed, with appropriate local flexibility, by the local crime committees proposed in the next chapter. That sentencing is too important to be left to the judges alone is a point being increasingly accepted by other criminal justice professionals, and it can be made without conceding any diminution of the constitutional safeguard of judicial independence. But when such independence becomes *carte blanche* for sentencers to do what they will within the very wide sentencing bands available in law even for relatively minor offences, when the financial cost of imprisonment is so high and met out of a limitless budget provided by the taxpayer, when there is so little reason to believe that sentences give value for money or even reflect the consistent application of agreed principles or objectives, when judges resent being called to account by those who pay their salaries and fund their disposals – when these happen there is proper cause for disquiet. We cannot forever permit a powerful profession, but one still variably trained in sentencing, to conceal its demand to be accountable to none but itself behind the smokescreen of a threat to civil liberties and a prospect of totalitarian tyranny.

Whether sentencing is an art or a science, it is a very much more private activity in Britain than elsewhere, and there is little reason to believe it to be better done as a result of that privacy. But as the training of judges was introduced in the 1980s in the face of opposition from some senior members of the judiciary (Devlin 1979), so will the 1990s (or at the latest the early years of the next century) see more fundamental reforms of the legal profession, including a scrutiny of sentencing by people other than sentencers. The case against such scrutiny is, in the final analysis, almost impossible to sustain.

## SOCIAL ENQUIRY REPORTS AND SENTENCING

This is not the place to provide a history of the social enquiry report. This task has already been accomplished in a number of ways (see for example Bottoms and McWilliams 1986; McWilliams 1986; Harris and Webb 1987; Bottoms and Stelman 1988). Recent history begins, in fact, with the Streatfeild Report (Home Office and Lord Chancellor's Office 1961), since at least part of the ensuing thirty years have been spent by Home Office and probation interests trying to beat a graceful retreat from the aspirations of that overly optimistic document.

The 1950s and early 1960s represented the apotheosis of positivistic optimism in penology and criminology: let us, it was thought, proceed with ever greater precision and confidence towards specifying what sentence will 'work' for what offender, and the ultimate outcome of our endeavours will be a crime-free society. The idea was not new, but involved extending to the world of adult offenders some of the reformative enthusiasm which had been a longstanding political, cultural and professional response to child care and juvenile delinquency (Harris and Webb 1987: Chapters 1–2). Increasingly accurate applications of scientific method to offenders would identify and eliminate the criminogenic aspects of their character, behaviour and environment. Though punishment would be a part of this process, the primary focus was on the elimination of causes by whatever combination of reward and punishment was necessary in a particular case.

Streatfeild, therefore, while not abandoning retributive questions of desert and culpability, was more interested in influencing future behaviour by deterrence or reformation. It follows, therefore, that as well as the knowledge about the offence available to the court from the evidence (which would be a sufficient basis for a retributive sentence) additional information about the individual offender was necessary in order that the most effective disposal could be selected. In this, the report writer and sentencer would be aided by an accumulation of knowledge about the application of prediction methods to particular cases. Streatfeild was aware of, and influenced by, a number of predictive studies, in particular the Mannheim–Wilkins scale (Mannheim and Wilkins 1955) which considered in some detail the proper use of case studies in criminology:

We regard it as the specific task of case histories presented in crime prediction studies

(a) to give concrete illustrations of the various score classes of success and failure as worked out in the statistical part of the enquiry, with particular emphasis on the variety of factors and the diverse combinations of factors which may produce a particular score. This could be achieved by presenting for each score class a number of cases to illustrate, first, the possible diversity of cases within the same score class, and, secondly, to compare cases of different score classes to see whether and how the statistical difference between these classes is reflected in individual cases.

(b) to pay attention to the emergence of typical patterns of cases and combinations of factors in order to work out a typology of cases related to the statistical score classes.

(c) to make a special study of typical cases and, in particular, of cases which do not seem to fit into their statistical score classes, i.e. of individuals who, according to their score class, should have become failures but were, in fact, successes ('over-achievers') or vice versa ('under-achievers').

(Mannheim and Wilkins 1955: 174)

This rational and scientific approach to human criminality makes a range of information about offenders necessary and helps explain why Streatfeild argued that social enquiry reports should contain not only offence-related information but advice to courts on how best to check a defendant's criminality and on what impact a specified sentence would have (Home Office and Lord Chancellor's Office 1961: para. 335). A steady supply of information from the Home Office and the research community to both report writers and sentencers would, therefore, continually refine decision-making. Both probation officers and sentencers would be able to address the questions of the *risk* posed by particular offenders on the basis of their psychological and social characteristics (a question of identifying criminogenic variables) and the *reductionist efficacy* of particular forms of penal treatment for certain kinds of offender. The accumulation of knowledge from research-based practice would lead to steady improvements in sentencing, while the continuing stress not only on these future-oriented decisions but also (though to a lesser degree) on culpability would ensure that scientific enthusiasm was not unyoked from procedural justice and political realism. An essentially British pragmatism, in short, was to hold in check any pressure towards scientific hegemony.

But this optimism was to founder on the theoretical critique of the new criminologists (Taylor, Walton and Young 1973) and the empirical critique of the effectiveness of penal methods in reducing crime. Most programmes have little predictable effect, and though in Robert Martinson's cautious words: 'while some programs are beneficial under certain conditions, others can be distinctly harmful' (Martinson 1979: 258), the numbers of intervening variables elsewhere in an offender's life and the low probability of apprehension for most offences combine to make the attainment of scientific perfection as infeasible in practice as the quest for it is incorrect in theory. So by 1978, Barbara Wootton, a member of the Streatfeild Committee, in a predominantly pessimistic retrospective on fifty years as a magistrate, was saying:

> I welcome social enquiry reports because they make me feel cosy, inasmuch as they transform a 'case' into a human being; but, sadly, I am driven to the conclusion . . . they do little to make me (or anybody else) in any sense a better sentencer.
>
> (Wootton 1978: 45)

So the contribution of the social enquiry report to a scientific penology is uncertain and probably slight:

> In the light of all this, and of the research reviewed in this paper, are social enquiry reports (along with much else done in the courts) indeed a 'monumental irrelevance'? None of the research reported in this paper shows clearly that they are not, but, equally, it does not prove that they are.
>
> (Bottoms and McWilliams 1986: 270)

But irrelevant to what? is the key question, and the 1980s saw a scaling down of the expectations of the social enquiry report. Empirical research into the quality, content, consistency and impartiality of social enquiry reports found them wanting (Perry 1974; Thorpe 1979; see also J.H. Curran 1983) and probably incomprehensible to their subjects, disappointingly few of whom possessed the social science degree which would have enabled them to have understood the more linguistically and conceptually complex of these documents (Horsley 1984).

The Home Office, in a series of circulars (Home Office 1983a; 1983b; 1986) which reflected its own increasing concern to prioritise the activities of the probation service, made the 'official' expectation of the social enquiry report increasingly clear. In essence the new themes were that reports should be costed more carefully and concentrate on cases where there was a risk of custody or where a probation order was a possible outcome. When reports *were* prepared they should focus on the offence, the offender's part in it and attitude towards it, and should contain recommendations supported by argument. The 1986 circular and the accompanying letter made the following main points:

● the social enquiry report is not concerned to establish guilt or the gravity of the offence;
● it is relevant for a particular occasion only and therefore of limited value on a subsequent occasion or for another purpose;
● it is not a plea in mitigation but an impartial professional consideration of the circumstances which led to the commission of the offence and of the scope for minimising the risk of future offending;

- it should be concise and well-expressed;
- irrelevant material should be removed through sifting;
- it should not confuse fact and opinion;
- it should not contain jargon or technical terms;
- for ethnic minority defendants in particular it should set their offending in a cultural context which might otherwise not be understood by the court;
- the report is a partial document in that it does not take into consideration all factors which influence the sentencer. It is, however, concerned with discouraging future crime, and should therefore assess to what extent particular disposals might achieve this end;
- the report should review the range of possible sentences and their likely impact on the offender;
- information should be verified where possible and the source of the information stated;
- where a not guilty plea is anticipated, reports should not normally be prepared routinely for magistrates' courts, but local arrangements should apply in Crown Courts where the desirability of addressing an offence has to be set against the desirability of speedy disposal. Where an offender pleading not guilty has within the previous three months been known to the probation service, a 'response to supervision' report should be prepared;
- stand-down reports may be either a substitute for social enquiry reports or a means of determining whether such a report is necessary;
- social enquiry reports should be subject to local discussion among sentencers, administrators, clerks and probation officers.

So the Home Office approach to the social enquiry report is a microcosm of its approach to criminal justice more generally: the articulation of broad brush policies involving prioritisation, economy of content and relevance to major sentencing concerns, but with policy implementation left to local negotiations. With the likely introduction, in the reasonably near future, of national standards for social enquiry reports, the balance between national policy development and local policy implementation will shift somewhat in the direction of the former, but it is inconceivable that a balance will not be retained: after all, as consumers of reports, there is every reason for local sentencers to have a significant say in the focus and orientation of the work of local probation staff, and they are unlikely to accept the relegation of the report to a pre-sentencing fact sheet.

## SOCIAL ENQUIRY REPORTS, COURTS AND PROBATION SERVICE

Social enquiry reports are the main vehicle for routine interchange between probation service and courts. As such, though the focus of the report is on the background, offence and prospective fate of a particular defendant, as the negotiated outcome of a range of formal and informal discussions, strategies and manoeuvres it reflects and perpetuates the broader relations between service and court. This social and organisational reality renders naive the 'official' view that the document is simply an 'impartial, professional consideration' of the offence. To make this point is not to deny that there are areas where 'impartiality' is present, but to acknowledge the function of the report as a 'strategic' document designed to create a particular impression in the mind of the sentencer. The 'tariff-minus-one' approach identified in Scottish research (Curran and Chambers 1982) aims to ensure that recommendations are simultaneously lenient and realistic, and the policy of the professional association and some local services not to 'recommend' prison brings the report very close to a piece of mitigation. All of which means, of course, that the earlier discussion about the 'right act' of the sentencer applies to the probation officer too. On the basis of what principles do – and should – they write their reports?

There are, of course, problems, both theoretical and practical, with the notion of impartial professionalism (for an excellent discussion of the complexity underlying the seemingly most straightforward 'accounts' see Stone 1987). Even in the event of impartial professionalism being possible in principle, to attain it in practice when recommending an individualised response to an offender would be singularly difficult. Again, though, can it be that, as with community sensitive sentencing, to seek consistent principles is to ask the wrong question? Could it be rather that the importance of the social enquiry report is primarily in its acknowledgement that the existence of liberal professionals providing sentencers with a rationale for leniency is simply in everybody's best interests, from the individual offender to the Home Office minister?

In good part the problem turns on the nature of the 'recommendation' (a term not used by Streatfeild, and seen by successive commentators (Harris 1985; Bottoms and Stelman 1988) as fundamentally misconceived). Everybody agrees that the basis of the social enquiry report is partial, excluding, for example, retribution, general deterrence and prophylaxis. The basis of sentencing, on the other hand, includes all these possible factors and involves weighing these potentially conflicting objectives and apportioning their relative significance in a particular case. This being so, it is obviously illogical for the probation officer, who properly ignores some of these considerations, to make a recommendation to a sentencer who has to take them all into account. Yet nor, seemingly, is the probation officer to ignore these factors, and courts get publicly cross with probation officers who do: after all, if the social enquiry report is a sentencing aid it is clearly not its job to 'recommend' a sentence which it is in practice impossible for a court to impose. On the other hand, if the social enquiry report involves the probation officer legitimating an undesirable but realistic sentence, the job is not really about making a 'recommendation' at all, but about oiling the wheels of the system.

These are murky waters indeed. Two significant, and not dissimilar proposals have been made to recast the function of the report and resolve these awkward problems. I developed the first in a paper given to an audience of juvenile justice experts as part of an argument that the 'justice versus welfare' debate in which many of them were then engaging had more than run its useful course. The paper was subsequently published in slightly revised form (Harris 1985) and argued that the *recommendation* should be replaced by an *opinion* (a word also used by Streatfeild), of two kinds:

> first, the likely social and personal consequences of particular sentencing options which might be chosen, and secondly, *in case the sentencer decided that the defendant's welfare was in this particular case his main consideration*, a statement agreed with the client as to what the client's needs were and a clear offer to the sentencer of a welfare 'package' (binding on worker to provide and client to accept) which would aim to meet some or all of these needs.
>
> (Harris 1985: 40–1. Italics original)

This conceptual framework remains feasible today, though its extension to adult offenders and the development of punishment in the community render the reference to 'welfare' obsolete. The argument was that it was demonstrably undesirable in anything other than a crude retributive sentencing system for a sentence to be imposed without the sentencer being offered an opinion on the likely consequences of that sentence for the offender. If in the light of this opinion the sentencer decided to proceed with what was termed a 'welfare package', the best option and a commitment from the defendant to cooperate with it would both be provided. The option derived from the concept of just welfare, which allowed that welfare might be positive (taking action) or negative (doing as little as possible), but that where positive welfare was chosen it should be subject to a test of proportionality and not involve an intervention out of proportion to the seriousness of the offence. Hence just welfare meets the desert theorists' test of just punishment: the scales of welfare, like those of justice, need to balance.

Bottoms and Stelman helpfully review the debate about 'recommendations' (Bottoms and Stelman 1988: 96–9) in a manner consistent with this approach and conclude that 'community options' should be the framework for what is currently the recommendation. The community option has the sense of an 'offer' about it just as the second limb of the just welfare 'opinion' has, and whatever differences of detail exist, the two approaches together offer an appropriate way forward for the social enquiry report.

## CONCLUSION

This chapter had a number of aims. Firstly, to categorise the literature about sentencing into philosophical/analytic, empirical, informational and reformist. I showed that sentencing may be looked at as an activity in its own right or as a particular case of the general relation between the state and the criminal. The limitations of this latter approach for helping us understand sentencing are, however, obvious, for the competing 'theories' of sentencing do not have any behavioural counterparts: a fine, prison sentence or community service order may in any case be retributive, deterrent or reformative in intent, or some combination of these. The fact that sentencers themselves are often unfamiliar with these categories adds the further problem that their activities are being considered by reference to a framework of which they themselves may have no knowledge.

This is not to say that the framework is unimportant for theoreticians, and indeed I returned to it at the end of the chapter to make sense of the notion of just welfare. Rather it is that if we wish to understand what sentencers do and why they do it, we need to turn to other bodies of knowledge, from which we learn that there is a range of practical disparities among sentencers which cannot be explained away by the use of legal variables. Different courts have different sentencing 'scales', and though justice may not, since there are reasonably high levels of consistency in sentencing within court areas, be entirely arbitrary, it does appear to be geographical, showing evidence of what in Chapter 6 we called disparity.

This being so, we looked at the proposals of sentencing reformers to make the sentencing task a more public one and I supported the formation of a sentencing council with academic and other non-judicial involvement, whose pronouncements would have the status of Practice Directions, with departures from them being appealable.

From sentencing generally I moved to consider social enquiry reports as an aid to it, and they too proved problematic. They have their roots in an approach to sentencing which is theoretically outdated and empirically bankrupt – the idea that crimes have external identifiable causes and that it is generally within the scope of a punishment system to eliminate them and so reform offenders. Added to this theoretical problem are the practical ones that the authors of the reports are frequently unsystematic in their inclusions and exclusions, and that they are frequently not the impartial, dispassionate professionals of official myth. These two problems together mean that to speak of reports as making sentencing 'recommendations' is misconceived, and the 'recommendation' should be replaced by an 'opinion'. This would entail firstly an assessment of the impact on an offender of any plausible sentence (but with particular reference to prison) and secondly an offer of a community option (now a better phrase than welfare package), proportional to the offence, and to which the defendant was committed. The detailed implementation of such a programme would be a matter for local negotiation on the basis of national guidance, and the existence of a sentencing council would enhance the quality of that guidance.

The social enquiry report almost certainly influences sentencers and normally towards leniency. There is nothing improper in this: on the contrary, if the report does, as Barbara Wootton inimitably put it, make her feel 'cosy' by turning a criminal into a person, then it is making the sentencing process more real and more human by creating a bridge between the worlds of sentencer and sentenced. This activity can be defended as an intrinsic good.

But if the reports are so variable in content and focus that their utility is unpredictable, the good that they do has to be set against the problem that they may be contributing to a process of erratic justice. There is, therefore, a need for standards to be introduced nationally, but interpreted, applied and monitored locally. The 'recommendation' should be removed, and the conclusion of the report be brought into line with its changing purpose. This can no longer sensibly be to cure offenders but to inform sentencers of the likely impact of (in particular) a prison sentence and to offer courts which wish not to impose such a sentence a realistic opportunity of avoiding doing so. Whether the sentencers take the option is their business not the probation officer's, but the existence of a local (as well as national) forum in which both community options and sentencing practice were discussed would increase the probability of the demands of the consumers for particular kinds of community facility being met by the providers. Once the demands of the consumers were met, pressure to use them would become considerable. But it is hard to proceed rationally along these lines if the guidelines are not available and openly debated, and if no local infrastructure for implementation and debate exists.

# Chapter 8

# Supervision in the community – towards delinquency management

In large American cities so many people are in a hurry and drive automobiles that traffic in the congested streets goes into slow motion. In England so many people want to live on the edge of the countryside that miles and miles of it disappear into the city . . . Just when Man thinks he can do everything, he finds himself helpless in the clutch of some unknown force. And in this ironic principle, which appears to govern so much of our lives, I find delight.

(J.B. Priestley: *Delight*)

'if probation and parole were done away with today, the crime rate in America would probably go up by about 2 percent. This 2 percent would be probation and parole administrators and line managers who turned to crime only because they could find no other suitable employment.'

(anonymous sociologist, cited in Champion 1988: 91)

## PREAMBLE: SOME CONTEMPORARY ISSUES IN PROBATION

This final chapter falls into two main parts. Firstly I consider aspects of the background to the current bipartisan concern to reduce the prison population and to use the probation service, and possibly private sector organisations, to take on the management of more serious offenders in the community. Secondly I examine some of the literature on supervision and delinquency management. While affecting the delinquent activities of supervised offenders is difficult and doomed to be variably successful, it is a proper objective for the probation service and other agencies of social control. To assume that this predominantly involves exercising personal influence over individual offenders is now old-fashioned, and probably the sooner the probation service ceases to regard its individual counselling or supervisory sessions with 'clients' as the core of its activities the better. Involvement in situational crime prevention, environmental amelioration, liaison with professional and volunteer groups, helping victims, communicating with the public on the realities of crime, risk and vulnerability, and becoming far more centrally involved in the workings of local criminal justice systems so as to maximise its influence over decision-making by police and sentencers are the priorities if the probation service is to become a more visible and effective participant in the fight against crime:

> Strategic thinking would seem to demand that there be one central, keystone purpose from which all other goals can be derived. Where crime response strategies are concerned, the central strategic goal must surely be to reduce crime.

> (Locke 1990: 246)

The probation service has frequently stayed somewhat aloof from other components of the criminal justice system and has characteristically demurred from pursuing any specific activity – such as crime reduction – wholeheartedly, because of its traditional function of balancing a range of contradictory aspirations involving care *and* control, liberation *and* constraint, calling offenders to account *and* demanding social reform. The problem of constructing a *modus operandi* which satisfies both the demands of Government that the probation service be unambiguously involved in crime management and the humanitarian reformist traditions of the service itself has been considerable. It has led to wide disparities in practice and philosophy (Harris 1980; Fielding 1984; Singer 1989), strident statements in support of the service's liberationist and social reform traditions from the probation officers' trade union (Whitehead 1990) and pressure from Government to play down the 'social work' dimensions of the job. This is not, however, the place to review these issues yet again; nor is it my intention to deny that they are, to a degree at least, intrinsic to the job. Indeed the more one knows about probation practice the less likely it appears that it lends itself to simplistic, regulation-driven solutions. As I have previously written:

> I wonder actually whether the authors of the Green Paper have ever actually met . . . any of the kind of people who are going to be subject to its requirements. Many of them are by nature or habit disorganised, resentful, overwhelmed by pressures which get in the

way of their leading ordered lives, unpredictable and irrational . . . the reluctant conscripts will have to be cajoled, encouraged, helped, threatened. There will be petty resentments to be ironed out, complicated and convoluted reasons why conformity is impossible. And in all this the conscripts will either be helped to limp through their community punishment or they will be returned to court and imprisoned. And then we are back precisely where we started.

(Harris 1989a: 31)

There is a need, however, to review such knowledge as we have about the capacity of correctional strategies to reduce criminal behaviour. Little of this has apparently been read by probation officers. Indeed a study of probation officers' professional reading habits (Davies 1989) reveals that the top book (McGuire and Priestley 1985) received almost as many citations as the remaining nine in the probation officers' top ten put together. From this we conclude not only that the social skills approach to managing offending behaviour espoused in that book is widely used by probation officers, but that this is the only professional book which most probation officers have recently read.

From this in turn there are two possible conclusions: that probation officers do not bother to read books which they believe could be helpful to them or that they have little confidence in the books themselves. Of these two possible conclusions, the latter is the more plausible, if only because indolence is likely to be an individual rather than a universal trait of probation officers. This lack of confidence in the books has in turn two possible causes: probation officers do not believe the books answer their professional questions or they do not believe there are answers to be had. The fact that the most popular book by far is one which claims to provide answers and also a simple technology to find them suggests that the quest for the magic solution, the 'panacea phenomenon' (Finckenauer 1982) is as popular as ever.

The extent of pessimism about the possibility of creating change should not, however, be underestimated. Until the 1960s the long-standing belief that exposure to good influence would change people's behaviour seemed self-evident. The 1970s, however, saw an attenuation of confidence in the therapeutic aspirations of the professionals. A predominantly, though not entirely, gloomy review of a number of American correctional programmes (Martinson 1974) was much misquoted (though little read) as saying that 'nothing works' in spite of the author's own subsequent clarification and partial withdrawal (Martinson 1979; see also Greenberg 1977a; Finckenauer 1982: 7).

Conservatives allied with libertarian socialists to reach the same conclusion for different reasons: whether rehabilitation was a 'soft' excuse which sought explanations outside of the will of the offender, or a covert form of social control of one class by another (Cohen 1985) it seemed not to work. This interesting political, philosophical and professional convergence inevitably provoked a crisis for the probation service (Harris and Webb 1987).

Beyond this, however, if clients are deemed responsible for their own destiny, the probation officer cannot share either in success or in failure: a client who offends does so for reasons beyond the officer's control, a client who does not is likewise acting other than under professional influence. And given the problems associated with official statistics, the probation officer is also faced with the awkward possibility that it may be the mere chance of apprehension which turns an official success into an official failure. Not surprisingly, existential questions about the purpose of professional life are asked, burnout among probation staff, at least in the United States, though by no means universal (Whitehead 1989), is not uncommon, and when it occurs it is associated with precisely this kind of problem. It is rare in the world of the human relations professions for consequences to have simple causes, and almost never the case that confident predictions about success or failure can be made. This provides some relief for probation officers whose clients misbehave, but there is a price to pay:

> Almost all supervision officers are concerned that they not be held accountable for their clients' misbehaviors; that it be recognized that supervision choices are extremely limited and may well be ineffectual. The result is that officers are frequently unsure of their supervision strategies and vacillate widely in their approaches . . . The alternative – to believe that each officer is in fact responsible for the failures that occur among clients in his or her caseload – is clearly intolerable . . . Thus the cynical view that clients determine their own outcomes, largely irrespective of probation, develops as a natural consequence of lack of meaningful feedback.
>
> (Clear and O'Leary 1983: 60)

So the distancing of probation officers from 'failure' also distances them from 'success'. This is partly a psychological necessity, partly an ethical imperative (based on the view that clients make their own choices) and partly commonsense. But in consequence it becomes hard to see how probation work is to develop on the basis of more secure knowledge. Evaluation is especially difficult, partly because there is no agreed criterion of success, partly because the most obvious and publicly promotable one (that offending is reduced) is hard to measure and often a matter of chance. Granted there is an undoubted utility in many situations of directly approaching and confronting offending behaviour (McGuire and Priestley 1985); nevertheless, there is little other technology to enable the officers to move confidently towards success, and it often seems that a debilitating sense of professional impotence and purposelessness is seldom far from the surface.

There is, therefore, a serious professional problem to address. To do so we need to make more and better use of *prediction*, for prediction, imprecise as it is, will at least enable professionals, by making more informed guesses than hitherto, both to impose some conceptual order on a confused world and, more mundanely, to allocate their time more rationally. It is important, however, to understand what crime prediction is. To predict recidivism is not to assume deterministic attributes of criminal behaviour, but to apply actuarial principles of probability to criminality. As Todd Clear has put it:

> Rather than trying to 'explain' human behavior in the same way that we use the laws of physical sciences to explain physical phenomena, we should think of the human sciences as ways to 'reduce our uncertainty' about human behavior. This concept of uncertainty reduction is critical to an understanding of what correctional prediction is all about.
>
> (Clear 1988: 4)

There are patterns in crime, and criminal justice professionals should be aware of them and relate them to their various activities. Prediction does not, in spite of the fears expressed by many, have specific implications for sentencing or social action: depending on one's political orientation, high probability levels can lead either to selective incapacitation or to the provision of additional state resources to ameliorate the social and family problems associated with (but which do not necessarily cause) criminality (West and Farrington 1977; West 1982; Greenwood 1986b). Nor can prediction scales be appropriately used to measure trivial offending, and it is now widely accepted that the use of a simple 'success rate' based on no offending of any kind is virtually meaningless. But as probation officers come to supervise more serious offenders, pressure to use prediction scales will increase, on the grounds of both efficiency and effectiveness. At present, while prediction scales are popular in relation to the sentencing behaviour of courts (Mair 1989), less use is made of predictors of criminality, partly as a result of concerns about validity (see, for example, Wright, Clear and Dickson 1984) and to what uses they may be put, and partly through ignorance. I return to prediction later in the chapter. Firstly, though, we consider other aspects of probation practice.

## ALTERNATIVES TO CUSTODY AND THE PROBATION SERVICE

The quest for alternatives to custody is not new. It is, however, being vigorously pursued by a Government struggling to square a circle which involves fiscal stringency, being seen to be 'tough on crime', solving the political problem of fear of crime, and dealing delicately with the popular equation of toughness with prison while knowing full well that prison does not reform those inside it. The strategy involves closing the gap between punitive prison and caring probation firstly by creating punitive probation; secondly by 'twin track sentencing', which involves a bifurcation of crimes into those serious enough to justify imprisonment and those which can be dealt with by punishment in the community; thirdly by increased private sector involvement in community punishment; and fourthly by the increased use of surveillance technology.

The policy involves *diversification* as a response to the problem of prison numbers. The belief is that to provide more sentencing options for courts will lead to sentencers, partly by a voluntary code of conduct and partly through guideline judgements from the superior courts, decanting people who would hitherto have been destined for prison into new facilities. This assumes that the problem is a lack of sentencing options, not sentencers' use of options currently available. This view has been questioned both academically (Harris 1988, 1989a) and by probation interests who may well feel that they are being selected by Government as softer targets than the judiciary, and that in being asked to solve an allocation problem when they are not allocaters they are being given an impossible task.

The issue is, however, more complex than that, stemming from the tendency to conflate two distinct policy objectives: reducing the prison population and decarcerating non-violent offenders. The former addresses the prison *population*, and the latter *receptions*. Twin-track sentencing, involving more lenient sentencing for one group of offenders and tougher sentencing for another, will not of itself necessarily reduce the prison population and, depending on the precise mathematics of crime and punishment involved, may well increase it.

After all, to double the average sentence for rape is, over time, to double the number of rapists in the prison population. If at the same time short sentence prisoners were decanted we should reduce receptions, but not necessarily the population, the effect on which would be determined primarily by the numbers of cleared-up rapes. And if further we assume that a policy of decarcerating serious non-violent offenders would, at least intermittently, run into serious political difficulties, with, in particular, the likelihood of strong pressure being exerted by senior judges, politicians, press and public to continue imprisoning most domestic burglars, one is left wondering who, precisely, is going to be left to be punished in the community. Car thieves, serious shoplifters, white collar criminals, non-domestic burglars, vandals? The political risks may not be great, but nor are the likely gains.

The recent history of 'alternatives to custody' has been fully rehearsed elsewhere (see for example Stanley and Baginsky 1984; Vass 1984; Harris and Webb 1987; Ryan and Ward 1990). It has not been an especially happy history, with a repeated tendency for things to go wrong, for strategies designed to empty the prisons serving to fill them (for the case of the suspended sentence, see Bottoms 1980; for community service, see Vass 1984; for more theoretical accounts of 'things going wrong', see Marx 1981; Doleschal 1982; Cohen 1985; Harris and Webb 1987). This means that for the present set of policies to succeed, certain new conditions must appertain. This is going to be difficult to achieve, but I intend to proceed by offering what may be the most effective strategy.

This strategy involves the creation of new structures as part of a multi-agency and systemic approach to crime control. In part this will involve improved information flow among the agencies, but in part a softening of some of the currently very firm agency boundaries so that the probation service becomes involved not just in the supervision of offenders but in a range of community strategies designed to create a safer and therefore healthier social environment. Agency sanction is of course important, but it is impossible to have a coherent system of criminal justice when the police so bitterly complain that CPS is undermining them, when probation provides community correctional facilities which the courts use for the wrong people, when magistrates are discouraged by clerks from visiting and becoming involved in the very facilities to which they are sentencing offenders, when the daily experience of the courts is of repeated remands because the right people are never available. Nor can it be proper for local community interests

– ethnic minorities, chambers of trade, rape crisis centres – not to have
a say and play a part in an integrated strategy involving crime
prevention, victim support and community involvement as well as the
management of offenders.

The necessity of developing punishment in the community has long
been recognised by some commentators, but the meaning of
'punishment' has seldom been clear and may in fact have been
deliberately obfuscated. After all, as we have seen, much of the utility of
the community service order is that it can be presented to different
audiences as hard labour, industrial training for the workshy, restitution
and therapy. Any policy which avoids the pitfalls of previous attempts
to reduce the prison population may have to depend on just this kind of
sleight of hand, for there is insufficient agreement among the different
interest groups involved to permit any approach which is either
simplistically punitive or simplistically caring. To the diversification of
penality which has already been created by Government, therefore,
must be added an *ambiguity of penality* of just the kind provided by
community service.

If punishment in the community is to be successful in decarcerating
non-violent offenders in a way that previous attempts have not, the key
factors include the use of the *victim interest* as a justification for
constructive non-custodial penalties, the judicious involvement of
*private sector organisations* to deal with the 'hard end' of punishment in
the community, the involvement of the probation service in *community
activities which are non offender-centred*, such as victim support, crime
prevention and general environmental amelioration, and its involvement in local *crime committees* (along the lines of the crime response
commissions suggested by Locke 1990). Also crucial is the central
involvement of sentencers alongside other professionals in joint strategies to respond to crime, for it cannot be said too often that without the
sentencers little can be achieved.

The strategic benefits for the probation service of extending its
services beyond those for offenders are considerable, and an involvement with *crime victims* should be a key part of any such diversification.
We have seen that victims have at present a useful but patchy network
of largely voluntary facilities provided by Victim Support, other victim
organisations and the women's movement; that the police have taken
considerable steps to improve their management of complaints by
women but that much still needs to be done; that the provisions of the
Criminal Injuries Compensation Board fall short of what many victims
wish; that the treatment of victims in court can be inept and insensitive;

that many members of the public favour reparative to non-reparative penalties; and that, perhaps because everyone is a potential, if not actual, victim of crime, identification with the plight of victims is almost universal, even though the identification is based on an incorrect stereotype of the victim. In the light of this, an exclusively offender-centred probation service is unlikely to trigger much popular sympathy for the depressing social circumstances of its errant charges.

Because other organisations are currently working with victims, however, the probation service must involve itself systematically with them, negotiating its role locally, but on the basis of national guidelines, and determining how its new grant-aiding powers will be exercised most appropriately and accountably. The roles it could agree with the voluntary organisations might include direct counselling for victims, supporting and supervising victim support workers, developing training initiatives, monitoring and developing the network of victim services, liaising with the police, communicating the work of the victim support agencies to sentencers and developing a range of reparative and restitutive forms of community punishment.

Similarly, if the service is to become seriously involved in attacking crime it must turn its attention to *crime prevention*, in relation to which it is, for a number of reasons, especially well placed to link with other professionals as well as relevant members of the community. In particular, to equate situational crime prevention with target hardening alone is to take a negative and ultimately self-defeating view, the logical conclusion of which is to manufacture a cure worse than the disease itself. Few of us would be willing to live in an environment characterised by video cameras, security police, locks, bolts, barbed wire and searchlights in order to reduce a risk of serious crime which, in most parts of the country, is already minimal. There is all the difference, however, between this fortress approach to crime prevention and encouraging people to take sensible precautions, providing correct information about risk and vulnerability, ensuring that appropriate advice about self-defence and self-protection are available where needed, and at the same time seeking to promote the forms of community cohesion which can result from a concerted response to a shared problem. It will be remembered that a major theme of Chapter 4 was the importance of moving towards a notion of crime prevention as a contributor to the development of community health. There is a need for defensive *and* ameliorative strategies, not for one at the expense of the other, and it is not easy to see how this combination can be developed without involving a 'bridging' agency such as the probation service.

The probation service has competence in community involvement and networking, environmental amelioration, dealing with people in their social context and in criminology and criminal justice. Its prime concern is not with thief catching, yet nor can it properly lie in protecting the interests of the offender to the exclusion of those of the actual or potential victim population. If the service is concerned with creating opportunity structures, enhancing choices, providing new options and with encouraging people to take responsibility for their own lives, it has a potentially important role in crime prevention work.

Nor should it be forgotten that offenders are themselves members of the community, and that if decarceration is successful the need for social reintegration will be all the greater. It is all too easy, in discussing crime prevention, to paint a picture of a law-abiding population at war with an inimical set of offenders. But as many probation officers will ruefully admit, offenders are as 'tough on crime' as anybody else, sustaining their own involvement by a combination of techniques of neutralisation (Sykes and Matza 1957) and protestations of future reformation. The probation service, in exercising its most traditional role of 'bridging' offender and society can, in what is only seemingly a paradox, harness the energy of offenders themselves in crime prevention.

Giving a central role in criminal justice to a small agency variably linked with other agencies and concerned predominantly with the welfare of offenders is no longer feasible. Linkages of the various correctional agencies will be necessary if a concerted attack on crime is to be made, and Government is going to have to devote considerable thought, as well as resources, to the creation of central and local administrative structures which will make a reality of its vision of a coordinated and integrated criminal justice policy. The need for local crime committees, as central parts of a strategic approach to criminal justice policy has been persuasively argued elsewhere (Locke 1990) and Government acknowledges the need for a formalisation of local relations, albeit in as non-bureaucratised a way as possible (Faulkner 1989: 7).

In these matters it is sometimes helpful to learn from others. The Home Office, in pondering the development of local structures, could usefully look not only at such groupings of criminal justice professionals as currently exist, such as court user groups and inter-agency committees on delinquency management, but also at the Department of Health's experience of developing mandatory *child protection committees* (Department of Health and Social Security 1988). These committees are coterminous with social services departments throughout England and

Wales, and though not without their problems of role, function, accountability and funding (Harris 1990a), do nevertheless require senior decision makers from the relevant agencies – normally health, education, social services, police, voluntary agencies and probation – to meet to develop and enforce local guidelines and procedures to protect children from abuse. The lesson from the most successful of these committees is that it is possible to obtain the correct balance between individual agency accountability and joint accountability, but that that balance will vary from area to area and can be developed only by detailed local work. Circular and legislation, though necessary, are not sufficient.

If child protection, which is, of course, a form of crime prevention (Harris 1990a) can bring senior managers together and spawn working groups involving individuals from all levels of seniority, so can crime policy more generally. That there is no mandatory forum for local meetings and decisions about the multi-agency approach to crime and criminals is surprising. To fail to require or encourage police, CPS, probation, magistrates, judges, justices' clerks, circuit administrators, local business and community relations interests to come together to address their problems and priorities is to miss the opportunity of providing an increasingly rational and participative basis for system development.

In such committees, any fears for the integrity of judicial independence will quickly evaporate (its desirability is, after all, scarcely controversial), and my own guess is that magistrates' independence of their clerks may prove a more contentious issue. There is, however, room for debate about many questions in relation to the performance of the courts and their relationship with the various criminal justice agencies. How do magistrates agree among themselves and communicate to the probation service their precise expectations of punishment in the community? How are serious and possibly idiosyncratic deviations from agreed policies to be discussed with criminal justice professionals? How is a rational and equitable local sentencing policy which has the support of local criminal justice agencies to be established? How are sentencers to receive comments from other local criminal justice experts on their practices? How are magistrates and court administrators to hear formally of the views of victims and witnesses about matters such as waiting facilities and timetabling? The days when magistrates, and especially clerks, could announce that they did not want this kind of information may well be numbered. No civil liberty worth having can possibly be threatened by sentencers talking to criminal justice experts, visiting projects, engaging in discussions about local crime problems and the proper response to them, and only good can come of exposing sentencers to wider knowledge and experiences than they normally acquire from their divisional training events.

And in all this there is a role for the probation service. The vacuum which must be filled in criminal justice is large; the probation service is ideally placed to fill at least part of it, but only if it ceases to regard itself as exclusively offender-oriented. But it cannot move far without a funding commitment. If Government genuinely envisages a concerted local policy on crime and criminal justice emerging there are major resource implications, and interested parties from the private and voluntary sectors as well as the probation service itself are likely to require reassurance that the lessons of the failure of Government's community care policies have been learned. Though the probation service may be uncertain whether it wishes to proceed down the path of major expansion, a clear commitment to fund a set of new activities would encourage those groups, particularly probation committees (Central Council of Probation Committees 1990), which see the social desirability of an integrated approach to crime control, and wish the probation service to play a part in it.

It is appropriate, however, to end this section with a cautionary footnote. Not everybody is unequivocally in favour of linkages (see, for example, Blagg, Pearson, Sampson, Smith and Stubbs 1988), and there is a proper concern, from a civil liberties perspective, about information flow among agencies and about the possible dangers of having the social workers speaking too readily to the police, the probation officers too hand in glove with the sentencers. This is a major subject which has been dealt with briefly elsewhere (Harris and Webb 1987: Chapter 7) and which transcends the precise issue of inter-agency collaboration. The main question is what price is to be paid, and by whom, for crime prevention? Video cameras in public places? Electronic security devices in undercover police operations? Curfew as an alternative to custody? Legislation to make reporting of certain known offences mandatory?

These issues arise inevitably from the development of agency linkages and from any reduction in the delicate equivocation traditionally associated with the probation service. They necessitate both academic and professional discussion but ultimately they are matters for national and, crucially, international law. But they do not of themselves constitute proper objections to linkages and information exchange; nor need they evoke images of the Big Brother of 1984. It is a poor sort of civil liberty which depends for its sustenance on the inefficiency of the agencies. The issue is not, therefore, whether the agencies should work together, but how the task of crime reduction is to be balanced against such competing political objectives as the maximisation of liberty and the enhancement of privacy (Harris 1990b). The manner in which this conflict is best resolved is a crucial subject, but for another book.

## PREDICTION AND PROBATION: SECONDARY CRIME PREVENTION AND DELINQUENCY MANAGEMENT

> . . . some approaches or methods work to prevent delinquency with some juveniles under some conditions – so we should not conclude that nothing works. Instead, we should ask what kinds of programs, under what conditions are effective with what juveniles, and with respect to what kinds of outcomes . . . We should lower our expectations . . . We need to avoid raising unrealistic goals and expectations that cannot be achieved.
>
> (Finckenauer 1982: 232)

> No one is predestined to criminal behavior, and no one is absolutely immune. The only kind of statement we can reasonably make is that some types of people are more likely to engage in crime than others. We can identify a variety of factors that raise or lower the probability somewhat, but at no time can we be certain about how particular people will behave in the future. This year's burglar can easily become next year's servant of God.
>
> (Greenwood 1986b)

The science of managing offenders in the community is inexact. As we have seen, the social scientist's laboratory lacks the predictability of that of the pure scientist. The social scientist can deal only in *probability*, and acquire and refine a range of *observational and interpretive skills* to apply the probability to a single case. This process can only be 'scientific' to a degree, as the variables which the social researcher freezes as a basis for prediction are forever shifting. Jobs are gained and lost, relationships formed and broken, mental health fluctuates, alcohol consumption varies with a bewildering rapidity which defies the most sophisticated research design.

It is because rules and regulations, formulae and exactitude are impossible that professionals are necessary (Harris 1989b). Professionals exercise judgement on the basis of a combination of observation, knowledge, skill and value which cannot be exact. In the social world, actions are taken on the basis of inexact knowledge, and in taking such action it is the duty of the professional firstly to do no harm (*primum non nocere*) and secondly to do better than the layman. Knowledge can only provide some pieces in the jigsaw: it can inform us about probabilities and hence our chances of being effective. But using probability to determine an action in a particular 'case' is not solely a matter of knowledge. How do you tell whether your 'client', a drug-abusing male burglar with criminal parents and a long record of solitary juvenile delinquency, is one of the majority of such people who will reoffend or one of the minority who will not? How do we identify those who, in the title of one study, have manifested an 'abandonment of delinquent behavior'? (Jenkins and Brown 1988).

There is a substantial literature on behavioural prediction, but few approaches have strong predictive power, and all of them present a number of largely unsolved methodological problems. Nor has the development of reliable indicators been assisted by the internecine warfare among advocates of actuarial, statistical and clinical prediction (for a helpful review of the battle-lines, see Clear and O'Leary 1983: 38; Gottfredson and Taylor 1986: 133–8). Conversely, critical criminologists have focused on structural variables such as poverty and inequality, racism and stigma as 'creating' criminality. These writers too have generally failed to establish strong causal relations between a structural variable (or gestalt of variables) and criminality. Once the the banal point that there is 'more crime' in 'poor areas' has been made and agreed, structural theorists are left with the problem of explaining differential crime rates, patterns and characteristics in different kinds of 'poor area' as well as dealing with problems such as the prevalence of white collar crime in 'rich areas' and the fact that even in 'poor areas' serious or repeated crime is the activity of a small minority. The unsolved theoretical problem for such theorists is how to explain mass conformity in conditions of poverty or exclusion from the social reward structure; while for many outside the critical tradition the suspicion is always that critical theories of crime are really thinly veiled political arguments for social reform.

Of course, it would be wrong to suggest that all structural or areal criminology falls into this kind of trap, and it would be unthinkable for professionals to focus only on decontextualised individuals. After all, most offenders are not detected most of the time, only a tiny minority of the tiny minority who are detected are likely to be amenable to the ministrations of the professionals, and only a tiny minority of these in turn are likely to receive the right treatment. If crime prevention and therefore a safe and healthy environment are to be attained, a broader canvas for professional action is needed: to work solely with individuals is a costly and ineffective secondary prevention strategy.

From the Chicago School onwards (see Shaw 1929, 1930; Shaw and Mackay 1942) there have been studies of 'crime-prone areas' reflecting such factors as housing tenure and reputation (Baldwin and Bottoms 1976) and architectural design (Newman 1972), moving, as the research has increased in sophistication, to an ecological perspective focusing not on individuals as autonomous units and not on neighbourhoods or structural variables as static givens, but on the point of interaction between individuals and their social environment. The work of Oscar Newman (Newman 1972) on 'defensible space' was a significant step in developing this approach in that it regarded this 'space' as both a physical and a psychological construct. Physical safety and privacy affect not only criminal opportunity structures (by removing surveillance-free zones) but also the collective subjectivity of the inhabitants.

Though Newman's work has not been persuasively validated empirically, it proved a potent and influential metaphor linking physical safety with psychological well-being. It also acted as a spur to the development of further neighbourhood-based research, including studies of such phenomena as local social ties (through which social control can be exercised and information about legitimate opportunity structures disseminated), attachment to locale (involving studies of participation levels in local events and personal commitment to the locality) and the extent and nature of local services, some of which may produce benefits such as support and material goods, while others may be criminogenic (see in particular Gottfredson and Taylor 1986).

The main advantage of this approach for the criminal justice professional is not that it provides hard information about the consequence for 'crime' of particular levels of, say, unemployment, ethnic mix or public house provision. Rather it invites professionals, as part of their task of general social enquiry, to explore and analyse the nature of 'neighbourhood' both materially (how it is characterised in terms of systems, structures and demography) and subjectively (how these characteristics are perceived by the inhabitants and significant others). We cannot assume a static or universal consequence of the presence (or absence) of, say, public houses, gambling dens or prostitution, but there is every reason to ensure that their social role, criminogenic or not, in local social and cultural life is fully understood. In one community the presence of a public house will apparently provoke alcohol-related crime, or will itself be a site for illegal acts such as the disposal of stolen goods or narcotics distribution; in another, the absence of a public house will mean that the community is denuded of a focal point and that, supposedly for want of anything else to do in the evening, crime levels are high and vandalism rife. In one community the existence of prostitution will lead to stigmatisation, with other forms of social nuisance following in its train: services may be withdrawn, credit disallowed, helping networks collapse and criminal elements infiltrate the area with the consequential collective demor-alisation of the inhabitants. Elsewhere prostitution may (rightly or wrongly) be perceived positively, with local businesses regenerated by an influx of money, or community confidence enhanced through an apparent reduction in sexual attacks.

Quantitative studies tell us what is generally probable, but only detailed local ethnography will tell us what local people believe actually occurs in particular places, how that belief reflects (or does not reflect) reality, how the locality has changed over time, what meaning the concept neighbourhood has for the people who live there and how criminal opportunities can be identified and eliminated. Ethnographic details of this kind can in practice be collected only by local professionals and agencies: because the nature of a neighbourhood is forever shifting, the visiting researcher can never understand it in the way that local professionals, and particularly local people, can. The augmentation of quantitative research and theoretical knowledge by appreciative yet systematic local enquiry is, therefore, a cornerstone of community-based criminal justice and in particular crime prevention work. The reluctance of Government adequately to fund, or agencies consistently to provide, effective local social monitoring is, to the interested academic, literally incomprehensible.

To stress the necessity of a community-based assault on crime is not to decry the importance of individual work too. But few individually-based treatment strategies affect the delinquent conduct of their consumers on a lasting basis: the potency of the new correctional variable interjected into the life of the delinquent fades with time. Thus David Greenberg, in a gloomy review of American correctional programmes notes:

> The diversity of programs showing an initially favorable effect which disappears after subjects have been released for some time suggests to me that the limited effects that programs do have may be achieved, not through the conventionally imagined therapeutic effects of the programs, but by increasing legitimate aspirations and commitment

to the avoidance of illegal behavior, probably as a result of social attention and, in some instances, possibly through special deterrence. That this effect slowly extinguishes . . . shows the limitations of an individual approach to the elimination of criminality.

(Greenberg 1977a: 141)

To affect crime other than marginally, therefore, necessitates community-based as well as individual strategies. It would be wrong to assume that these strategies should necessarily involve injecting material resources for generalised social amelioration: one lesson of the poverty programmes of the Kennedy and Johnson administrations is that the ill-focused distribution of material resources is ineffective in crime reduction and may be counterproductive. Once one accepts the logic of the poverty programme, enough resources are never provided, discontent and frustration increase and welfare bureaucracies grow exponentially but with few demonstrable benefits for the majority of the intended beneficiaries. To be empirically sound as well as economically responsible, resources for crime prevention and delinquency management need to be precisely targeted and clearly distinguished from resources for income support and the redistribution of wealth. Both crime prevention and the redistribution of wealth may well be desirable, but they have different empirical, moral and political justifications. Put bluntly, if the aim is to reduce crime, attacking poverty is neither the most effective nor the most economical way of going about it. A much more precisely targeted approach is likely to yield better dividends more cheaply.

This precision of focus is also appropriate at a level of individual work. In the United States it is stark:

any assistance rendered an offender must be reasonably related to a crime reduction goal. A supervision agency is not a welfare agency, and an extension of its activities beyond a crime control focus is both inappropriate and dangerous.

(O'Leary and Clear 1984: 18)

So bald a distinction is historically inappropriate in the United Kingdom, but for the British probation officer the 'client' is still properly the court, and it is reasonable to expect that the prime purpose of the organisation will also be crime reduction. It is perfectly consistent with that purpose for the probation officer to work to open new opportunity structures, to help offenders manage their lives better, control alcohol consumption, withstand temptation and generally lead a more ordered existence. Nor is it other than intrinsically desirable to show a humane and genuine interest in their lives and a concern for their well-being, though if an extraneous justification is needed, it is that the large majority of probationers are themselves lacking in opportunities for success, either by chance or through their own actions, and that it is proper for there to be a professional to help them maximise their capacity for rational and autonomous action (Harris 1985, 1989b). But such concerns need to co-exist with the crime control function, and the commitment of the probation service to social reform *per se* cannot replace it without an unbridgable disjunction emerging between purpose and practice.

It is in this sense that crime prevention is a logical and appropriate task for the probation service. It has self-evident skills in working with individuals, and although those skills need redirecting to maximise the chances of secondary prevention, the service's work with disadvantaged offenders can be defended by the sympathetic as an intrinsic good and would probably have a wider legitimacy if it devoted time, skills and resources to victims too. But I have also argued that the service has a range of skills which make it uniquely suited to involvement in community-based criminal justice work. Probation officers learn skills of community involvement and development, of management and organisation, of mobilising people to help themselves, of general social enquiry and social research. They know how to analyse statistical data, to engage in socially ameliorative activities and to liaise with other professionals. In all these areas there is a major job as yet undone.

But if the service does embrace the role Government has in mind for it, it will have to address systematically certain prerequisites for effective delinquency management and crime reduction, of which there are two in particular – risk assessment and private sector involvement.

## Risk assessment

A three part typology of risk has been devised by American criminal justice researchers (Clear and O'Leary 1983; O'Leary and Clear 1984). Though the determination of what constitutes the legitimate management of different categories of offender will properly be defined by legislation, the interpretation and implementation of statute will fall to whatever local crime committees are instituted. The crucial technical problem in community-based strategies is, of course, to avoid 'soft' supervision being extended inappropriately to cover a wide range of marginal offenders whose need is not great and who present minimal risk to the community. In this context Clear and O'Leary define three principles for risk control: *controlling the net, guaranteeing due process* and *sustaining the capacity for change* (Clear and O'Leary 1983: 8-9):

> Our fundamental aim is to develop a fair system of community protection in which incapacitative and treatment measures used to control risk are employed rationally. It is a system constrained by the notion of desert, which fixes the range of acceptable punishment and encourages the use of such devices as restitution and community service.
>
> (Clear and O'Leary 1983: 27)

It follows that in delinquency management, though crime control must be the central purpose, it cannot be the only one, existing unconstrained by contrary pulls. In this it is precisely akin to situational crime prevention as described in Chapter 4. If one objective, however intrinsically desirable, is pursued at the expense of other competing objectives, we are on the road to the tyranny of impossible obsessionalism. In crime control as in any other socio-political activity, there is an opportunity cost, and if community corrections are to be effective, their opportunity cost must be significantly less than that of the prison. What the scale of risk and control must be is a decision which is not simply technical, but moral, political and professional, one in which local discussion is as crucial as national policy and legislation.

Risk control involves developing a *program plan profile* (or PPP) for each offender: there are four essential steps:

1. Determining the degree of supervision emphasis (and coercion) a client should receive, depending on the risk level represented by that client
2. Analyzing the problems that affect the client's risk to the community
3. Specifying the client's behavioral objectives in order to control risk
4. Specifying resources (techniques or interventions) to be used in regard to each objective.

(Clear and O'Leary 1983: 68)

There is, of course, a range of intensive supervision models available, particularly in the United States, as a possible basis for experimentation. These include Ohio's shock probation (short incarceration followed by probation) and Georgia's intensive probation supervision (IPS) (Conrad 1985), involving almost daily contact with the supervising officer, community service, curfew and unannounced spot checks at the workplace.

In the case of IPS, daily checking is carried out by a relatively low level surveillance officer accountable to a probation officer. The probation officer operates as case manager, with an assessment, monitoring and trouble-shooting role.

Obviously such schemes would be strongly resisted by the probation service on a number of grounds, primarily the use to which they would be put by sentencers. This objection is entirely proper and highlights again the fact that the sentencing problem is one for Government to address, preferably both by means of a sentencing commission and by local crime committees with the mandatory membership of sentencers in both lower and higher courts. I do believe this latter step is a prerequisite for the success of the present commitment to reducing the prison population. At present the integrated structure necessary is simply not available and the proposals will suffer the same fate as their various predecessors.

### Private sector involvement

The reluctance of the probation service to engage with the forms of management and surveillance which Government has in mind has probably contributed to private sector involvement in criminal justice becoming, as it is in the United States, a question of not 'whether' but 'how' and 'how much' (Champion 1988: 86). Much of the work involved will be routine, its nature governed by national and international statements of legal rights rather than by the 'values' of probation officers. Though such involvement is regarded as wrong in principle by some commentators on the left (Ryan and Ward 1989) their objection seems difficult to sustain unless we are clear what privatisation means. If, as seems probable, it primarily involves subcontracting routine tasks and drawing on specific technical contributions, with the state still responsible for their effective and efficient implementation (Home Office 1990d), the more important concerns are with inspection and monitoring, practicality and economy (Demone and Gibelman 1990). Though the emotive issue of electronic tagging tends to dominate professional discussions, it is probably on these more mundane grounds that the argument among proponents (Champion 1988), opponents and agnostics (Lilly 1989) will be resolved.

### CONCLUSION

The stage on which the dramas of delinquency management in the community are to be acted out in the future will be larger than in the past, with more actors in the cast and bigger parts to be had. If the probation service is to hold centre stage it is going to have to grow into one of these bigger parts. If it chooses not to do so, the part will be played by someone else.

This would not *necessarily* be a bad thing, of course. The service may choose to continue to identify itself as a proponent of social and penal reform, injecting reformist, humanitarian and sometimes liberationist values into the system, taking the view that its capacity to continue with this honourable tradition will be compromised by the new controlling functions planned for it. Such a stance seems unlikely to be wise, however. When in 1977 I argued that there should indeed be a 'split' between care and control, with the probation service assuming responsibility for the former, leaving the latter to another criminal justice agency, the political world was not that of the 1990s, and the conceptual logic of the case I argued then can, ironically, only be followed by arguing almost (though not quite) for the reverse of this. For the deprived, distressed but marginal offender, love and compassion can no longer be provided by the probation service. Perhaps we need to turn the wheel full circle and reinvent the Police Court Mission to provide the necessary voluntary help and care which once such people received. The policy vacuum which exists in criminal justice is at present huge, and the probation service should be involved in filling it.

The worlds of social work and criminal justice, as the Home Office has rightly observed (Home Office 1990d), changed remarkably in the 1980s. The emphasis of social work too has shifted towards case management and developing multi-disciplinary initiatives. The therapeutic aspirations of the 1970s have given way to concern with the efficient delivery of those accountable, focused and realistic services specified by law and policy. The notion that social work is mandated in some extra-legal manner to act as a generalised liberal conscience can no longer be sustained. The experience of multi-disciplinary work, in child protection and juvenile justice for example, has reminded many social workers that their 'values', far from being unique to them, are basic to civilised social and political relations, and as evident among other professionals as among themselves. Hence, as David Faulkner has observed, probation officers can no longer properly regard themselves as the 'good guys' of the criminal justice system (Faulkner 1989). What is important is that the system as a whole should be 'good' and the probation service has an integral role in helping make it so.

The probation service is being asked to embark on a set of activities which may be beyond it or anybody. But once crime reduction becomes a central and shared objective of all elements of the criminal justice system, and once all elements of that system, including the probation service, operate *as* a system, some of the sense of being asked to do the impossible will be reduced by dint of its very cooperation with other services, and in particular by the protection which results from operating in an integrated local network.

This book has sought to adumbrate a conceptual framework within which the service can take on some of these functions. It outlines the knowledge base necessary for the job, but as it is decidedly not a blueprint for action I do not address issues of funding, accountability and prioritisation. Broadly based probation work, I have argued, must be central to criminal justice if we are to move away from prisoncentricity. But managing large numbers of more serious offenders in the community has major implications – and not only of resources. From time to time there will be embarrassments, indeed disasters. There will be lapses by staff, offenders undergoing punishment will commit serious crimes, there will be Press campaigns, sentencers will make intemperate comments and the edifice will start to shake. When that happens, if the overall strategy is not to be destroyed, a collective response from the criminal justice professionals is going to be needed, and that will only be obtained if they too are involved in and committed to it. Press campaigns are run not only against probation officers but against magistrates and the police too, and though I am asking that the probation service surrender some of its exclusivity, in doing so it will gain an entry to other areas of criminal justice where it has a contribution to make. If the service can engage increasingly with police, sentencers, victims and others, it has a real opportunity to develop community-based criminal justice provisions which may, with a fair wind, make a contribution to reducing the use of prison.

This surrender of exclusivity, therefore, applies to the other agencies too, and gives the probation service an emergent role in the areas I have been writing about – work with victims, crime prevention, dealing with fear of crime, community involvement – as well as in the management of offenders. Local crime committees will, if they come about, create a new participatory structure involving both professionals and community representatives and will represent one of the first coherent community responses to adult crime known in this country. And the problems to be solved will be considerable, including the development of community corrections for women and girls, dealing appropriately with ethnic minority crime, advising and supporting local crime prevention and victim support initiatives, developing sentencing strategies and planning the community surveillance and management of high risk offenders to name but six. These are not problems that any one agency need try to solve alone once the different skills of police, probation, courts and the community are pooled.

There are many problems to be resolved and pitfalls to be avoided, not least in relation to resourcing, accountability and the complexities of partnership, the independence of the judiciary and the relationship between consistent central and flexible local policy development. These are issues primarily for Government and the services themselves, however, not the interested academic. But if probation officers support the possibility of decarceration it would be regrettable if they were unwilling to share part of the cost which must accompany it. Decarceration is no different from any other cake: one can choose to have it or to eat it but not both, and though there is always the third alternative of having nothing to do with it, the fate of the person making that choice is usually to experience prolonged and increasingly distressing pangs of hunger.

# Notes

## 1 Criminal statistics – some themes and issues
1 By 'criminal statistics', I mean the annual publications *Criminal Statistics, England and Wales*, and *Prison Statistics, England and Wales*, both published by HMSO, but not other forms of data gathered by 'official' sources, such as the British Crime Survey or its American counterpart the National Crime Survey, which are discussed in Chapter 2. There is no detailed discussion of the statistics themselves in this chapter, and for such a discussion you are recommended to read a definitive commentary already available (Bottomley and Pease 1986) as well, of course, as the primary sources themselves.

## 2 Counting crime – beyond the official statistics
1 Other methods, which include a 'confessional' or 'biographical' approach to the undetected crimes of known criminals and a 'documentary' approach to police and other records have a number of fundamental flaws and are now little used for academic (as opposed to journalistic) purposes. A more complex approach to undetected criminality is to be found in observational (including participant) work, where rich data have been uncovered about, in particular, gang processes (see, for example, Yablonsky 1962; Patrick 1973; Parker 1974; Campbell 1984), place of employment criminality (Taylor and Walton 1971; Ditton 1977) and, in a celebrated and astonishing study, importuning in public lavatories (Humphreys 1970). For a classic early attempt at theorising schoolchildren's deviant behaviour by creating deviant opportunities while ostensibly subjecting the children to educational tests, see Hartshorne and May 1928.

## 3 Fear, victims and community
1 And, to squash one particular stereotype, by far the safest part of the UK is Northern Ireland. Even in relation to 'assaults with force' the province is well below the international average, with a figure over the five year period of only just over one third of that of Australia, the highest risk country.

## 4 The probation service and situational crime prevention
1 It is important not to conflate 'displacement' in this sense with its Freudian derivative, involving as that does the idea that an unconscious drive must out, if

not in one place then in another. This failure to dissassociate the rational from the intrapsychic may have led to scepticism about situational crime prevention on the part of psychotherapeutically influenced social workers and other professionals (Clarke and Cornish 1985: 155).

## 5  Women and girls, criminal justice and the probation service

1  An interesting side-issue from this study is that, contrary to hypothesis, there was a direct relationship between social class and the likelihood of arrest. Whereas store detectives were likely to feel sympathy for poorly dressed thieves, one in particular 'recalled with obvious pleasure an occasion when she had apprehended and charged a person who had arrived at the store in a chauffeur-driven luxury car' (Feuerverger and Shearing 1982: 285).

2  It should, however, be noted that since many of these prisoners are foreigners arrested at ports and airports it is strictly inaccurate to 'count' them as a proportion of the British population. Their removal does, of course, reduce considerably the striking overrepresentation of black women *as a proportion of that population*.

## 6  Race, criminal justice and the probation service

1  This is, however, a sensitive issue: see Gilroy 1987: 114 for the view that it reflects the 'twin racist stereotypes of the quiescent Asian victim and the criminally inclined West Indian street youth'.

2  I am using this phrase to connote what in the classification are termed 'West Indian, Guyanese, African'. I am omitting reference here to all other ethnic groups, partly because the overrepresentation is greatest with Afro-Caribbeans and partly because of the counting system which classifies 'refusals' as part of the 'other' category, thereby rendering that column meaningless.

3  It is theoretically possible that there are hard determinants, of course, and positivist researchers, most significantly the indefatigable Sheldon and Eleanor Glueck (see for example Glueck and Glueck 1950, 1956) have devoted themselves to computing the right combinations of variables which will translate probability into certainty. Whether this quest is ever likely to prove fruitful is a question which can, fortunately, be avoided here.

4  My approach to this section has much benefited from supervisory discussions with two former students, Robert Waters and Keith McInniss. A revised version of Waters's M.Phil thesis, *Race on Probation: the Criminal Justice System and Ethnic Minorities* (University of Leicester 1987) has now been published in book form, and is cited in the bibliography. McInniss's unpublished MA thesis, *Race and the Criminal Justice System* (University of Hull 1989), is not cited in the bibliography but is lodged in the University's Brynmor Jones Library. As is the way of these things, this chapter doubtless contains a number of Waters's and McInniss's thoughts, just as one or two of mine are, I think, recognisable in their theses.

## 7  Sentencing practice and the social enquiry report

1  It should be noted that the contemporary use of the phrase 'a deterrent sentence' as synonymous with a 'tough sentence', in that it departs from this principle, is technically incorrect.

# Bibliography

I'm saving Virginia Woolf for when I'm dead.

(Julian Barnes: *Flaubert's Parrot*)

Abel, R.L. (ed.) (1982) *The Politics of Informal Justice*. New York: Academic Press.

Adler, F. (1975) *Sisters in Crime*. New York: McGraw-Hill.

Advisory Council on the Penal System (1970) *Non-Custodial and Semi-Custodial Penalties*. (Wootton Report) London: HMSO.

Agopian, M.W., Chappell, D. and Geis, G. (1977) 'Black Offender and White Victim: a Study of Forcible Rape in Oakland, California'. In D. Chappell, R. Geis and G. Geis, (eds) *Forcible Rape: the Crime, the Victim, and the Offender*. New York: Columbia University Press.

Ainsworth, P.B. and Pease, K. (1987) *Police Work*. London: British Psychological Society and Methuen.

Alaszewski, A. and Harrison, L. (1988) 'Literature Review: Collaboration and Co-ordination Between Welfare Agencies'. *British Journal of Social Work* 18: 635–47.

Allen, H. (1987) *Justice Unbalanced: Gender, Psychiatry and Judicial Decisions*. Milton Keynes: Open University Press.

Ashworth, A. (1983) *Sentencing and Penal Policy*. London: Weidenfeld and Nicolson.

Ashworth, A. (1987) 'Devising Sentencing Guidance for England'. In K. Pease and M. Wasik (eds) *Sentencing Reform: Guidance or Guidelines?* Manchester: Manchester University Press.

Ashworth, A. (1989) 'Policy, Accountability and the Courts'. In R. Shaw and K. Haines (eds) *The Criminal Justice System: a Central Role for the Probation Service*. Cambridge: University of Cambridge Institute of Criminology.

Audit Commission (1989) *The Probation Service: Promoting Value for Money*. London: HMSO.

Baldwin, J. (1979) 'Ecological and Areal Studies in Great Britain and the United States'. In N. Morris and M. Tonry (eds) *Crime and Justice: an Annual Review of Research*, Vol. 1. Chicago: University of Chicago Press.

Baldwin, J. and Bottoms, A.E. (1976) *The Urban Criminal*. London: Tavistock Publications.

Bean, P. (1976) *Rehabilitation and Deviance*. London: Routledge and Kegan Paul.

Bean, P. (1981) *Punishment: a Philosophical and Criminological Inquiry.* Oxford: Martin Robertson.

Bean, P. and Whynes, D. (eds) (1986) *Barbara Wootton: Social Science and Public Policy: Essays in Her Honour.* London: Tavistock Publications.

Bell, M. and Bell, M. (1987) '"Crime Control", Deterrence and Target Hardening'. In E. Johnson (ed.) *Handbook on Crime and Delinquency Prevention.* New York: Greenwood Press.

Belson, W.A. (1975) *Juvenile Theft: the Causal Factors.* London: Harper and Row.

Bennett, T. (1990) 'Tackling Fear of Crime'. *Home Office Research Bulletin* 28: 14–19.

Bentham, J. (1789) *An Introduction to the Principles of Morals and Legislation.* (London: Thos. Payne.) (Reprinted 1948: Oxford: Basil Blackwell.)

Benyon, J. (1986) 'Policing in the Limelight: Citizens, Constables and Controversy'. In J. Benyon and C. Bourn (eds) *The Police: Powers, Procedures and Proprieties.* Oxford: Pergamon Press.

Benyon, J. and Bourn, C. (eds) (1986) *The Police: Powers, Procedures and Proprieties.* Oxford: Pergamon Press.

Berlins, M. and Dyer, C. (1982) *The Law Machine.* Harmondsworth: Penguin Books.

Bhat, A., Carr-Hill, R. and Ohri, S. (eds) (1988) *Britain's Black Population: a New Perspective.* 2nd Edn. Aldershot: Gower.

Bienvenue, R. and Latife, A.H. (1975) 'Arrests, Dispositions and Recidivism: a Comparison of Indians and Whites'. In R. Silverman and J. Teevan (eds) *Crime in Canadian Society.* Toronto: Butterworth (Canada).

Blagg, H., Pearson, G., Sampson, A., Smith, D. and Stubbs, P. (1988) 'Inter-agency Coordination: Rhetoric and Reality'. In T. Hope and M. Shaw (eds) *Communities and Crime Reduction.* London: HMSO.

Blair, I. (1985) *Investigating Rape: a New Approach for Police.* London: Croom Helm.

Blom-Cooper, L. (ed.) (1974) *Progress in Penal Reform.* Oxford: Clarendon Press.

Bolton, F.G., Morris, L.A. and MacEachron, A.E. (1989) *Males at Risk: the Other Side of Child Sexual Abuse.* Beverly Hills, CA: Sage Publications.

Bottomley, A.K. and Coleman, C.A. (1981) *Understanding Crime Rates.* Farnborough: Gower Press.

Bottomley, A.K. and Pease, K. (1986) *Crime and Punishment: Interpreting the Data.* Milton Keynes: Open University Press.

Bottoms, A.E. (1980) *The Suspended Sentence after Ten Years.* Leeds: University of Leeds Centre for Social Work and Applied Studies.

Bottoms, A.E. (1989) 'The Concept of Intermediate Sanctions and its Relevance for the Probation Service'. In R. Shaw and K. Haines (eds) *The Criminal Justice System: a Central Role for the Probation Service.* Cambridge: University of Cambridge Institute of Criminology.

Bottoms, A.E. and McWilliams, W. (1986) 'Social Enquiry Reports Twenty-Five Years After the Streatfeild Report'. In P. Bean and D. Whynes (eds) *Barbara Wootton: Social Science and Public Policy: Essays in Her Honour.* London: Tavistock Publications.

Bottoms, A.E. and Stelman, A. (1988) *Social Inquiry Reports: a Framework for Practice Development.* Aldershot: Wildwood House.

Box, S. (1983) *Power, Crime and Mystification*. London: Tavistock Publications.

Box, S. (1987) *Recession, Crime and Punishment*. London: Macmillan.

Box, S. and Hale, C. (1984) 'Liberation/Emancipation, Economic Marginalization, or Less Chivalry'. *Criminology* 22: 473–97.

Braithwaite, J. (1981) '"The Myth of Social Class and Criminality" Reconsidered'. *American Sociological Review* 46: 36–57.

Braithwaite, J. (1989) *Crime, Shame and Reintegration*. Cambridge: Cambridge University Press.

Braithwaite, J., Biles, D. and Whitrod, R. (1982) 'Fear of Crime in Australia'. In H.J. Schneider (ed.) *The Victim in International Perspective*. Berlin: de Gruyter.

Brake, M. (1985) *Comparative Youth Culture*. London: Routledge and Kegan Paul.

Bridge, Lord (1978) *Report of the Working Party on Judicial Studies and Information*. London: HMSO.

Brody, S.R. (1976) *The Effectiveness of Sentencing: a Review of the Literature*. Home Office Research Study No. 35. London: HMSO.

Burney, E. (1979) *J.P.: Magistrate, Court and Commmunity*. London: Hutchinson.

Burrows, J., Ekblom, P. and Heal, K. (1979) *Crime Prevention and the Police*. Home Office Research Study No. 55. London: HMSO.

Burrows, J. and Tarling, R. (1982) *Clearing Up Crime*. Home Office Research Study No. 73. London: HMSO.

Button, J.W. (1978) *Black Violence: Political Impact of the 1960s Riots*. Princeton, NJ: Princeton University Press.

Buzawa, E.S. and Buzawa, C.G. (1990) *Domestic Violence: the Criminal Justice Response*. Beverly Hills, CA: Sage Publications.

Byrne, J.M. and Sampson, R.J. (eds) (1986) *The Social Ecology of Crime*. New York: Springer-Verlag.

Cain, M. (1973) *Society and the Policeman's Role*. London: Routledge and Kegan Paul.

Campbell, A. (1981) *Girl Delinquents*. Oxford: Basil Blackwell.

Campbell, A. (1984) *The Girls in the Gang*. Oxford: Basil Blackwell.

Carlen, P. (1983) *Women's Imprisonment: a Study in Social Control*. London: Routledge and Kegan Paul.

Carlen, P. and Worrall, A. (eds) (1987) *Gender, Crime and Justice*. Milton Keynes: Open University Press.

Carr-Hill, R. and Drew, D. (1988) 'Blacks, Police and Crime'. In A. Bhat, R. Carr-Hill and S. Ohri (eds) *Britain's Black Population: a New Perspective*. 2nd Edn. Aldershot: Gower.

Central Council of Probation Committees (1987) *Crime Prevention: a Role for Probation Committees*. London: Central Council of Probation Committees.

Central Council of Probation Committees (1990) *Probation: the Key to Change*. Working Party Report. London: Central Council of Probation Committees.

Champion, D.J. (1988) *Felony Probation: Problems and Prospects*. New York: Praeger.

Chappell, D., Geis, R. and Geis, G. (eds) (1977) *Forcible Rape: the Crime, the Victim, and the Offender*. New York: Columbia University Press.

Christie, N. (1977) 'Conflicts as Property'. *British Journal of Criminology* 17: 1–19.

Christie, N. (1981) *Limits to Pain*. Oxford: Martin Robertson.

Clark, J.P. and Tifft, L.L. (1966) 'Polygraph and Interview Validation of Self-Reported Deviant Behavior'. *American Sociological Review* 31: 516–23.

Clarke, R.V.G. (1983) 'Situational Crime Prevention: Its Theoretical Basis and Practical Scope'. In M. Tonry and N. Morris (eds) *Crime and Justice: an Annual Review of Research*. Vol. 4. Chicago: University of Chicago Press.

Clarke, R.V.G. and Cornish, D.B. (1985) 'Modeling Offenders' Decisions: a Framework for Research and Policy'. In M. Tonry and N. Morris (eds) *Crime and Justice: an Annual Review of Research*. Vol. 6. Chicago: University of Chicago Press.

Clarke, R.V.G., Ekblom, P., Hough, M. and Mayhew, P. (1985) 'Elderly Victims of Crime and Exposure to Risk'. *Howard Journal of Criminal Justice* 24: 81–9.

Clarke, R.V.G. and Mayhew, P.M. (eds) (1980) *Designing Out Crime*. London: HMSO.

Clear, T.R. (1978) 'Correctional Policy, Neo-Retributionism, and the Determinate Sentence'. *The Justice System Journal* 4/1: 26–48.

Clear, T.R. (1985) 'Managerial Issues in Community Corrections'. In L.F. Travis III (ed.) *Probation, Parole, and Community Corrections: a Reader*. Prospect Heights, IL: Waveland Press.

Clear, T.R. (1988) 'Statistical Prediction in Corrections'. *Research in Corrections* 1: 1–40.

Clear, T.R. and O'Leary, V. (1983) *Controlling the Offender in the Community*. Lexington, MA: D.C. Heath.

Cleaver, E. (1968) *Soul on Ice*. New York: McGraw-Hill

Cloward, R.A. and Ohlin, L.E. (1960) *Delinquency and Opportunity: a Theory of Delinquent Gangs*. Glencoe, IL: Free Press.

Cohen, J.E. (1983) 'Incapacitation as a Strategy for Crime Control: Possibilities and Pitfalls'. In M. Tonry and N. Morris (eds) *Crime and Justice: an Annual Review of Research*. Vol. 5. Chicago: University of Chicago Press.

Cohen, L.E. and Land, K.C. (1984) 'Discrepancies Between Crime Reports and Crime Surveys'. *Criminology* 22: 499–530.

Cohen, S. (ed.) (1971) *Images of Deviance*. Harmondsworth: Penguin Books.

Cohen, S. (1985) *Visions of Social Control*. Cambridge: Polity Press.

Conklin, J.E. (1975) *The Impact of Crime*. New York: Macmillan.

Conrad, J.P. (1985) *The Dangerous and the Endangered*. Lexington, MA: D.C. Heath.

Cook, D. (1987) 'Women in Welfare: In Crime or Injustice?' In P. Carlen and A. Worrall (eds) *Gender, Crime and Justice*. Milton Keynes: Open University Press.

Cook, F.L. and Cook, T.D. (1976) 'Evaluating the Rhetoric of Crisis: a Case Study of Criminal Victimization of the Elderly'. *Social Science Review* 50: 632–46.

Cornish, D.B. and Clarke, R.V.G. (1986) 'Situational Prevention, Displacement of Crime and Rational Choice Theory'. In K. Heal and G. Laycock (eds) *Situational Crime Prevention: from Theory into Practice*. London: HMSO.

Council of Europe (1984) *Participation of the Public in Crime Policy*. Report of the European Committee on Crime Problems. Strasbourg: Council of Europe.

Covington, J. (1984) 'Insulation from Labeling'. *Criminology* 22: 619–43.

Crow, I. and Cove, J. (1984) 'Ethnic Minorities and the Courts'. *Criminal Law Review* 413–17.

Curran, D.A. (1983) 'Judicial Discretion and Defendant's Sex'. *Criminology* 21: 41–58.

Curran, J.H. (1983) 'Social Enquiry Reports: a Selective Commentary on the Literature'. In J. Lishman (ed.) *Social Work with Adult Offenders*. Research Highlights 5. Aberdeen: University of Aberdeen Department of Social Work.

Curran, J.H. and Chambers, G.A. (1982) *Social Enquiry Reports in Scotland*. Scottish Office Social Research Study. Edinburgh: HMSO.

Curtis, L.A. (1975) *Violence, Race and Culture*. Lexington, MA: D.C. Heath.

Davidoff, L. and Dowds, L. (1989) 'Recent Trends in Crimes of Violence against the Person in England and Wales'. *Home Office Research Bulletin* 27: 11–17.

Davies, M. (1989) *Probation Reading: an Empirical Bibliography*. Norwich: Social Work Monographs.

Davis, K.C. (1971) *Discretionary Justice: a Preliminary Inquiry*. Urbana: University of Illinois Press.

Demone, H.W., Jr and Gibelman, M. (1990) '"Privatizing" the Treatment of Criminal Offenders'. *Journal of Offender Counseling, Services and Rehabilitation* 15 (2): 7–25.

Department of Health and Social Security (1972) *Intermediate Treatment: a Guide for the Regional Planning of New Forms of Treatment for Children in Trouble*. London: HMSO.

Department of Health and Social Security (1988) *Working Together*. London: HMSO.

Departments of Health, Social Security, Scottish and Welsh Offices (1989) *Caring for People: Community Care in the Next Decade and Beyond*. London: HMSO.

Devlin, P. (1979) *The Judge*. Oxford: Oxford University Press.

Ditton, J. (1977) *Part-time Crime: an Ethnography of Fiddling and Pilferage*. London: Macmillan.

Ditton, J. (1978) *Controlology: Beyond the New Criminology*. London: Macmillan.

Dobash, R.P., Dobash, R.E. and Gutteridge, S. (1986) *The Imprisonment of Women*. Oxford: Basil Blackwell.

Doleschal, E. (1982) 'The Dangers of Criminal Justice Reform'. *Criminal Justice Abstracts* 14: 133–52.

Doyal, L. and Harris, R. (1986) *Empiricism, Explanation and Rationality*. London: Routledge and Kegan Paul.

Drapkin, I. and Viano, E. (eds) (1974a) *Victimology*. Lexington, MA: D.C. Heath.

Drapkin, I. and Viano, E. (eds) (1974b) *Victimology: a New Focus*. Vol. 1. Theoretical Issues in Victimology. Lexington, MA: D.C. Heath.

Drapkin, I. and Viano, E. (eds) (1974c) *Victimology: a New Focus*. Vol. 2. Society's Reaction to Victimization. Lexington, MA: D.C. Heath.

Drapkin, I. and Viano, E. (eds) (1975a) *Victimology: a New Focus*. Vol. 3. Crimes, Victims, and Justice. Lexington, MA: D.C. Heath.

Drapkin, I. and Viano, E. (eds) (1975b) *Victimology: a New Focus*. Vol. 4. Violence and its Victims. Lexington, MA: D.C. Heath.

Drapkin, I. and Viano, E. (eds) (1975c) *Victimology: a New Focus*. Vol. 5. Exploiters and Exploited. Lexington, MA: D.C. Heath.

Eaton, M. (1986) *Justice for Women? Family, Court and Social Control*. Milton Keynes: Open University Press.

Edwards, S. (1984) *Women on Trial*. Manchester: Manchester University Press.

Elliott, D. (1988) *Gender, Delinquency and Society*. Aldershot: Gower.

Elliott, D.S., Huizinga, D. and Ageton, S.S. (1982) *Explaining Delinquency and Drug Use*. Boulder, CO: Behavioral Research Institute.

Ellis, T. (1989) 'The Safer Cities Programme: Profiles, Surveys and Evaluation'. *Home Office Research Bulletin* 27: 21–4.

Ennis, P.H. (1970) 'Estimates of Crime from Victim Survey Research'. In A. Guenther (ed.) *Criminal Behavior and Social Systems*. Chicago: Rand McNally.

Erickson, M.L. and Empey, L.T. (1963) 'Court Records, Undetected Delinquency and Decision-Making'. *Journal of Criminal Law, Criminology, and Police Science* 54: 456–69.

Farrington, D.P. (1985) 'Delinquency Prevention in the 1980s'. *Journal of Adolescence* 8: 3–16.

Farrington, D.P and Dowds, E.A. (1985) 'Disentangling Criminal Behaviour and Police Reaction'. In D.P. Farrington and J. Gunn (eds) *Reactions to Crimes: the Police, Courts and Prisons*. Chichester: John Wiley.

Farrington, D.P. and Gunn, J. (eds) (1985) *Reactions to Crimes: the Police, Courts and Prisons*. Chichester: John Wiley.

Farrington, D.P. and Morris, A.M. (1983) 'Sex, Sentencing and Reconviction'. *British Journal of Criminology* 23: 229–48.

Farrington, D.P., Osborn, S. and West, D. (1978) 'The Persistence of Labelling Effects'. *British Journal of Criminology* 18: 277–84.

Faulkner, D. (1989) 'The Future of the Probation Service: a View from Government'. In R. Shaw and K. Haines (eds) *The Criminal Justice System: a Central Role for the Probation Service*. Cambridge: University of Cambridge Institute of Criminology.

Ferdinand, T.N. (1970) 'Demographic Shifts and Criminality: an Inquiry'. *British Journal of Criminology* 10: 169–75.

Feuerverger, A. and Shearing, C.D. (1982) 'An Analysis of the Prosecution of Shoplifters'. *Criminology* 20: 273–89.

Field, S. (1984) *The Attitudes of Ethnic Minorities*. Home Office Research Study No. 80. London: HMSO.

Fielding, N. (1984) *Probation Practice: Client Support Under Social Control*. Aldershot: Gower Press.

Figueira-McDonough, J., Barton, W.H. and Sarri, R.C. (1981) 'Normal Deviance: Gender Similarities in Adolescent Subcultures'. In M.Q. Warren (ed.) *Comparing Female and Male Offenders*. Beverly Hills, CA: Sage Publications.

Finckenauer, J.O. (1982) *Scared Straight! and the Panacea Phenomenon*. Englewood Cliffs, NJ: Prentice-Hall.

Findlay, M. and Hogg, R. (eds) (1988) *Understanding Crime and Criminal Justice*. Sydney: The Law Book Company.

Finkelhor, D. (ed.) (1986) *A Sourcebook on Child Sexual Abuse*. Beverly Hills, CA: Sage Publications.

Flowers, R.B. (1988) *Minorities and Criminality*. New York: Greenwood Press.

Forst, M.L. (ed.) (1982) *Sentencing Reform: Experiments in Reducing Disparity*. Beverly Hills, CA: Sage.

Foucault, M. (1977) *Discipline and Punish: The Birth of the Prison*. Harmondsworth: Allen Lane.

Furstenberg, F.F. Jr (1971) 'Public Reactions to Crime in the Streets'. *American Scholar* 40: 601–10.

Garofalo, R. (1914) *Criminology*. Boston, MA: Little, Brown.

Gaskell, G. (1986) 'Black Youth and the Police'. *Policing* (2) 1: 26–34.

Gelsthorpe, L. (1989) *Sexism and the Female Offender*. Aldershot: Gower Press.

Genders, E. and Player, E. (1987) 'Women in Prison: the Treatment, the Control and the Experience'. In P. Carlen and A. Worrall (eds) *Gender, Crime and Justice*. Milton Keynes: Open University Press.

Gibson, J.L. (1977-8) 'Race as a Determinant of Criminal Sentences: a Methodological Critique and Case Study'. *Law and Society Review* 12: 455–78.

Giller, H. and Morris, A. (1981) *Care and Discretion: Social Workers' Decisions with Delinquents*. London: Burnett Books in association with Andre Deutsch.

Gilroy, P. (1987) 'The Myth of Black Criminality'. In P. Scraton (ed.) *Law, Order and the Authoritarian State: Readings in Critical Criminology*. Milton Keynes: Open University Press.

Gladstone, F.J. (1980) *Co-ordinating Crime Prevention Efforts*. Home Office Research Study No. 62. London: HMSO.

Glueck, S. and Glueck, E.T. (1950) *Unraveling Juvenile Delinquency*. Cambridge, MA: Harvard University Press.

Glueck, S. and Glueck, E.T. (1956) *Physique and Delinquency*. New York: Harper.

Goffman, E. (1968) *Stigma: Notes on the Management of Spoiled Identity*. Harmondsworth: Penguin Books.

Goffman, E. (1971) *The Presentation of Self in Everyday Life*. Harmondsworth: Penguin Books.

Gold, M. (1966) 'Undetected Delinquent Behavior'. *Journal of Research in Crime and Delinquency* 13: 27–46.

Gomes-Schwartz, B., Horowitz, J.M. and Cardarelli, A.P. (1990) *Child Sexual Abuse: the Initial Effects*. Beverly Hills, CA: Sage Publications.

Gottfredson, M.R. (1984) *Victims of Crime: the Dimensions of Risk*. Home Office Research Study No. 81. London: HMSO.

Gottfredson, S.D. and Taylor, R.B. (1986) 'Person–Environment Interactions in the Prediction of Recidivism'. In J. Byrne and R. Sampson (eds) *The Social Ecology of Crime*. New York: Springer-Verlag.

Government Statistical Service (1989a) *Prison Statistics England and Wales 1988*. Cm 825. London: HMSO.

Government Statistical Service (1989b) *Criminal Statistics England and Wales 1988*. Cm 847. London: HMSO.

Government Statistical Service (1990a) *Social Trends* 20. London: HMSO.

Government Statistical Service (1990b) *Prison Statistics England and Wales 1990*. Cm 1221. London: HMSO.

Graham, J. (1989) 'Families, Parenting Skills and Delinquency'. *Home Office Research Bulletin* 26: 17–21.

Green, R. (1987) 'Racism and the Offender: a Probation Response'. In J. Harding (ed.) *Probation and the Community: a Practice and Policy Reader*. London: Tavistock Publications.

Greenberg, D.F. (1977a) 'The Correctional Effects of Corrections: A Survey of Evaluations'. In D.F. Greenberg (ed.) *Corrections and Punishment*. Beverly Hills, CA: Sage Publications.

Greenberg, D.F. (ed.) (1977b) *Corrections and Punishment*. Beverly Hills, CA: Sage Publications.

Greenberg, D.F. and Humphries, D. (1980) 'The Cooptation of Fixed Sentencing Reform'. *Crime and Delinquency* 26: 206–25.

Greenwood, P.W. (ed.) (1986a) *Intervention Strategies for Chronic Juvenile Offenders: Some New Perspectives*. New York: Greenwood Press.

Greenwood, P.W. (1986b) 'Predictions of Chronic Criminal Behavior'. In P.W. Greenwood (ed.) *Intervention Strategies for Chronic Juvenile Offenders: Some New Perspectives*. New York: Greenwood Press.

Greenwood, P.W. with Abrahamse, A. (1982) *Selective Incapacitation*. Prepared for the National Department of Justice, U.S. Department of Justice, Santa Monica, CA: Rand Corporation.

Grupp, S.E. (ed.) (1971) *Theories of Punishment*. Bloomington, IN: Indiana University Press.

Guenther, A.L. (ed.) (1970) *Criminal Behavior and Social Systems*. Chicago: Rand McNally.

Hakim, S. and Regert, G.F. (1981) *Crime Spillover*. Beverly Hills, CA: Sage Publications.

Hall, S., Critcher, C., Jefferson, T. and Roberts, B. (1978) *Policing the Crisis*. London: Macmillan.

Hanmer, J. and Saunders, S. (1984) *Well Founded Fear: a Community Study of Violence to Women*. London: Hutchinson.

Harding, C. and Koffman, L. (1988) *Sentencing and the Penal System: Text and Materials*. London: Sweet and Maxwell.

Harding, J. (1982) *Victims and Offenders: Needs and Responsibilities*. NCVO Occasional Paper No. 2. London: Bedford Square Press.

Harding, J. (ed.) (1987) *Probation and the Community: a Practice and Policy Reader*. London: Tavistock Publications.

Harris, B. (1987) 'Sentencing Guidance in the Magistrates' Court'. In K. Pease and M. Wasik (eds) *Sentencing Reform: Guidance or Guidelines?* Manchester: Manchester University Press.

Harris, R. (1977) 'The Probation Officer as Social Worker'. *British Journal of Social Work* 7: 433–42.

Harris, R. (1980) 'A Changing Service: the Case for Separating "Care" and "Control" in Probation Practice'. *British Journal of Social Work* 10: 163–84.

Harris, R. (1985) 'Towards Just Welfare: a Consideration of a Current Controversy in the Theory of Juvenile Justice'. *British Journal of Criminology* 25 (1): 31–45.

Harris, R. (1988) 'The Place of the Probation Service in the Criminal Justice System'. In Central Council of Probation Committees, *The Madingley Papers*. London: Central Council of Probation Committees.

Harris, R. (1989a) 'Social Work in Society or Punishment in the Community?'. In R. Shaw and K. Haines (eds) *The Criminal Justice System: a Central Role for the Probation Service*. Cambridge: University of Cambridge Institute of Criminology.

Harris, R. (1989b) *Suffer the Children: the Family, the State and the Social Worker*. Hull: Hull University Press.

Harris, R. (1990a) 'The Role and Task of the Area Child Protection Committee'. In Department of Health Children Services Division *Chairing an Area Child Protection Committee: 'Making it Work'*. Conference Proceedings. London: Department of Health. Mimeograph.

Harris, R. (1990b) 'A Matter of Balance: Power and Resistance in Child Protection Policy'. *Journal of Social Welfare Law* 5: 332–40.

Harris, R. and Webb, D. (1987) *Welfare, Power and Juvenile Justice: the Social Control of Delinquent Youth*. London: Tavistock Publications.

Hartshorne, H. and May, M.A. (1928) *Studies in Deceit*. Book One: 'General Methods and Results'. New York: Macmillan.

Haskell, M.R. and Yablonsky, L. (1970) *Crime and Delinquency*. Chicago: Rand McNally.

Haxby, D. (1978) *Probation: a Changing Service*. London: Constable.

Heal, K. and Laycock, G. (eds) (1986) *Situational Crime Prevention: from Theory into Practice*. London: HMSO.

Heidensohn, F. (1987) 'Women and Crime: Questions for Criminology'. In P. Carlen and A. Worrall (eds) *Gender, Crime and Justice*. Milton Keynes: Open University Press.

Heidensohn, F. (1989) *Crime and Society*. London: Macmillan.

Henderson, P. (1986) 'Community Work and the Probation Service'. *Home Office Research Bulletin* 20: 13–16.

Henham, R. (1986) 'The Influence of Sentencing Principles on Magistrates' Sentencing Practices'. *Howard Journal of Criminal Justice* 25 (3): 190–8.

Henig, J. and Maxfield, M.G. (1978) 'Reducing Fear of Crime: Strategies for Intervention'. *Victimology* 3: 297–313.

Hentig, H. von (1941) 'Remarks on the Interaction of Perpetrator and Victim'. Reprinted in I. Drapkin and E. Viano (1974a) *Victimology*. Lexington, MA: D.C. Heath. pp. 45–53.

Hindelang, M.J., Gottfredson, M.R. and Garofalo, J. (1978) *Victims of Personal Crime: an Empirical Foundation for a Theory of Personal Victimization*. Cambridge, MA: Ballinger.

Hindus, M.S. (1980) *Prison and Plantation: Crime, Justice and Authority in Massachusetts and South Carolina, 1767–1878*. Chapel Hill, NC: University of North Carolina Press.

Hirschi, T. (1969) *Causes of Delinquency*. Berkeley, CA: University of California Press.

Hirschi, T. and Hindelang, M.J. (1977) 'Intelligence and Delinquency: a Revisionist View'. *American Sociological Review* 42: 571–87.

Hoff, L.A. (1978) *People in Crisis*. Monterey, CA: Addison-Wesley.

Hogarth, J. (1971) *Sentencing as a Human Process*. Toronto, Ont.: University of Toronto Press.

Home Office (1983a) *Social Inquiry Reports: General Guidance on Contents*. Circular 17/1983. London: Home Office (mimeograph).

Home Office (1983b) *Social Inquiry Reports: Recommendations Relevant to Sentencing*. Circular 18/1983. London: Home Office (mimeograph).

Home Office (1984a) *Probation Service in England and Wales: Statement of National Objectives and Priorities*. London: Home Office (mimeograph).

Home Office (1984b) *The Probation Rules 1984*. Statutory Instrument 1984 No. 647. London: Home Office (mimeograph).

Home Office (1986) *Social Inquiry Reports*. Circular 92/1986. London: Home Office (mimeograph).

Home Office (1989) *Tackling Crime*. London: Home Office.

Home Office (1990a) *Crime, Justice and Protecting the Public*. Cm 965. London: HMSO.

Home Office (1990b) *Victim's Charter: a Statement of the Rights of Victims of Crime*. London: Home Office.

Home Office (1990c) *Supervision and Punishment in the Community: Framework for Action*. Cm 966. London: HMSO.

Home Office (1990d) *Partnership in Dealing with Offenders in the Community*. A Discussion Paper. London: Home Office (mimeograph).

Home Office and Lord Chancellor's Office (1961) *Report of the Inter-departmental Committee on the Business of the Criminal Courts*. (Streatfeild Report.) Cmnd. 1289. London: HMSO.

Home Office Standing Conference on Crime Prevention (1989) *Report of the Working Group on the Fear of Crime*. London: Home Office.

Honderich, T. (1969) *Punishment: the Supposed Justifications*. London: Hutchinson.

Hood, R. (ed.) (1989) *Crime and Criminal Policy in Europe: Proceedings of a European Colloquium*. Oxford: University of Oxford Centre for Criminological Research.

Hood, R. and Sparks, R. (1970) *Key Issues in Criminology*. London: Weidenfeld and Nicolson.

Hope, T. (1984) 'The First British Crime Survey: Current and Future Research'. *Home Office Research Bulletin* 18: 12–15.

Hope, T. (1985) *Implementing Crime Prevention Measures*. Home Office Research Study No. 86. London: HMSO.

Hope, T. (1986) 'Council Tenants and Crime'. *Home Office Research Bulletin* 21: 46–51.

Hope, T. (1986) 'School Design and Burglary'. In K. Heal and G. Laycock (eds) *Situational Crime Prevention: from Theory into Practice*. London: HMSO.

Hope, T. (1987) 'Residential Aspects of Autocrime'. *Home Office Research Bulletin* 23: 28–33.

Hope, T. (1988) 'Support for Neighbourhood Watch: a British Crime Survey Analysis'. In T. Hope and M. Shaw (eds) *Communities and Crime Reduction*. London: HMSO.

Hope, T. and Shaw, M. (eds) (1988) *Communities and Crime Reduction*. London: HMSO.

Hopkirk, M. (1949) *Nobody Wanted Sam*. London: John Murray.

Horsley, G. (1984) *The Language of Social Inquiry Reports*. Norwich: Social Work Monographs.

Hough, M., Clarke, R.V.G. and Mayhew, P. (1980) 'Introduction'. In R. Clarke and P. Mayhew (eds) *Designing Out Crime*. London: HMSO.

Hough, M. and Lewis, J. (1986) 'Penal Hawks and Penal Doves: Attitudes to Punishment in the British Crime Survey'. *Home Office Research Bulletin* 21: 5–9.

Hough, M. and Mayhew, P. (1983) *The British Crime Survey: First Report*. Home Office Research Study No. 76. London: HMSO.

Hough, M. and Mayhew, P. (1985) *Taking Account of Crime: Key Findings from the 1984 British Crime Survey*. Home Office Research Study No. 86. London: HMSO.

Hough, M. and Mo, J. (1986) '"If at First You Don't Succeed": BCS Findings on Attempted Burglaries'. *Home Office Research Bulletin* 21: 10–13.

Hough, M. and Moxon, D. (1985) 'Dealing with Offenders: Popular Opinion and the Views of Victims'. *Howard Journal of Criminal Justice* 24: 160–75.

Hough, M. and Sheehy, K. (1986) 'Incidents of Violence: Findings from the British Crime Survey'. *Home Office Research Bulletin* 20: 22–6.

Hudson, B. (1987) *Justice Through Punishment*. London: Macmillan.

Hudson, B. (1989) 'Discrimination and Disparity: Researching the Influence of Race on Sentencing'. Paper presented to the British Criminology Conference, Bristol.

Hudson, J. (ed.) (1976) *Restitution in Criminal Justice*. St Paul, MN: Minnesota Department of Corrections.

Humphreys, L. (1970) *Tearoom Trade*. London: Duckworth.

Husain, S. (1988) *Neighbourhood Watch in England and Wales: a Locational Analysis*. Crime Prevention Unit Paper No. 12. London: Home Office.

Hyman, R. and Price, B. (1979) 'Labour Statistics'. In J. Irvine, I. Miles and J. Evans (eds) *Demystifying Social Statistics*. London: Pluto Press.

Ignatieff, M. (1978) *A Just Measure of Pain*. London: Macmillan.

Irvine, J., Miles, I. and Evans, J. (eds) (1979) *Demystifying Social Statistics*. London: Pluto Press.

Jacob, B. (1976) 'The Concept of Restitution: an Historical Overview'. In J. Hudson (ed.) *Restitution in Criminal Justice*. St Paul, MN: Minnesota Department of Corrections.

James, A.L., Wilson, K. and Parry, M.L. (eds) (1988) *Social Work in Family Proceedings: a Practice Guide*. London: Routledge.

Jeffery, C.R. (1971) *Crime Prevention through Environmental Design*. Beverly Hills, CA: Sage Publications.

Jenkins, R.L. and Brown, W-K. (eds) (1988) *The Abandonment of Delinquent Behavior: Promoting the Turnaround*. New York: Praeger.

Johnson, E.H. (ed.) (1987) *Handbook on Crime and Delinquency Prevention*. New York: Greenwood Press.

Johnson, K.A. and Wasielewski, P.L. (1982) 'A Commentary on Victimization Research and the Importance of Meaning Structures'. *Criminology* 20: 205–22.

Jones, A.E. (1945) *Juvenile Delinquency and the Law*. Harmondsworth: Penguin Books.

Jones, R. and Kerslake, A. (1979) *Intermediate Treatment and Social Work*. London: Heinemann Educational Books.

Jones, T., Maclean, B. and Young, J. (1986) *The Islington Crime Survey*. Aldershot: Gower Press.

Junger, M. (1989) 'Ethnic Minorities, Crime and Public Policy'. In R. Hood (ed.) *Crime and Criminal Policy in Europe: Proceedings of a European Colloquium*. Oxford: University of Oxford Centre for Criminological Research.

Kant, I. (1887) *Philosophy of Law* (trans.W. Hastie). Edinburgh: T. & T. Clarke.

Kelling, G. (1986) 'Neighbourhood Crime Control and the Police: a View of the American Experience'. In K. Heal and G. Laycock (eds) *Situational Crime Prevention: from Theory into Practice*. London: HMSO.

King, M. and May, C. (1985) *Black Magistrates: a Study of Selection and Appointment*. London: Cobden Trust.

Kinsey, R., Lea, J. and Young, J. (1986) *Losing the Fight against Crime*. Oxford: Basil Blackwell.

Kitsuse, J.I. and Cicourel, A.V. (1963) 'A Note on the Uses of Official Statistics'. *Social Problems* 11: 131–9.

Kleck, G. (1981) 'Racial Discrimination in Criminal Sentencing: a Critical Evaluation of the Evidence with Additional Evidence on the Death Penalty'. *American Sociological Review* 46: 783–805.

Kleck, G. (1985) 'Life Support for Ailing Hypotheses: Modes of Summarizing the Evidence for Racial Discrimination in Sentencing'. *Law and Human Behavior* 9 (3): 271–85.

Klein, D. (1973) 'The Etiology of Female Crime: a Review of the Literature'. *Issues in Criminology* 8: 3–30.

Klemke, L.W. (1978) 'Does Apprehension for Shoplifting Amplify or Terminate Shoplifting Activity?' *Law and Society Review* 12 (3): 391–403.

Kluckhohn, C. (1949) *Mirror for Man*. New York: McGraw-Hill.

Kothari, M. and Mehta, L. (1988) 'Violence in Modern Medicine'. In A. Nandy (ed.) *Science, Hegemony and Violence: a Requiem for Modernity*. Tokyo and Delhi: United Nations University and Oxford University Press.

Labour Party (1990) *A Safer Britain: Labour's White Paper on Criminal Justice*. London: Labour Party.

Landau, S.F. (1981) 'Juveniles and the Police'. *British Journal of Criminology* 21: 143–72.

Landau, S.F. and Nathan, G. (1983) 'Selecting Delinquents for Cautioning in the London Metropolitan Area'. *British Journal of Criminology* 23: 128–49.

Launay, G. (1985) 'Bringing Victims and Offenders Together: a Comparison of Two Models'. *Howard Journal of Criminal Justice* 24: 200–12.

Lavrakas, P.J. and Herz, E.J. (1982) 'Citizen Participation in Neighborhood Crime Prevention'. *Criminology* 20: 479–98.

Laycock, G. and Pease, K. (1985) 'Crime Prevention within the Probation Service'. *Probation Journal* June: 43–7.

Lea, J. and Young, J. (1984) *What is to be Done about Law and Order?* Harmondsworth: Penguin Books.

LeBeau, J.L. (1987) 'Environmental Design as Prevention Rationale'. In E. Johnson (ed.) *Handbook on Crime and Delinquency Prevention*. New York: Greenwood Press.

Lemert, E.M. (1967) *Human Deviance, Social Problems and Social Control*. Englewood Cliffs, NJ: Prentice Hall.

Lewis, C.S. (1948/49) 'The Humanitarian Theory of Punishment'. *20th Century* 3 (3): 5–12. Reprinted in S. Grupp (ed.) (1971) *Theories of Punishment*. Bloomington, IN: Indiana University Press.

Lewis, H. and Mo, J. (1986) 'Burglary Insurance: Findings from the British Crime Survey'. *Home Office Research Bulletin* 22: 33–6.

Light, R. (ed.) (1989) *Prisoners' Families*. Bristol: Bristol and Bath Centre for Criminal Justice.

Lilly, J.R. (1989) 'A Brief and Speculative Comparison of "House Arrest" and Electronic Monitoring in the U.S. and Britain'. Unpublished Paper delivered to the British Criminology Conference, Bristol Polytechnic.

Lindquist, J.H. and Duke, J.M. (1982) 'The Elderly Victim at Risk'. *Criminology* 20: 115–26.

Lipton, D., Martinson, R. and Wilks, J. (1975) *The Effectiveness of Correctional Treatment*. New York: Praeger.

Lishman, J. (ed.) (1983) *Social Work with Adult Offenders*. Research Highlights 5. Aberdeen: University of Aberdeen Department of Social Work.

Lloyd, C. and Walmsley, R. (1989) *Changes in Rape Offences and Sentencing*. Home Office Research Study No. 105. London: HMSO.

Locke, T. (1990) *New Approaches to Crime in the 1990s: Planning Responses to Crime*. London: Longman.

Lopez-Rey, M. (1970) *Crime: an Analytical Approach*. London: Routledge and Kegan Paul.

Lymbery, R. (1989) 'The Future of the Probation Service: a View from the Courts'. In R. Shaw and K. Haines (eds) *The Criminal Justice System: A Central Role for the Probation Service*. Cambridge: University of Cambridge Institute of Criminology.

McConville, M. and Baldwin, J. (1982) 'The Influence of Race on Sentencing in England'. *Criminal Law Review* 652–8.

McGuire, J. and Priestley, P. (1985) *Offending Behaviour: Skills and Stratagems for Going Straight*. London: Batsford Books.

MacLeod, E. (1982) *Women Working: Prostitution Now*. London: Croom Helm.

McLeod, M. (1983) 'Victim Noncooperation in the Prosecution of Domestic Assault'. *Criminology* 21: 395–416.

McWilliams, W. (1986) *The English Social Inquiry Report: Development and Practice*. Unpublished Ph.D. Thesis. Sheffield: University of Sheffield.

Maguire, M. and Corbett, C. (1986) *The Effects of Crime and the Work of Victims Support Schemes*. Aldershot: Gower Press.

Maguire, M. and Pointing, J. (eds) (1988) *Victims of Crime: a New Deal?* Milton Keynes: Open University Press.

Mair, G. (1986) 'Ethnic Minorities, Probation and the Magistrates'. *British Journal of Criminology* 26: 147–55.

Mair, G. (ed.) (1989) *Risk Prediction and Probation: Papers from a Research and Planning Unit Workshop*. Research and Planning Unit Paper No. 56. London: Home Office.

Mannheim, H. and Wilkins, L.T. (1955) *Prediction Methods in Relation to Borstal Training*. London: HMSO.

Marris, P. and Rein, M. (1967) *Dilemmas of Social Reform*. New York: Atherton Press.

Marshall, T.F. (1985) 'British Initiatives in Mediation and Dispute Resolution'. *Home Office Research Bulletin* 19: 5–8.

Marshall, T.F. (1987) 'Mediation: a New Mode of Establishing Order in Schools'. *Howard Journal of Criminal Justice* 26: 33–46.

Martin, J.P. (1962) *Offenders as Employees*. London: Macmillan.

Martinson, R. (1974) 'What Works? Questions and Answers about Prison Reform'. *The Public Interest* 35: 22–54.

Martinson, R. (1979) 'Symposium on Sentencing, Part II: New Findings, New Views: A Note of Caution Regarding Sentencing Reform'. *Hofstra Law Review* 7 (2): 243–58.

Marx, G. (1981) 'Ironies of Social Control: Authorities as Contributors to Deviance through Escalation, Nonenforcement and Covert Facilitation'. *Social Problems* 28: 221–46.

Matthews, J. (1983) *Forgotten Victims*. London: National Association for the Care and Resettlement of Offenders.

Matthews, J., Barnard, B. and Stern, V. (1988) 'Encouraging Alternatives to Custody'. In A. Morris and C. Wilkinson (eds) *Women and the Penal System*. Cambridge: University of Cambridge Institute of Criminology.

Matza, D. (1964) *Delinquency and Drift*. New York: John Wiley.

Mawby, R.I. and Gill, M.L. (1987) *Crime Victims: Needs, Services and the Voluntary Sector*. London: Tavistock Publications.

Mawby, R. McCullough, J.W. and Batta, I.D. (1979) 'Crime among Asian Juveniles in Bradford'. *International Journal of the Sociology of Law* 7: 297–306.

Maxfield, M.G. (1984) *Fear of Crime in England and Wales*. Home Office Research Study No. 78. London: HMSO.

Mayhew, P. (1987) 'How are we Doing on the Burglary Front? A Comparison with the USA and Canada'. *Home Office Research Bulletin* 23: 42–7.

Mayhew, P., Elliott, D. and Dowds, L. (1989) *The 1988 British Crime Survey*. Home Office Research Study No. 111. London: HMSO.

Mendelsohn, B. (1963) 'The Origin of the Doctrine of Victimology'. Reprinted in I. Drapkin and E. Viano (1974a) Victimology. Lexington, MA: D.C. Heath. pp. 3–11.

Menninger, K. (1966) *The Crime of Punishment*. New York: Viking Press.

Mezey, G. (1988) 'Reactions to Rape: Effects, Counselling and the Role of Health Professionals'. In M. Maguire and J. Pointing (eds) *Victims of Crime: a New Deal?* Milton Keynes: Open University Press.

Miers, D. (1978) *Responses to Victimization*. Abingdon: Professional Books.

Miles, R. (1989) *Racism*. London: Routledge.

Morris, A.M. and Wilkinson, C. (eds) (1988) *Women and the Penal System*. Papers Presented to the 19th Cropwood Round-Table Conference. Cambridge: University of Cambridge Institute of Criminology.

Morris, N. and Hawkins, G. (1970) *The Honest Politician's Guide to Crime Control*. Chicago: University of Chicago Press.

Morris, N. and Tonry, M. (eds) (1979) *Crime and Justice: an Annual Review of Research*. Vol. 1. Chicago: University of Chicago Press.

Mott, J. (1985) 'Self-Reported Cannabis Use in Great Britain in 1981'. *British Journal of Addiction* 80: 37–43.

Moxon, D. (ed.) (1985) *Managing Criminal Justice*. London: HMSO.

Moxon, D. (1988) *Sentencing Practice in the Crown Court*. Home Office Research Study No. 103. London: HMSO.

Muehlenhard, C.L. (1989) 'Misinterpreted Dating Behaviors and the Risk of Date Rape'. In M. Pirog-Good and J. Stets (eds) *Violence in Dating Relationships: Emerging Social Issues*. New York: Praeger.

Myren, R.A. (1988) *Law and Justice: an Introduction*. Monterey, CA: Brooks/Cole.

Nagel, I.H. and Hagan, J. (1983) 'Gender and Crime: Offense Patterns and Criminal Court Sanctions'. In M. Tonry and N. Morris (eds) *Crime and Justice: an Annual Review of Research*. Vol. 4. Chicago: University of Chicago Press.

Nandy, A. (ed.) (1988) *Science, Hegemony and Violence: a Requiem for Modernity*. Tokyo and Delhi: United Nations University and Oxford University Press.

Nellis, R.M. (1990) *Intermediate Treatment and Juvenile Justice in England and*

*Wales 1960–1985*. Unpublished Ph.D. Thesis. Cambridge: University of Cambridge Institute of Criminology.

Nettler, G. (1974) *Explaining Crime*. New York: McGraw-Hill.

Newburn, T. and Peyrecave, H. de (1988) 'Victims' Attitudes to Courts and Compensation'. *Home Office Research Bulletin* 25: 18–21.

Newman, G.R. (ed.) (1980) *Crime and Deviance: a Comparative Perspective*. Beverly Hills: Sage Publications.

Newman, O. (1972) *Defensible Space*. New York: Collier.

Nicolson, P. and Bayne, R. (1990) *Applied Psychology for Social Workers*. 2nd Edn. London: Macmillan.

O'Brien, R.M. (1985) *Crime and Victimization Data*. Beverly Hills, CA: Sage Publications.

O'Dwyer, J., Wilson, J. and Carlen, P. (1987) 'Women's Imprisonment in England, Wales and Scotland: Recurring Issues'. In P. Carlen and A. Worrall (eds) *Gender, Crime and Justice*. Milton Keynes: Open University Press.

O'Leary, V. and Clear, T.R. (1984) *Directions for Community Corrections in the 1990s*. Washington, DC: US Government Department of Justice.

Oppenlander, N. (1982) 'Coping or Copping Out: Police Service Delivery in Domestic Disputes'. *Criminology* 20: 449–65.

Painter, K. (1988) *Lighting and Crime Prevention: the Edmonton Project*. London: Middlesex Polytechnic.

Parker, H. (1974) *View from the Boys*. Newton Abbott: David and Charles.

Parry, G. (1990) *Coping With Crises*. London: Routledge.

Parry, M. (1988) 'The Legal Framework of Practice, Principles and Issues'. In A. James, K. Wilson and M. Parry (eds) *Social Work in Family Proceedings: a Practice Guide*. London: Routledge.

Patrick, J. (1973) *A Glasgow Gang Observed*. Bristol: Eyre Methuen.

Paulos, J.A. (1989) *Innumeracy: Mathematical Illiteracy and its Consequences*. London: Viking Books.

Pearson, G. (1983) *Hooligan: a History of Respectable Fears*. London: Macmillan.

Pease, K. (1985) 'Obscene Telephone Calls to Women in England and Wales'. *Howard Journal of Criminal Justice* 24: 275–81.

Pease, K. and Wasik, M. (eds) (1987) *Sentencing Reform: Guidance or Guidelines?* Manchester: Manchester University Press.

Pepinsky, H.E. (1980) *Crime Control Strategies*. New York: Oxford University Press.

Perry, F.G. (1974) *Information for the Court: a New Look at Social Inquiry Reports*. Cambridge: University of Cambridge Institute of Criminology.

Peters, R.S. (1970) *Ethics and Education*. London: Allen & Unwin.

Pinder, R. (1982) 'On What Grounds? Negotiating Justice with Black Clients'. *Probation Journal* 29: 19–23.

Pirog-Good, M.A. and Stets, J.E. (eds) (1989) *Violence in Dating Relationships: Emerging Social Issues*. New York: Praeger.

Pithouse, A. (1987) *Social Work: The Social Organisation of an Invisible Trade*. Aldershot: Gower Press.

Pitts, J. (1988) *The Politics of Juvenile Crime*. London: Sage.

Pointing, J. (ed.) (1986) *Alternatives to Custody*. Oxford: Basil Blackwell.

Porterfield, A.L. (1946) *Youth in Trouble: Studies in Delinquency and Despair: With Plans for Prevention*. Fort Worth, TX: Leo Potishman Foundation.

President's Commission on Law Enforcement and the Administration of Justice (1967) *The Challenge of Crime in a Free Society*. Washington, DC: United States Government Printing Office.

Prins, H. (1982) *Criminal Behaviour*. 2nd Edn. London: Tavistock Publications.

Radzinowicz, L. and King, J. (1979) *The Growth of Crime: the International Experience*. Harmondsworth: Penguin Books.

Ramsay, M. (1986) 'Preventing Disorder'. In K. Heal and G. Laycock (eds) *Situational Crime Prevention: from Theory into Practice*. London: HMSO.

Ramsay, M. (1989) 'Crime Prevention: Lighting the Way Ahead'. *Home Office Research Bulletin* 27: 18-20.

Reasons, C.E. and Kuykendall, J.L. (eds) (1972) *Race, Crime and Justice*. Pacific Palisades, CA: Goodyear Publishing.

Reiner, R. (1985) *The Politics of the Police*. Brighton: Harvester Wheatsheaf.

Riley, D. (1985) 'Drinking Drivers: the Limits to Deterrence'. *Howard Journal of Criminal Justice* 24: 241–56.

Riley, D. and Shaw, M. (1985) *Parental Supervision and Juvenile Delinquency*. Home Office Research Study No. 83. London: HMSO.

Rosenbaum, D.P. (ed.) (1986) *Community Crime Prevention: Does it Work?* Beverly Hills, CA: Sage Publications.

Rosenbaum, D.P. (1988) 'A Critical Eye on Neighbourhood Watch: Does it Reduce Crime and Fear?' In T. Hope and M. Shaw (eds) *Communities and Crime Reduction*. London: HMSO.

Roshier, B. (1989) *Controlling Crime: the Classical Perspective in Criminology*. Milton Keynes: Open University Press.

Rossi, P.H. (ed.) (1970) *Ghetto Revolts*. New York: Aldine Publishing.

Rutherford, A. (1986) *Growing Out of Crime*. Harmondsworth: Penguin Books.

Rutter, M. and Giller, H. (1983) *Juvenile Delinquency: Trends and Perspectives*. Harmondsworth: Penguin Books.

Ryan, M. and Ward, T. (1989) *Privatization and the Penal System: the American Experience and the Debate in Britain*. Milton Keynes: Open University Press.

Ryan, W. (1972) *Blaming the Victim*. New York: Vintage Books.

Sagarin, E. (1980a) 'Taboo Subjects and Taboo Viewpoints in Criminology'. In E. Sagarin (ed.) *Taboos in Criminology*. Beverly Hills, CA: Sage Publications.

Sagarin, E. (ed.) (1980b) *Taboos in Criminology*. Beverly Hills, CA: Sage Publications.

Scarman, Lord (1981) *The Brixton Disorders, 10–12 April 1981*. (Scarman Report.) Cmnd. 8427. London: HMSO.

Schafer, S. (1960) *Restitution to Victims of Crime*. London: Stevens and Sons.

Schneider, H.J. (ed.) (1982) *The Victim in International Perspective*. Berlin: de Gruyter.

Schur, E.M. (1965) *Crimes Without Victims*. Englewood Cliffs, NJ: Prentice Hall.

Schur, E.M. (1973) *Radical Non-Intervention*. Englewood Cliffs, NJ: Prentice Hall.

Schweinhart, L.J. and Weikart, D.P. (1980) *Young Children Grow Up: the Effects of the Perry Preschool Program on Youths Through Age 15*. Ypsilanti, MI: High/Scope Educational Research Foundation.

Scraton, P. (ed.) (1987) *Law, Order and the Authoritarian State: Readings in Critical Criminology*. Milton Keynes: Open University Press.

Sellin, T. (1928) 'The Negro Criminal: a Statistical Note'. *Annals of the American*

*Academy of Political and Social Science* 140: 52–64.

Shapland, J. (1978) 'Self-Reported Delinquency in Boys aged 11 to 14'. *British Journal of Criminology* 18: 255–66.

Shapland, J. (1981) *Between Conviction and Sentence: the Process of Mitigation.* London: Routledge and Kegan Paul.

Shapland, J., Willmore, J. and Duff, P. (1985) *Victims in the Criminal Justice System.* Aldershot: Gower Press.

Shaw, C.R. (1929) *Delinquency Areas.* Chicago: University of Chicago Press.

Shaw, C.R. (1930) *The Jack-Roller: a Delinquent Boy's Own Story.* Chicago: University of Chicago Press.

Shaw, C.R. and Mackay, H. (1942) *Juvenile Delinquency and Urban Areas.* Chicago: University of Chicago Press.

Shaw, G.B. (1946) *The Crime of Punishment.* New York: Philosophical Library.

Shaw, R. (1987) *The Children of Imprisoned Fathers.* London: Hodder and Stoughton.

Shaw, R. and Haines, K. (eds) (1989) *The Criminal Justice System: a Central Role for the Probation Service.* Cambridge: University of Cambridge Institute of Criminology.

Sheleff, L. (1974) 'The Criminal Triad: Bystander, Victim and Criminal'. In I. Drapkin and E. Viano (eds) *Victimology: a New Focus.* Vol. 1. Lexington, MA: D.C. Heath.

Silverman, R.A. and Teevan, J.J. Jr (eds) *Crime in Canadian Society.* Toronto: Butterworth (Canada).

Simon, R.J. (1975) *Women and Crime.* Lexington, MA: D.C. Heath.

Singer, L.R. (1989) *Adult Probation and Juvenile Supervision: Beyond the Care–Control Dilemma.* Aldershot: Avebury.

Small, S. (1983) *Police and People in London.* Vol. 2. *A Group of Young Black People.* London: Policy Studies Institute.

Smart, C. (1976) *Women, Crime and Criminology: a Feminist Critique.* London: Routledge and Kegan Paul.

Smith, A.D. (1974) 'The Woman Offender'. In L. Blom-Cooper (ed.) *Progress in Penal Reform.* Oxford: Clarendon Press.

Smith, D. and Visher, C. (1980) 'Sex and Involvement in Deviance/Crime: a Quantitative Review of the Empirical Literature'. *American Sociological Review* 45: 697–701.

Smith, D.J. (1983) *Police and People in London.* Vol.1. *A Survey of Londoners.* London: Policy Studies Institute.

Smith, D.J. and Gray, J. (1983) *Police and People in London.* Vol. 4. *The Police in Action.* London: Policy Studies Institute.

Smith, L.J.F. (1988) 'Images of Women – Decision-Making in Courts'. In A. Morris and C. Wilkinson (eds) *Women and the Penal System.* Cambridge: University of Cambridge Institute of Criminology.

Smith, L.J.F. (1989) *Concerns about Rape.* Home Office Research Study No. 106. London: HMSO.

Smith, L.J.F. and Burrows, J. (1986) 'Nobbling the Fraudsters: Crime Prevention Through Administrative Change'. *Howard Journal of Criminal Justice* 25: 13–24.

Southgate, P. (1987) 'Behaviour in Police-Public Encounters'. *Howard Journal of Criminal Justice* 26: 153–63.

Southgate, P. and Ekblom, P. (1986) *Police–Public Encounters.* Home Office

Research Study No. 90. London: HMSO.

Sparks, R. (1981) 'Surveys of Victimization: an Optimistic Assessment'. In M. Tonry and N. Morris (eds) *Crime and Justice*. Vol. 3. Chicago: University of Chicago Press.

Sparks, R., Genn, H. and Dodd, D. (1977) *Surveying Victims*. Chichester: Wiley.

Stafford, M.C. and Galle, O.R. (1984) 'Victimization Rates, Exposure to Risk, and Fear of Crime'. *Criminology* 22: 173–85.

Stanko, E.A. (1985) *Intimate Intrusions: Women's Experience of Male Violence*. London: Routledge and Kegan Paul.

Stanko, E.A. (1988) 'Hidden Violence Against Women'. In M. Maguire and J. Pointing (eds) *Victims of Crime: a New Deal?* Milton Keynes: Open University Press.

Stanley, S. and Baginsky, M. (1984) *Alternatives to Prison*. London: Peter Owen.

Staplehurst, A. (1983) *Working with Young Afro-Caribbean Offenders*. Social Work Monographs No. 20. Norwich: University of East Anglia.

Steffensmeier, D.J. (1978) 'Crime and the Contemporary Woman: an Analysis of Changing Levels of Female Property Crime, 1960–75'. *Social Forces* 57: 566–84.

Steffensmeier, D.J. and Harer, M.D. (1987) 'Is the Crime Rate Really Falling? An "Aging" U.S. Population and its Impact on the Nation's Crime Rate, 1980–1984'. *Journal of Research in Crime and Delinquency* 24: 23–48.

Stern, V. (1987) 'Crime Prevention – the Inter-Organizational Approach'. In J. Harding (ed.) *Probation and the Community: a Practice and Policy Reader*. London: Tavistock Publications.

Stets, J.E. and Straus, M.A. (1989) 'The Marriage License as a Hitting License: a Comparison of Assaults in Dating, Cohabiting, and Married Couples'. In M. Pirog-Good and J. Stets (eds) *Violence in Dating Relationships: Emerging Social Issues*. New York: Praeger.

Stevens, P. and Willis, C.F. (1979) *Race, Crime and Arrests*. Home Office Research Study No. 58. London: HMSO.

Stone, N. (1987) 'Sentencing Reform and the Probation Service'. In K. Pease and M. Wasik (eds) *Sentencing Reform: Guidance or Guidelines?* Manchester: Manchester University Press.

Stookey, J.A. (1976) 'The Victim's Perspective on American Criminal Justice'. In J. Hudson (ed.) *Restitution in Criminal Justice*. St Paul, MN: Minnesota Department of Corrections.

Stubbs, J. and Wallace, A. (1988) 'Protecting Victims of Domestic Violence?' In M. Findlay and J. Hogg (eds) *Understanding Crime and Criminal Justice*. Sydney: The Law Book Company.

Sugarman, D.B. and Hotaling, G.T. (1989) 'Dating Violence: Prevalence, Context, and Risk Markers'. In M. Pirog-Good and J. Stets (eds) *Violence in Dating Relationships: Emerging Social Issues*. New York: Praeger.

Sutherland, E.H. (1941) 'Crime and Business'. *Annals of the American Academy of Political and Social Sciences* September: 112–18.

Sutherland, E.H. (1949) *White Collar Crime*. New York: Dryden Press.

Sykes, G. and Matza, D. (1957) 'Techniques of Neutralization: a Theory of Delinquency'. *American Sociological Review* 22: 664–70.

T., Anna (1988) 'Feminist Responses to Child Sexual Abuse: the Work of the Birmingham Rape Crisis Centre'. In M. Maguire and J. Pointing (eds)

*Victims of Crime: a New Deal?* Milton Keynes: Open University Press.

Tarling, R. (with Weatheritt, M.) (1979) *Sentencing Practice in Magistrates' Courts.* Home Office Research Study No. 56. London: HMSO.

Tarling, R., Moxon, D. and Jones, P. (1985) 'Sentencing of Adults and Juveniles in Magistrates' Courts'. In D. Moxon (ed.) *Managing Criminal Justice.* London: HMSO.

Taylor, I. (1981) *Law and Order: Arguments for Socialism.* London: Macmillan.

Taylor, I., Walton, P. and Young, J. (1973) *The New Criminology.* London: Routledge and Kegan Paul.

Taylor, I., Walton, P. and Young, J. (eds) (1975) *Critical Criminology.* London: Routledge and Kegan Paul.

Taylor, L. and Walton, P. (1971) 'Industrial Sabotage: Motives and Meanings'. In S. Cohen (ed.) *Images of Deviance.* Harmondsworth: Penguin Books.

Taylor, W. (1981) *Probation and After-Care in a Multi-Racial Society.* London: Commission for Racial Equality.

Thomas, D.A. (1970) *Principles of Sentencing.* London: Heinemann.

Thornberry, T.P. (1973) 'Race, Socio-Economic Status and Sentencing in the Juvenile Justice System'. *Journal of Criminal Law and Criminology* 64: 90–8.

Thornberry, T.P. (1979) 'Sentencing Disparities in the Juvenile Justice System'. *Journal of Criminal Law and Criminology* 79: 164–71.

Thorpe, D.H., Smith, D., Green, C.J. and Paley, J.H. (1980) *Out of Care: the Community Support of Juvenile Offenders.* London: Allen and Unwin.

Thorpe, J. (1979) *Social Inquiry Reports: a Survey.* Home Office Research Study No. 48. London: HMSO.

Tobias, J.J. (1967) *Crime and Industrial Society in the Nineteenth Century.* London: Batsford Books.

Tonry, M. (1987) 'Sentencing Guidelines and Sentencing Commissions: the Second Generation'. In K. Pease and M. Wasik (eds) *Sentencing Reform: Guidance or Guidelines?* Manchester: Manchester University Press.

Tonry, M. and Morris, N. (eds) (1981) *Crime and Justice: an Annual Review of Research.* Vol. 3. Chicago: University of Chicago Press.

Tonry, M. and Morris, N. (eds) (1983a) *Crime and Justice: an Annual Review of Research.* Vol. 4. Chicago: University of Chicago Press.

Tonry, M. and Morris, N. (eds) (1983b) *Crime and Justice: an Annual Review of Research.* Vol. 5. Chicago: University of Chicago Press.

Tonry, M. and Morris, N. (eds) (1985) *Crime and Justice: an Annual Review of Research.* Vol. 6. Chicago: University of Chicago Press.

Tonry, M. and Zimring, F. (eds) (1983) *Reform and Punishment: Essays on Criminal Sentencing.* Chicago: University of Chicago Press.

Trasler, G. (1986) 'Situational Crime Control and Rational Choice: a Critique'. In K. Heal and G. Laycock (eds) *Situational Crime Prevention: from Theory into Practice.* London: HMSO.

Travis, L.F. III (ed.) (1985) *Probation, Parole, and Community Corrections: a Reader.* Prospect Heights, IL: Waveland Press.

Tuck, M. and Southgate, P. (1981) *Ethnic Minorities, Crime and Policing: a Survey of the Experiences of West Indians and Whites.* Home Office Research Study No. 70. London: HMSO.

Van Dijk, J.J.M., Mayhew, P. and Killias, M. (1990) *Experiences of Crime Across the World: Key Findings from the 1989 International Crime Survey.* Daventer,

Netherlands: Kluwer Law and Taxation.

Vass, A.A. (1984) *Sentenced to Labour: Close Encounters with a Prison Substitute*. St Ives: Venus Academica.

Visher, C.A. (1983) 'Gender, Police Arrest Decisions, and Notions of Chivalry'. *Criminology* 21: 5–28.

Von Hirsch, A.(1985) *Past or Future Crimes: Deservedness or Dangerousness in the Sentencing of Criminals*. New Brunswick, NJ: Rutgers University Press.

Von Hirsch, A. (1987) 'Guidance by Numbers or Words? Numerical Versus Narrative Guidelines for Sentencing'. In K. Pease and M. Wasik (eds) *Sentencing Reform: Guidance or Guidelines?* Manchester: Manchester University Press.

Walker, H. and Beaumont, B. (1981) *Probation Work: Critical Theory and Socialist Practice*. Oxford: Basil Blackwell.

Walker, N. (1969) *Sentencing in a Rational Society*. Harmondsworth: Allen Lane.

Walker, N. (1971) *Crimes, Courts and Figures*. Harmondsworth: Penguin Books.

Walker, N. (1985) *Sentencing: Theory, Law and Practice*. London: Butterworth.

Walklate, S. (1989) *Victimology: The Victim and the Criminal Justice Process*. London: Unwin Hyman.

Wallerstein, J.A. and Wyle, C.J. (1947) 'Our Law-Abiding Law Breakers'. *Federal Probation* 25: 107–12.

Walsh, A. (1984) 'Gender-Based Differences'. *Criminology* 22: 371–87.

Warr, M. (1982) 'The Accuracy of Public Beliefs about Crime'. *Criminology* 20: 185–204.

Warren, M.Q. (eds) (1981) *Comparing Female and Male Offenders*. Beverly Hills, CA: Sage Publications.

Wasik, M. and Pease, K. (1987) 'Discretion and Sentencing Reform: the Alternatives'. In K. Pease and M. Wasik (eds) *Sentencing Reform: Guidance or Guidelines?* Manchester: Manchester University Press.

Wasik, M. and Von Hirsch, A. (1988) 'Non-Custodial Penalties and the Principle of Desert'. *Criminal Law Review* 555–72.

Waters, R. (1988) 'Race and the Criminal Justice Process'. *British Journal of Criminology* 28: 82–94.

Waters, R. (1990) *Ethnic Minorities and the Criminal Justice System*. Aldershot: Avebury.

Webb, D. and Harris, R. (1984) 'Social Workers and Supervision Orders: a Case of Occupational Uncertainty'. *British Journal of Social Work* 14: 579–99.

Weiss, R.P. (1987) 'Community and Prevention'. In E. Johnson (ed.) *Handbook on Crime and Delinquency Prevention*. New York: Greenwood Press.

Werner, E.E. and Smith, R.S. (1982) *Vulnerable but Invincible*. New York: McGraw-Hill.

West, D.J. (1967) *The Young Offender*. Harmondsworth: Penguin Books.

West, D.J. (1969a) *Present Conduct and Future Delinquency*. London: Heinemann Educational Books.

West, D.J. (ed.) (1969b) *Criminological Implications of Chromosome Abnormalities*. Cropwood Conference Proceedings No. 4. Cambridge: University of Cambridge Institute of Criminology.

West, D.J. (1982) *Delinquency: Its Roots, Careers and Prospects*. London: Heinemann Educational Books.

West, D.J. and Farrington, D.P. (1973) *Who Becomes Delinquent?* London:

Heinemann Educational Books.
West, D.J. and Farrington, D.P. (1977) *The Delinquent Way of Life*. London: Heinemann Educational Books.
White, R.A.C. (1985) *The Administration of Justice*. Oxford: Blackwell.
Whitehead, J.T. (1989) *Burnout in Probation and Corrections*. New York: Praeger.
Whitehead, P. (1990) *Community Supervision for Offenders*. Aldershot: Avebury.
Whitehouse, P. (1983) 'Race, Bias and Social Enquiry Reports'. *Probation Journal* 30: 43–9.
Wilkins, L.T. (1964) *Social Deviance: Social Policy, Action, and Research*. London: Tavistock Publications.
Wilkins, L.T. (1980) 'World Crime: to Measure or not to Measure?'. In G. Newman *Crime and Deviance: a Comparative Perspective*. Beverly Hills, CA: Sage Publications.
Williams, J.R. and Gold, M. (1972) 'From Delinquent Behavior to Official Delinquency'. *Social Problems* 20: 209–29.
Wilson, J.Q. and Herrnstein, R.J. (1985) *Crime and Human Nature: the Definitive Study of the Causes of Crime*. New York: Simon and Schuster.
Wolfe, D.A. (1987) *Child Abuse: Implications for Child Development and Psychopathology*. Beverly Hills, CA: Sage Publications.
Wolfgang, M.E. and Cohen, B. (1972) 'Seeking an Explanation'. In C.E. Reasons and J.L. Kuykendall (eds) *Race, Crime and Justice*. Pacific Palisades, CA: Goodyear Pubishing.
Wolfgang, M.E., Figlio, R.F. and Sellin, T. (1972) *Delinquency in a Birth Cohort*. Chicago: University of Chicago Press.
Wolfgang, M.E. and Riedel, M. (1977) 'Race, Rape and the Death Penalty'. In D. Chappell, R. Geis and G. Geis (eds) *Forcible Rape: the Crime, the Victim, and the Offender*. New York: Columbia University Press.
Wooden, K. (1976) *Weeping in the Playtime of Others*. New York: McGraw-Hill.
Wootton, B. (1978) *Crime and Penal Policy*. London: Allen and Unwin.
Worrall, A. (1987) 'Sisters in Law? Women Defendants and Women Magistrates'. In P. Carlen and A. Worrall (eds) *Gender, Crime and Justice*. Milton Keynes: Open University Press.
Worrall, A. (1990) *Offending Women*. London: Routledge.
Worrall, A. and Pease, K. (1986) 'Personal Crime against Women: Evidence from the 1982 British Crime Survey'. *Howard Journal of Criminal Justice* 25: 118–24.
Wright, K.N., Clear, T.R. and Dickson, P. (1984) 'Universal Applicability of Probation Risk-Assessment Instruments: a Critique'. *Criminology* 22 (1): 113–34.
Wright, M. (1982) *Making Good: Prisons, Punishment and Beyond*. London: Burnett Books.
Wyatt, G.E. and Powell, G.J. (eds) (1988) *Lasting Effects of Child Sexual Abuse*. Beverly Hills, CA: Sage Publications.
Yablonsky, L. (1962) *The Violent Gang*. New York: Macmillan.
Yin, P.P. (1980) 'Fear of Crime Among the Elderly: Some Issues and Suggestions'. *Social Problems* 27: 492–504.
Yin, R.K. (1986) 'Community Crime Prevention: a Synthesis of Eleven Evaluations'. In D. Rosenbaum (ed.) *Community Crime Prevention: Does it Work?* Beverly Hills, CA: Sage Publications.
Young, J. (1971a) *The Drugtakers: the Social Meaning of Drug Use*. London:

MacGibbon and Kee.

Young, J. (1971b) 'The Role of the Police as Amplifiers of Deviancy, Negotiators of Reality and Translators of Fantasy: Some Consequences of Our Present System of Drug Control as Seen in Notting Hill'. In S. Cohen (ed.) *Images of Deviance*. Harmondsworth: Penguin Books.

Young, J. (1975) 'Working-Class Criminology'. In I. Taylor, P. Walton and J. Young (eds) *Critical Criminology*. London: Routledge and Kegan Paul.

Young, J. (1988) 'Risk of Crime and Fear of Crime: a Realist Critique of Survey-Based Assumptions'. In M. Maguire and J. Pointing (eds) *Victims of Crime: a New Deal?* Milton Keynes: Open University Press.

Young, W. (1979) *Community Service Orders: The Development and Use of a New Penal Measure*. London: Hutchinson.

# Name index

# Subject index

abuse: child 21–2, 104; sexual 44, 104–6; *see also* rape
advertisements 53, 54
Afro-Caribbeans 35–6, 109, 122–3
agencies: bias in statistics 9–11; inter-agency collaboration 75–6, 164–5; multi-agency approach 159–60, 162–4, 173; relationships with courts 163–4
American National Crime Survey 24
arrests: and gender 94–5
Asians 35–6
Association of Chief Officers of Probation 84
Australian Law Reform Commission 142

British Crime Survey: attitudes to punishment 36–7; distortions 44; findings 33–40; risk of crime 52; victimisation and lifestyle 37–40
bystanders 59

capitalism: and racism 113
Chicago School 40, 167
children: crime prevention 68–9; protection committees 75, 162–3; sexual abuse 21–2, 104
Children Act (1989) 28
chivalry 95–6, 97
Clark, Ramsey 30
class, social: crime prevention 80; delinquency 27; racism 113; warfare 41
clear-up rates 18–19

collusion, victim 14
communities: crime prevention schemes 54, 71, 76–81; fear of crime 49–55; supervision in 153–75; victims in 55–65; *see also* environment; inner cities
community service: factors for success 160; support for 36–7; underused for female offenders 102
compensation 60, 62
concern 42–3, 44, 67
correctional programmes 155–6, 168–9
courts: disparity 123; gender differences 93–100; relationship with agencies 163–4; social enquiry reports 148–50; *see also* sentencing
crime: clear-up rates 18–19; committees 162–4, 174–5; control 159–65; gender differences 90–3, 100; by girls 87–90; official statistics 1–22; organized 10–11; prediction 157–8; and race 108–16, 125–8; records 17–18; reports 13–17, 35; and social environment 40–2, 167–8; trends in 1980s 35; unofficial statistics 23–45; unrecorded 31; white-collar 10–11, 42; by women 90–102; *see also* criminal justice system; fear; victims
Crime Commission 24
crime prevention: advice on 57–9; child protection 75, 162–3;